Before, During and After My Falklands War

Terence Victor Barnes

ISBN: 9798743010486

DEDICATION

For Sharon, Sarah and Duchess the dog; thanks for sharing my life.

The Royal Marines Family; 'OARMAARM'.

CONTENTS.

ACKNOWLEDGMENTS

Amazon for their easy guide, Chris Pretty and Ged Herd for their conversations and last but not least Sharon and Sarah for their support, encouragement and patience.

Forward.

All I felt was a numbness, an empty, black void. If you had passed by me and looked you would have seen a middle-aged man, poker faced, eyes seemingly blank and simply focused ahead. I was on auto pilot.

Time seemed to have stopped, I couldn't remember a single thing about driving along the A14 on my way to work that day, my mind was absent of all thoughts and feelings. I had felt this sense of detachment before, in 1982, during the Falklands War.

The traffic hold ups on a Monday morning were normal but today was particularly bad. I pulled into the college carpark feeling frustrated, thinking what a great way to start the working week. 'Hello Mr Barnes and a happy 50th birthday to you!' was the greeting I received on entering the trendy, open planned, but bland, staff room that I shared with approximately thirty other lecturers. A bloody nightmare environment when you are trying to get any privacy and paperwork done. 'Any cakes?' I was asked even before I put my bags down. Unlike anywhere else in England, it is a strange tradition for people in my hometown of Ipswich (and in fact, the whole of Suffolk), where it is expected of you, not your colleagues, on your celebration day, to buy the cakes.

'Life begins at 50' an elderly lecturer called from a distant desk. Now, normally I would have ignored this cry of 'youthism' but it was 08.20, I had just spent almost an hour stuck in traffic, also there was a pile of paperwork left on my desk to sort out before my first lesson started at 09.00. Informal jollities I could do without. A dark, uncontrollable, but familiar anger rose inside of me, another unpleasant consequence and now a permanent attribute that I 'contracted' and have not been able to shake off since the Falklands War. I really wanted to go over to him and smash him in the face but instead clenched my fists to help divert my temper. I had visions of wasting him with a shot through the forehead from a Browning 9mm pistol. In reality the answer I hurled back at a surprisingly high level of decibels was 'No it didn't, it started 50 years ago you moron'. This frequently used statement 'life begins at ....(any age over 30)' gave me a cold shudder down my spine. I questioned myself, ' Is more than half of my life really over?'

Anyway, this seemingly bland comment was the kick start I

needed for me to begin writing my autobiography (well at least part of it). Why? Good question. To self-indulge in a blanket of reminiscence? To demonstrate to the world what a wonderful life I have lived so far? Or was it to show off in some literate manner? – Well no! Let me use an analogy (and a true one too) to help explain why. During the mid-1970's, in my final year of primary school (I believe now known as year 6), my peers and I were sat in regimental lines, on uncomfortable chairs, behind single wooden desks with ink wells on the lids, left from a bygone age. All set in a spacious classroom that was well lit by natural light streaming in from very large windows. These windows allowed us to look out onto the playground and if other classes were outside taking part in physical exercise lessons, we would often be distracted. Up at the front, facing us, was our teacher, Mrs Swift. Behind her, a very large chalk board and various wall displays for us to use as points of reference e.g. the twelve times table and a map of the world.

Robert Matuzczyk, my future best man, was located to my right, Joseph Tynan, one of three of the headmaster's sons that attended the school, to my left. We were at least three rows back from the front, which gave us suitable cover for any devious exploits we wished to covertly execute; well out of sight and hearing distance from the teacher. In the row in front from me and one desk to the right, sat Steven Tinsley. Steven was one of those boys you could only describe as 'strange'. Strange in manner and strange in physique. What he had inherited from the gene pool was a personality that bordered on a psychopath and a body shape that would not be lost in the stick insect tank at Bristol Zoo, or a look alike competition for Basil Fawlty. To compound his ill-fated appearance, his ears were not large, large would be a misuse of the word, colossus would be more appropriate. Let me put it this way, large Wedgewood dinner plates would have been eclipsed behind the circumference of his lobes!

Steven had the imagination of an out of date banana, unlike Robert. It was conceived in a moment of genius by him that the back of Steven's ears were a perfect blank canvas for any aspiring artist. While Mrs Swift was distracted writing on the chalkboard or by one of us three acting up which caused the rest of the class to riot, on a daily basis over two weeks we scribbled, sketched, and painted the back of Steven's ears with absolutely no response or complaints from the recipient. However, all was to come to an end. On a Monday morning at the start of the third week of our artistry on his ears, unknown to us, Steven's father had burst into the Headmaster's Office. He complained on behalf of his wife that she could no longer scrub clean the collars on her son's shirts and that the skin on Steven's ears was red raw because washing powder was the only thing that had enough abrasive action to remove the indelible ink and paint.

The guilty three of Joseph, Robert and myself were summoned from our classroom and led away by the school secretary like lambs to the slaughter. One at a time we entered the head's office to receive our verbal bashing and physical punishment - the dreaded hand smack on the backside (physical chastisement was legal in those days). The technique used by the headmaster was always the same. Standing, we were clasped on the back of the neck, bent over, eyes looking at the ground, legs straight and feet apart. Then on execution, from a great height the headmaster's hand came thundering down, making contact with the buttocks. A thwacking sound could be heard by any bystanders. This punishment resulted in us feeling some pain, pins and needles as the blood returned to our buttocks and trying to 'brave it out' by not crying. Afterwards, we, the poor 'sinners,' were questioned together on why we had defaced Stevens ears and committed such a hideous crime. With no respect left, I simply looked down at the floor in a manner in which all scolded children tend to do. On the third time of asking 'Why did you do this, why did you scrawl on his ears?' Joseph, to his credit and our defence, replied with an adaption of Mallory's famous quote, 'Because they were there'. And there you have it – why have I decided to write my autobiography, well it's quite simple, because I was there, and you weren't! I say autobiography but really, I should like to mention that this is a semi or part autobiography. Hopefully I have many more years and experiences yet to come. On a serious point I believe it is timely to release this book because soon it will be the fortieth Falklands War Anniversary and I would hope to remind the general public of this date.

I have now reached the stage in life when I go upstairs (no, I'm not quite in a bungalow, yet!) walk into a bedroom, look around and forget what the purpose of my visit was. Is this the start of Alzheimer's? I used to live in the comfort of happily knowing that I could class myself as a T.O.G. (Terry's old Geezers and Gals). However since Terry Wogan's death in 2016 and the demise of the TOG community I feel I am alone. The 8 million or so morning, weekday listeners of Radio 2 Terry Wogan's show will know what I'm rambling on about. Just in case you are unaware of what a TOG is, Terry Wogan helped clarify this when he was interviewed on Radio 4's Desert Islands Discs programme. 'You know you are a TOG when you are proud to show off your lawn mower and can live without sex but not your glasses, that's if you can find them!' I have to ask myself the question, have my mental faculties declined in their abilities as quickly as my physical? What I am implying is that as I get older, I need other people to jolt my memories, to get the brain cells firing again and reignite past experiences. I need verbal conversation to recall stories that I have long forgotten. Oh, how I wish I could turn back time!

I have surreptitiously questioned friends, family, and colleagues to get going on this journey of writing my autobiography. Why this subterfuge? Well, the truth is that I felt embarrassed at the thought of telling everyone that I was attempting to write my autobiography in case I didn't succeed. I was truly concerned that once started I would not be able to complete my work; yes, I feared failure. When reading the following chapters please consider my socioeconomic background, in plain words, my working class upbringing. During my pre university days, a majority of the people I met, (and that includes some of my family), thought that to be a 'pen pusher' or an academic you had to be from the bourgeoisie, a 'posh bastard' and were just lucky to be born into wealth. Labouring on a building site, working in the local bakery, factory, or a garage (if you had some mechanical brains) or any other manual employment was considered a proper man's job. Being a manager, doctor or teacher for example, was regarded as a profession for the rich, well to do individuals, with absolutely no street credibility. These 'types' didn't really want or need paid employment but did it as some sort of charity work. I was worried about the ridicule from some, and the snide comments like 'I wish I had time to sit on my arse all day'. Perhaps I'm being oversensitive?

Apart from asking questions face to face with the poor people that had shared my experiences, or in some cases, suffered, another method of jolting my grey matter to help me recall my journey through this life so far and putting it down on paper, was sifting through photographs. I thought that by including some of my pictures in the book it will help you to visualise some scenarios. Or at worse, give the reader the chance to skip through what they might perceive as the boring bits (I hope you don't have to do this!).They say that a picture paints a thousand words, let's see!

For some perplexing reason I have very few photographs of me growing up in the 1960's and 70's. Did this absence of pictures indicate a shunning because of the lack of potential I had shown up until then and possibly what I was going to achieve in my future, nothing? I'd like to think not! To be fair on my parents and myself, we had very little money to buy luxury goods like cameras, besides paying to develop the film. In contrast, today digital cameras, mainly on mobile phones, are taken everywhere. Any excuse to take a snap of something remotely interesting is so widespread it drives me crazy, as well as slowing down my laptop due to its storage capacity disappearing as my daughter downloads endless 'selfies' on it! Photographs were and still should be looked upon as something to be treasured, tangible, a part of history, unique, and rare, not to be easily discarded at a touch of a button.

I have only once previously attempted to record my life's daily activities in a diary. It lasted for approximately four months and unsurprisingly, typically for a fourteen-year-old boy, was brief in vocabulary, description, and word count. For three pages, about three and a half weeks' worth, I repeatedly referred to 'the first snog' I ever had. I was blatantly showing off in my discourse just in case, or perhaps I was hoping for, one of my friends to get 'accidently' hold of the diary, read my scribbles, and tell others that I wasn't a 'kissing virgin,' (I wouldn't have minded if they had because my street credibility would have gone up!).

The only other records I have are sports certificates for my athletic endeavours at school, however no teachers progress reports. Probably because I forgot, on purpose, to take any of them home or just binned them. Now this could be deemed as unfortunate or perhaps, reflecting on my lack of academic progress and poor behaviour at the time, fortunate. I could say that part of my life is forever locked in the fabric of history, underground in a landfill somewhere in Ipswich where I intended the reports to go!

With the help of one of the subsequent headmasters, Mr Smith, I was able to look at my primary school's diary during the years I attended, written by hand by the then serving headmaster, Mr Tynan. There were only two references relating to me. On 5th May 1972, banging my leg on a bench and needing medical treatment, and 27th June 1973 when the school was closed in the afternoon for Ipswich sports day, I quote' Terence Barnes (3rd Year Junior) 2nd in high jump (1m 23cm)'. The only other thing of substance about my family was on April 19th 1971, Ruth, my older sister, passed her eleven plus and was accepted into a grammar school - I didn't and wasn't!

In later life, with great organisational support from my wife Sharon, we have stockpiled anything of interest and importance that has happened to us during our lives. I have several A4 sized lever arch files of memorabilia, containing certificates, medals and a suitcase with my old military clothes issued to me when I left the Royal Marines. On emptying the contents of my 'Pussers' (MOD issued kit) suitcase I found it contained the following: denim trousers, 2, green shirts, 2, socks, 2 pairs, jumper and commando flashes, 1, boots high leg, one pair, mug, knife, fork and spoon, 1, and of course my 'green lid' the famous green beret worn by every Royal Marines Commando. God help us if I was ever recalled should there be a national crisis and I had to put on my uniform. It is astonishing how over time, after leaving the Royal Marines, I have gained size and weight. Once I thought that I would give it a go and put some of the garments on. I was shocked that I could not even get the woolly pully jumper over my head let alone belly. Was I really once that slim? I still think I am, though my body knows I am not! For me, just seeing this clothing can be very nostalgic and I could spend a long time reflecting on my career in the Royal Marines. The passage of time unfortunately hasn't stood still since I left the Corps, but my memories have, just like the clothes' size in my Pussers suitcase!

As I have previously cited, to assist me in completing this book, I have talked with other people face to face that have shared some of my life stories, wholly or in part. This has helped me gather information and recall events and details that I had long forgotten. Here are some examples of where I have obtained material (if you decide to write your own story I would recommend going to as many gatherings as possible!); two school reunions, (one primary the other secondary), several Falklands reunions (Operation Corporate) in the UK and one visit back to the Islands, a few top tables, a formal, all day leaving party in the Senior Non-Commissioned mess at CTCRM and RM Poole – free drink and food included!

During one Falklands reunion Charlie Company were toasting those that had 'crossed the bar' (passed on). At the end of the list the speaker finished by saying 'Please forgive me but I hope I haven't absently minded missed anyone out'. There was a call from the crowd 'What about Tony 'Buster' Brown?' My colleague Jock Hepburn shouted back, 'But he's not dead'. The person who had made the claim questioned, 'How do you know?' The reply from Jock had us all in fits of laughter, 'Because he's standing over there you idiot!' and he pointed to the bar where Buster was with a pint of beer in his hand and a smile on his face!

By giving you an insight to some of my resources and background before, during and after the Falklands War, I hope that I have succeeded in enticing you to read on and/or write your own story. I did not set out to make this book humorous but some things or scenarios you might find amusing, some unbelievable and some sad or thought provoking. You, the reader, might have had similar experiences and therefore a shared empathy with me. Everything is true as I can recall, the only thing I have changed are some of the names. I have done this to prevent any unintentional embarrassment to individuals, alive or relatives of the dead, and of course in case anyone should feel a sudden urge to take any legal action against me!

How would I describe the contents of this book? Well simply, the life (at least the first part) of a 'Normal bloke' or if you live on the other side of the Atlantic Ocean 'A regular guy'. 'They tell me' (Who exactly **they** are, I do not know) there's a book waiting to be written in everyone .... let's see.....? Just thinking out aloud here; are **they** the same bastards that wake up every person in the neighbourhood, including all of my household, by letting fireworks off at midnight, causing my dog to go off on a barking frenzy for the next two hours! Because if it is and I find them, I'll let you know who **they** are, so we all can go around to their house and give them a bloody good kicking!

For chapter one, I had some difficulty deciding on the title, indeed whether to bother with chapter headings at all. There were two headings I agonised over. My final options were 'In the Beginning' which I felt was used too often and implied that my family, past and present have had some great impact on the world stage, just like the First Testament of the Bible. Secondly 'Blood Ties' but this was too vulgar in the sense of gory and blood thirsty. Eventually, I decided on neither of these!

Can I just say, oh dear I cannot believe I have included that phrase. During some of the meetings I have had to attend over the years in education, I sat in classrooms, listening to pointless discussions which could have been finished in half the time. When all of a sudden, I think, 'Great, finished' someone comes out with 'Can I just say…'. And then they carry on blathering about a microscopic point that will have very little impact on the outcome and diverts us away from the main agenda. Is this person a 'do gooder' or a revolutionist thinker, outside the box (oh dear here I go again with the same old cliches) or do they just like the sound of their own voice or trying to score brownie points? I really don't know or care. All I want to do is escape from the meeting, get in my car, drive home and have my dinner!

Rant over. What I really wanted to say is does the title really matter? Surely it is the content that is important. I make no apology for having no fancy title for chapter one, and no, I'm not lazy!

Why have I included two chapters on my heritage and up-bringing? To complete an autobiography and get a holistic picture I believe it is essential to know where the author comes from. It is to give you, the reader, some insight into my background and to be honest, it helped me recall some great facts and stories, passed on to me when I was so young that I had forgotten. Also it has reminded me of how relationships, particularly family ones, can greatly influence what path(s) you have taken and may decide to take in your future life. What comes to mind is the famous quote by the American poet Maya Angelou;

'If you don't know where you've come from, you don't know where you're going'.

1. My Family History.

My Parents.

My parents were married in October 1957 at St Pancras RC Church, Ipswich. Both of my parents have a mixed geographical background. My father was born in 1935 and spent the early part of his life in Mazagaon, an area just outside Bombay (now Mumbai), India. He arrived in England at the age of fifteen on a P&O ship that docked at Tilbury, Essex, in the early months of 1951. What his first impressions of 'our clouded hills and dark satanic mills' were, I do not know, suffice to say that it was definitely a change from the warm climatic conditions he had experienced in India.

My father was one of eleven children (sadly, two infant girls died in India). Some of his siblings, along with his mother, uncles, and aunties, had made the move to England before my father had left India. I suppose it was a kind of 'Wind Rush' occasion, but obviously not from the Caribbean. Dad went on from Tilbury to Ipswich to be met by his family.

My Dad's relations were not unique in their migration from India to 'Blighty' during this period. I believe there are quite a few famous individuals that followed this pattern of movement; Spike Milligan, Cliff Richard and Felicity Kendal (who was actually born in Warwickshire but grew up in India) to name a few. The title Anglo – Indian is often used to categorise the British people who worked in India or had a mixed heritage.

In the 1950's my dad spent some time in the British Army travelling to the Far East and reached the dizzy heights of corporal. On his return to England, he married Brenda and subsequently left the Army to become a manager at a local tannery where they processed sheep's skin. To make ends meet, he also worked at weekends in men's clothing stores in Ipswich town centre. He was made redundant in his late fifties and tried in vain to find meaningful employment up to his retirement at sixty five.

My father constantly kept us on our toes after his retirement. His escapades are on par with Peter Sellers' Inspector Clouseau of the French Sûreté (now known as 'Police Nationale'), whose comical police investigations are marked with turmoil and destruction caused by himself. Once my dad received in the post, a voucher for a free set of lenses for his glasses from Spec Savers. My mother took my father by car and dropped him off in Ipswich town centre and arranged to meet him later. He walked into a shop and queued for approximately twenty minutes. Eventually he got to the counter and asked for a fitting for his free lenses and produced his voucher. The young girl serving said, 'Sorry sir you cannot use that coupon in here'. Now my father is not one to back down, especially if something is free (a trait I have inherited, just ask my friends from Charlie Company) and there is an audience, like the one that was in line behind him. He raised his voice saying 'I demand to see the manager. The voucher here says that I am entitled to my free lenses and I want a fitting now!' The poor young lady, by now very embarrassed, lent over the counter and said, 'Sir this is the Lloyds Bank, the opticians is on the corner of the next street!' We only knew about this story because after waiting sometime in the car, my mother gave up, went to find him, and after some searching, succeeded. She saw him just about to leave the bank and other customers staring at him. She questioned him on what had happened. There are so many other stories I have of my father's mishaps, here are a few that I have cut short, but I think you might enjoy.

Carrying out his driving test while in the Army and based in

Malaya during the 1950's, he was driving along in a Land Rover on an untarmacked track which was full of cyclists. My father hit a bike, sending the cyclist flying into the air and, after rolling several times, the poor soul eventually landed in a ditch. All the British Army driving examiner said was, 'For god's sake don't stop!' Unbelievably, my father still passed his test and was given a licence.

He didn't drive for years after he left the Army. In the 1980's he decided he wanted to start again, so he sent off his old, tatty, military paper licence to the DVLA and a few weeks later received a brand new one. He then purchased a car. Every night without fail he would take the battery out, top it up with distilled water and put it on charge. Well, in no time the battery completely died, and so he replaced it. This happened several times until one day he spilt acid on the carpet and my mother went crazy at him.

If there was any sign of rust on the car, my Dad would go and get his brush and tin of white gloss wood paint out of the shed and use it to cover the worst parts up. He never sanded and primed the area nor stirred the paint, as instructed to do so on the tin. My father was such a poor painter. He just slapped it on and, in some areas, he left large drip marks that were highly visible because of the brown/yellow oil on top of the paint in the tin had not been mixed in. Also, in no way did the colour of the paint match the original one on the car and it never adhered to the metal surface. After only a week or so the rust returned and the paint work looked like the face of a Caucasian youth suffering from severe acne, red with yellow spots on a white background.

In winter to stop the engine from getting cold overnight he would cover it with a blanket, then replace the bonnet. One day he went driving off down the busy road where he lives, and suddenly thick, dense, acrid, black smoke poured out from the bonnet. He had left the blanket on.

It wasn't just the car where his misfortunes occurred. One day my 'well to do' auntie went to visit my Mum and Dad at their bungalow (bungalow is actually an Indian word). She sat in the front room on a settee (settee may also be another Indian word! Sorry, I'm losing the plot) and was discussing and showing off her new hair style, while sipping tea and nibbling on biscuits with my mother. At this point my father decided to go up into the loft. A few moments later there was a sudden and almighty crash, as dust and debris came cascading down from the ceiling into the front room, landing directly on top of my aunt's head. Her new hair style was a mess. My mother looked up and saw a foot dangling through! Next year, while retrieving the Christmas decorations he did exactly the same thing, luckily this time with no one below.

We went to a suit fitting for a wedding at a very posh outfitter in Ipswich. There were about ten of us waiting; the groom, best man, my brother, my father, myself and others. There was only one changing room. So one at a time we had to go and try on the suit while the others in the group just waited near a desk on the far side of the sales floor. On the way walking from the desk where we stood to the changing room, we had to pass through a narrow section with shelves and displays on the walls. When it was my turn, I left the others and went to have my fitting. I was just trying on my jacket when I heard someone knocking on the changing room door. I opened it and saw my dad standing there holding his suit. I told him that he would have to wait and asked him if he had heard the instructions, he replied with just a grunt. I closed the door. The next minute I heard an enormous boom and the smashing of breaking glass. Shocked, I stopped getting dressed, opened the changing room door, and saw my father walking back towards the group. There was a raucous of laughter from them. In my father's wake was chaos. Shelves and their contents had fallen to the floor. Items such as a glass chess set lay shattered along with plates and a very large dent on the side of a silver tankard. My father, the only one that had been anywhere near the shelves continued walking muttering 'It's nothing to do with me'. The poor lad serving us was almost in tears.

For my father's birthday present our family clubbed together and brought him a leather reclining chair. He placed the chair by his living room window so he could see out on to the road and watch life as it went by. While going for a walk I used to frequently go past his bungalow, see him sitting in his chair, and rather than stopping, I would just give him a wave. One early morning I went past on the way out as well as on the way back home and just gave him the customary wave. I did this several times in the day while walking the dog. I was just pleased to see that he appeared to be okay. At night we got a call from my mother who had been out shopping in London. She had returned to find that my father hadn't moved all day. He had reclined the chair, and then still sitting in it he tried to get it back in the upright position but couldn't, only succeeding in getting it halfway. The result was that his body had been stuck in the chair in a V position all day. Every time he waved at me, he was actually gesturing for help!

Regrettably my father has recently been diagnosed with Alzheimer's and this debilitating illness resulted in him being taken into care. Since the outbreak of the Coronavirus, I have not been able to visit him for what seems to be a very long fourteen months.

My mother Brenda Barnes was born in 1938, in Ipswich and is almost three years younger than my father. She was brought up with her two sisters, living in a two up, two down terraced house on Bond Street, in what was called the sub-district of Ipswich Western. She went to school locally and soon after leaving met my father and was married. She often says 'I have done nothing in my life' however that is not true. For me she has fulfilled the roles of a loving mother, wife to my father and housekeeper, all without any financial reward.

She worked parttime at weekends and evenings during the week, leaving as soon as my father returned home from work. I used to accompany her on Saturdays to the local YMCA where she cooked and served in the café. At the time there were a lot of American servicemen living there. This was because there was a United States Air Force Base, Bentwaters, located close to Ipswich and accommodation was short on the camp. I used to watch them play on the pin ball machine and often they would leave me free games to play. One thing I used to look forward to when my mother worked in the evenings was that I could stay up late and she often brought home chips and ice cream as a treat. My mother's cooking was not bad, it was just a bit strange in the way she would combine food types. One of her dishes used to be mashed potatoes and a green salad, and that was it! No ham slices, chicken, or pork pie, it was totally absent of any meat. A very bland meal even if you were a vegetarian, I wasn't!

My mother always washed our clothes in the kitchen sink,

often in cold water causing her hands to turn purple when the hot from the storage tank ran out. Don't forget this was in the 1960's and a washing machine was relatively expensive, classed as an unnecessary luxury (certainly by my father) and therefore rare in working class homes. She would hang the clothes on the washing line out in the back garden to dry. Because of the wet weather, they would stay there for days or eventually be brought in when my father lit the open fire in the front room, the only form of heating in the house. Frequently my mother had to go outside in the mornings to bring in the washing when there had been an overnight frost. She would return with a hand full of clothes that looked like rigor mortis had set in. They were as stiff as a board. She would place them in front of the fire on clothes rails until they dried. This used to annoy me because all of the heat radiating from the fire was blocked from getting to me. However at least the condensation made droplets of water on the windows for me to draw patterns on.

During my childhood there was one other thing that froze in the back garden, in this case to death, my older sister Ruth's pet rabbit. It stayed outside throughout the year, in a hutch on top of a concrete coal bunker with only old newspaper for its bedding. My father was never one for pets, so it wasn't allowed in the house, even during the cold, dark months of winter. My father went to feed it one day and brought it back in to show us that it was dead and as stiff as my mother's washing had been on those frosty mornings. The rabbit looked like it had just been pulled out of a freezer. It was completely solid, and my father thought it was hilarious as he lifted it up by its hind legs and spun it around like a wind vane.

I'm not trying to make out that my family had it hard in the past, we lived like most working class people in the 1960's. But as a child I will never forget having to venture out on cold, wet nights by myself to the outside toilet. While sitting there watching an array of spiders hanging from the ceiling I would pray that one wouldn't drop down onto my head or worse, that I would get kidnapped by a passer-by!

As I have already implied, my father never had much time, sympathy and/or money for animals. When I was about nine years old, he sent me with our unwell Welsh Border Collie dog, Sheba, to the RSPCA, simply because he would not pay for any veterinary fees. I had to walk the three miles there and back. The vet examined the dog and said, 'She is very ill and you will need to bring her back for me to put her down, after you have spoken to your parents'. On my return home my father said to me 'Oh well, you'll have to take her'. The next day he left it for me to walk Sheba to her final resting place. After the vet took poor Sheba from me, I started to walk home feeling absolutely devastated. I found it hard to hold back the tears, the beech trees on the side of the road casting a shadow that reached right down into my heart. I had been attached to the dog and found it very hard to cope with not having her anymore. When I got home my father didn't even ask how I got on. I'm sure he had a smirk on his face because of his financial savings. He was pleased possibly because he wouldn't have to pay for any more dog food and had saved on veterinary fees by using the ploy of sending his youngest son to the vet, so that the story of our family having no money for the treatment on Sheba was more plausible.

Raising four children and working part time was hard enough, but my mother also had to suffer the psychological stress of seeing both her sons go off to join the Royal Marines Commandos at a time when the 'Troubles' in Northern Ireland (NI) were still on going. To make things worse, she had to endure the pain as I went off to war at the age of nineteen. For both my parents it must have been torturous to watch the Falklands War nightly reports on television by John Nott, the then Secretary for defence, and praying that I was safe. Now she has another battle, to watch as my father deteriorates with his Alzheimer's.

<u>My Paternal Grandfather.</u>

It is impossible to trace my father's ancestry. His father William Charles Barnes was an orphan in India, from what I had been led to believe was of English descent, but after some recent family gossip it could be German. My great grandfather allegedly had an affair with his secretary, an Indian woman. The result, an illegitimate child, my grandfather. If you take a minute to look at the photograph a few pages on of my paternal grandfather, you can make your own conclusions. With the smart but non ostentatious suit jacket, combed straight black hair and a delicately groomed moustache, he appears to me to have a strange resemblance to the picture of Adolf Hitler, when he is with British Prime Minister Neville Chamberlain at their handshake on Sept 23rd, 1938, allegedly bringing home to the UK 'peace in our time'.

Why my grandfather was an outcast is unclear, but I have heard some of my relations refer to him as a bastard (this was not meant in a derogatory manner). My alleged illegitimate grandfather married another Anglo Indian, possibly of Irish origins with the maiden name of Keenan. I recently carried out some research and have found that her great grandfather enlisted in D Troop, The Horse Artillery, aged nineteen. William Keenan had joined in Dublin and embarked for the Madras on February 24, 1825. He was later invalided out, as a bombardier, on 31st October 1838 and passed away in July 1862 aged 57. Why mention my grandmother now? Well, she was a Roman Catholic, her husband converted and subsequently I was brought up within this religious backdrop, one that has had an influence on my life.

I have no affinity to Ireland and would class myself as English – yes, a rarity, an English Roman Catholic (RC). I believe that RC's only make up approximately nine percent of the UK population. The fact that I was a religious minority never entered my thoughts, until I was a teenager. As I was growing up, for a majority of the time, I played on what was a waste land area (now owned by the council and described as an urban wildlife site) with some local boys, exploits to be discussed later. The site was about a mile away from where I lived with my parents. Walking home one summer's evening with a newfound friend who attended the local secondary school, he fired a question at me that was to ignite the bushes of religious discrimination awareness inside me. The query was 'are you a racist?' I replied very proudly 'No, I'm a Roman Catholic'. The boy turned his head, stared me in the eye and said, 'Oh dear', ran off and never spoke to me again. At the time there were three burning questions or issues that arose from this incident. What was a 'racist?' I didn't know, were they some rival gang of boys or even worse, Norwich City football supporters? The second was, wasn't he a RC as well, isn't everyone? Lastly, why did he run off like that?

It wasn't until some months later that I discovered, by looking in a dictionary, what a racist was and thought oh no, I'm not one of those! I couldn't stop laughing to myself about my misunderstanding of the word and the confusion it had caused me. What a pillock! The lad that had asked me the question must have thought I had gone mad.

When I discovered that most of my friends outside of school were non-Catholics, questions entered my mind about who I was and what others thought of me. This led to some loss of confidence. I thought I was different because I attended church and a different school. I can remember one lad saying that I went to a 'Special School' and therefore was 'mental'. Another person said to me that Catholics don't allow blood transfusions and when I pointed out that that was Jehovah Witness's I could feel myself getting angry at his ignorance. I wondered what some people were told about RC's; devil worshippers, witches or even politicians infiltrating the very structure of Great Britain, of free will itself, with a hidden agenda to rule the country if not the world? But to be fair, most of my close friends never mentioned anything about religion to me. Also, something else I found out and thought was funny was that the boy who had asked me the question 'was I a racist' had ran off because he realised that he was late for his dinner and panicked! Apparently, he was 'grounded' for two weeks, blamed me for walking too slow on our way home, and that was the reason for him not talking to me since!

My religious upbringing did lead to some moral questioning by me in future years. One was seeing the religious symbols carried or worn by some of the Argentine soldiers during the Falklands War. In my mind I had a bit of an internal conflict with Catholicism and my role at the time, but, as a professional soldier, I brushed these thoughts aside.

Returning back to my paternal grandfather. With eleven children I should imagine that he had very little leisure time or financial resources to spend on himself. My father has very few memories of him in India except that he enjoyed a drink and shooting. I was told that the alcoholic drink he consumed was a concoction made of any vegetable available at the time, normally potatoes, sugar and other bits and pieces that were fermented in jars and made somewhere in the city of Bombay. The spirit was stored in a bicycle inner tube, and would be brought in person by a cyclist, slung around his waist. The bottom end was tightly tied in a knot, the upper end with a tie made of string that could open for easy access to pour out the contents. The Russian Soldiers, during their relatively short tours of Afghanistan from 1979 to 1989, reportedly drank antifreeze taken from vehicles. This contained a small percentage of alcohol and was downed to dull their mostly negative experiences. The Russians only had to sustain this drink and war footing for as long as their posting lasted. My poor grandfather on the other hand had no reprieve, no choice, his situation was permanent. William Charles Barnes' escape was to drink this spirit with an 'essence of Dunlop' or nothing. Imagine the taste, especially after it had been wrapped around someone's sweaty waist as they cycled from one house to the next!

After a belly full of this alcoholic beverage, my Grandad, armed with his double-barrelled shot gun went off shooting. He shot at any unsuspecting duck, wild boar, or snake that crossed his path. With no care for public safety, he took aim and dispatched any fauna off to its maker. I'm only pleased that in his drunken stupor he didn't wander off into the jungle where tigers roamed. The consequence would have been fatal for the tiger or Grandad or both!

Sadly William Charles Barnes died of tuberculosis shortly after arriving in England in 1953, at the age of 54 years, leaving nine children and a wife, Lillian Beatrice Barnes, ten years his younger. One of the grievances I have with my maker is that I never had the opportunity to meet my paternal grandfather and this has left a bit of an empty space, a void, an incomplete part of my life I will never be able to fill.

Below, my paternal grandfather William Charles Barnes, who regrettably, I was never to meet.

My Paternal Grandmother.

Lillian Beatrice Barnes was a quiet lady who rarely spoke. When she did talk she did so softly and with a hint of an Indian accent. Often she would just smile at me rather than make conversation. The other thing I remember is that she kept budgies in a cage in the living room and sometimes let them out so they could spread their wings, oh and do a poo behind the bookshelves! My family frequently went to her house in the late 1960's early 70's where she lived with her two sons Richard and Reggie. The rest of their siblings had left home. Sometimes she would cook for us mouth-watering, authentic Indian curries and rice with side dishes like samosas. This tradition thankfully was continued long after her death, by my aunties.

In the overgrown grass in her unkept back garden, my older brother Gavin found a tortoise. We named him Henry and he became a part of the family for over thirty years, until Sharon my wife fed him, and he died the next day. He obviously didn't have the same constitution as me!

For some reason, from an early age I was given tea to drink by the adults in my family. Why this hot beverage I'm not sure, perhaps a reminder of India? Once, my grandmother left my older brother and myself in her kitchen, each with a cup of tea and a large bowl of sugar. The cups were made of clear glass, so you could see their contents. As a child I had and still have today, a very sweet tooth. Leaving a full bowl of sugar out on a table in front of me was fatal and a temptation I could not resist. I poured half the bowl into my cup, spilling the rest everywhere. A few minutes later Nanna Barnes returned to the kitchen and started to complain loudly about the amount of sugar I had used. I thought she was grumbling about the sugar spilt all over the table and floor. She however, had spotted the sugar, undissolved, taking up about three quarters of my cup. Nanna Barnes started shouting, so in came my parents to see what was happening. They saw my cup and the sugar, of course I blamed my brother!

After the death of her husband in 1953, Lillian Beatrice Barnes continued living in council housing in Ipswich, until she passed away in July,1980.

My Maternal Grandmother.

My maternal Grandmother Lillian (yes, the same first name as Nanna Barnes) was caring, helpful, loving and, above all, fun. She too, like my other grandmother, was slight in stature, and wore her hair cut short. Nanna was of local Suffolk stock and had a dislike of people waffling on. She was a mean force for a small lady. At 14 years old she was sent to Essex to work as a maid at St Osyth Priory, which contained a large house and estate. Transport was haphazard and costly. In those days, the 27 miles from Ipswich was like being deported to Australia. She had left her family and friends for the first time and I can remember her telling me of the tiny room she stayed in and that she was very home sick at first.. As a maid she had to work long hours for little pay or holiday. My mother always equated this work to slavery, but this was the 'norm' for working class girls in the early part of the twentieth century. In fact, she was grateful for having employment.

I have fond memories of Nanna or 'Bingo Lill' as she was known by many in her later years. This given nick name was because she frequently visited bingo halls, particularly at weekends. After the death of her husband Victor in 1980, going to bingo was her means of socialising with friends and getting out of the council flat she lived in on her own.

Hours before the bingo hall doors opened, she would make her way to the centre of Ipswich carrying her pens, flask and a pack of playing cards. Sitting outside the entrance to the bingo hall playing card games was used by her and her friends not only to pass the hours away before opening and the stampede for the best and luckiest chairs, but also to do a little fun gambling. About three to four old women could be seen with their heads down, playing cards in their hands, as bets were placed. On one occasion a police constable on foot stopped and observed what was going on. He informed the ladies that betting on the street was illegal and asked them to stop. He then went on his way. As soon as the constable had gone out of sight, the playing cards reappeared and the betting continued. Unluckily for Nanna and her friends, a few minutes later the same police officer returned and they were caught 'flagrante delicto,' arrested and taken to the central police station. She and her friends were fined and bound over not to bet again in a public space. In her late seventies she now had a criminal record! Not what she had envisaged as she set off to play bingo on a Sunday afternoon. Another vice she had was smoking. She continued this habit until she passed away at the age of eighty-nine.

My Maternal Grandfather.

My maternal grandfather was, as a current fast-food chain might use the term, a 'go large' person. Victor Arthur was well over six feet tall and had a considerable presence about him. He had shovel sized hands and wore shoes that the QE2 could have docked in. If I was ever sitting in a room with him, I was aware of this enormous silent aura flowing from his body saying, 'I'm watching you'. This was not unnerving for me, rather, as a young child I found it quite comforting; this paternal figure looking after me. I suppose I stood in awe of him. His physical appearance was typical of a person brought up during both world wars. With a clean-shaven face and head, he always wore a suit with shirt and tie, immaculately polished shoes and smoked a pipe. He had a John Wayne walking gait with the swagger to match as he moved and would never step out of the way for people he would pass head on, on the pavement. He used to say, 'if he ain't moving nor am I' and because of his size it could be quite intimidating for the person walking towards him. Often I would see others sidestep or individuals that had encountered him before cross over the road.

Victor's verbal communication, again like my paternal grandmother, was limited. In fact he rarely spoke. He was very happy left alone sitting in his armchair and smoking his pipe. He was a very solitary, unassuming man who enjoyed quietness and his own company. Let me give you an example of how silent he would be. During my childhood, on summer Sunday afternoons my grandad and I would go fishing. We walked from my parents' house the half mile to a pond on the site of an old, abandoned quarry. I sensed that he used the fishing trips as an excuse to escape the noise and chat caused by my family back home. The only discourse we had on our fishing trip, week after week went like this;

Granddad: 'nothing caught again this week'.

My reply: 'yes Grandad'.

Grandad: 'time to go then'

Me: 'yes Grandad'

And off we went, walking back home in the silence of our own thoughts.

Only once did our conversation go beyond this. It was a very hot afternoon, kids were paddling, making waves and throwing stones in the pond near my float. Because of this I thought that I had no chance of catching anything. What did annoy me was they kept on saying to me and my silent grandad, that we were stupid and that there were no fish in the pond. After about an hour, without a hint of any fish taking a bite, I thought 'one last cast' and then we would pack up and go. My float had been stationary for about ten minutes, then without any warning it took a dive. I had to strike quickly and to my surprise, and the amazement of the doubting on lookers, I reeled in a Perch that for its large size, looked out of proportion to its small surroundings. I have a vivid memory of my grandad's eyes and mouth widen and he shouted, 'My god'. On the way back home he never stopped smiling and kept repeating 'You showed 'em my boy!'

2. GROWING UP.

My Childhood.

When my primary school, St Pancras RC, celebrated its fiftieth year in existence on its current site, I was asked if I could go into the school and do a talk on what it was like when I had been a pupil there in the late 1960's early 70's and how things have changed since. I decided to take up their request.

I really enjoyed my time talking to different aged groups. They were fun, and one cohort particularly liked my story about school meals. I had explained to them how strict things were compared to today. At lunch, we had to sit on a designated table and chair, were allowed only one cup of water to drink and had to eat everything up. I told the class that the one meal I really disliked was the Lamb and even today I can't stand the sight of it, let alone the taste. The food St Pancras received was cooked at a nearby secondary school and brought in by a van. It often arrived cold and could not be reheated because there were no ovens (microwaves had been invented but were not freely available in the UK). The Lamb contained hardly any meat, it was mainly gristle, bathed in its own fat that gave it an anaemic appearance. I really didn't think it had been cooked long enough. You had to chew on it for ages to try and break it down into swallowable pieces. To me the taste and texture were disgusting. It was like a mixture of cod liver oil and a lump of lard slowly working its way down my gullet. This sluggish movement was made worse because I only had that one glass of water to help speed it on its way.

Before we were allowed to go out and play for the rest of the lunch time, we had to leave our table, approach the dinner lady (and it was always a female) and show her our empty plates. There was no chance of hiding behind a fellow pupil and slipping your plate on the collection trolley before she saw you because we were only permitted to go up one at a time. I couldn't stomach the Lamb, it made me want to retch. Rather than eating it, I decided to hide it in my mouth by pushing it into the sides of my cheeks like a hamster would store its food, sometimes even under my tongue if I was given a particularly large portion. There was no other way. I thought about putting it in my trouser pockets when no one was watching, but the consistency of the meat combined with the gravy would leave a smelly, wet patch and having to try and concoct a story for my mother when I got home as to why my trousers were in such a state was too much of a burden for me. I was never a good liar! So up I marched to the dinner lady, my jaws clenched tightly, careful not to let any seepage from the sides of my mouth, praying that no one asked me a question and wanted a response.

Feeling nervous, I presented my empty plate and thankfully was given the all clear. I ran out of the hall, found the nearest lavatory and spat the lamb into a toilet bowl, flushed it, washed my mouth out and went outside to play, feeling quite pleased with myself!

The children and the form teacher, all who were listening to my story, fell about laughing at this before I continued. About ten minutes later I finished my talk, had a coffee in the teacher's staff room, then left to walk home, thinking nothing else of it. Several weeks later I was in the school playground, waiting to pick up my daughter, when the form teacher of the class I had spoken to previously approached me. 'Mr Barnes I've got something to show you'. As we walked to his classroom, he explained that after my talk he had asked each pupil to draw a picture of one thing that they remembered about the changes that had happened at the school over the years. In the classroom, spread out on Mr Glower's desk were their pictures. A few had drawn a computer, or calculator, things we never had available in the 1960/70's. However, a great many had drawn a stickman, leaning over a toilet, vomiting food into it. One even had a bubble above the stickman's head with the word's 'Horrible lamb!'

Mr Tynan, the headmaster of St Pancras R C school was a devout Roman Catholic, brought up in Yorkshire, had a no-nonsense approach and a bit of a temper, hence the nick name 'Time Bomb Tynan'. As I have already mentioned, Mr Tynan had three sons at the school during the time I was there, Joseph (Joe) was in my class. On more than one occasion Joe and I were sent out of class by the teacher to see the headmaster because of our bad behaviour. One memorable time, the pair of us waited for ages outside Mr Tynan's office and when he eventually arrived, the pair of us got the giggles. Exactly why, I can't remember. To me this humorous situation escalated when the headmaster said to Joe 'Wait until I get you home and tell your mother'. As Joe and I watched each other receive his punishment, the dreaded 'smack' on the backside, far from making us regret our actions, it made us laugh uncontrollably. Upholding his nick name, Mr Time Bomb Tynan lost his temper. This loss of control manifested itself in a raised voice and, by the sight of the redness in his face, blood pressure too. After a shouting frenzy in which he almost exploded and possibly due to a sore hand, Time Bomb gave up and sent us back to class.

The main hall, in fact the only hall in the school, was entered by double doors from the main atrium. The hall was square and measured approximately ten by ten metres and five in height. As you entered the hall, on the far wall facing you there was a large cross placed there just to remind you that this was a catholic school and we are all sinners! Below this was a stage with a piano facing it and to the right a kitchen with a varnished wooden roller shutter which was only opened up at lunch time. On the far left wall there were two large windows strategically placed there, I guess, to let in some natural light. To the left of the doorway in which you entered was a recess. In this gap was a small library with shelves at various heights on all three walls and several mobile trolleys full of books. The floor was made of stone block bricks placed in a straight stack bond fashion (parallel lines) and was highly polished every day by the caretaker. The main hall had a variety of uses: assemblies, school mass, canteen, physical education, music lessons and watching television. There was only one black and white TV in the whole school. With every pupil in attendance I can remember watching the first landing on the moon, July 20th 1969, and Mr Tynan getting overly excited, shouting ' Watch children, this is it, this is it!' as Neil Armstrong made that first historical step on to the moon surface.

My classes' music lessons at St Pancras were during the winter term, timetabled once a week, and just after our first break in the morning. At the time, no permanently employed teachers could play the piano so they paid a middle aged, short, plumb, spinster, Ms Stubbs to do so. For music lessons, my cohort were escorted into the main hall by Miss Swift, our personal tutor, and sat on the ground, in nice, neat rows in front of the piano. Miss Swift would then go back to the classroom and leave us under the supervision of the music teacher.

I never knew why, but for some reason the piano was always left facing the stage, therefore Ms Stubbs played the piano with her back to us. Anyhow, I would always plan to be in the back row so I could mime and pretend to sing, but also participate in and try to win a game that we had invented. The idea of this game was that you slowly, but surely, made your way to the back of the hall, furthest from the piano. The winner was the first person to reach the library recess and hide behind the book trolleys before Ms Stubbs knew you were missing. We did this while sitting, slowly pushing backwards with our two feet at the same time on the ground, extending our legs so our bottom slid along the highly polished floor. Then bringing our legs back up towards our body and repeating the process in a caterpillar like fashion. In between songs Ms Stubbs would turn from her seat at the piano to speak to the class but she never clicked on to what we were doing. Surely she must have noticed as the back row of kids slowly moved off in the distance, getting further away and some eventually disappearing? All I knew was she wore glasses, possibly because she was severely short sighted!

One day in a desperate attempt to win the race, I cheated. The rest of the class, apart from the back row of course, were happily singing and Ms Stubbs was banging away on the old 'ivories'. I spotted that Robert Matuzczyk, my fellow 'back rower' was getting close to the library. I looked forward checking that all was clear, jumped to my feet, turned, ready to run the last few steps to reach the library first and win. Alas I didn't check behind me before I stood up. As I took a step forward with my head down, I smashed straight into an unknown object and landed on top of it. Mr Tynan, the headmaster, lay horizontal on the floor with me just to his side. I was so close to him that I could smell his breath and felt the bristle of his beard on my face. I'm sure I heard him swear! I was smacked on the arse again and told I was beyond redemption. During another music lesson, we soon became bored and made up a new game. It wasn't really a game with rules and regulations or teams, it was simply throwing things at each other. After playing football on the grass during morning break time just before the music lessons, our shoes would be covered in dirt. We entered the main hall straight after play without cleaning our footwear off. If it had been raining, the soles would be caked in wet mud, particularly where the heel joins the sole. We would peel this mud off and make balls from it. Then we would throw it, not just at those participating in the 'war,' but also pupils on the front rows, aiming for the back of their heads. One 'nutter' in the group threw a mud ball at Ms Stubbs while she was playing the piano. It was a good shot and hit her right on the shoulder. Still sitting, she turned around to face the class to see who the culprit was. At the same time her right hand slipped, knocked the heavy wooden piano keyboard cover on to her left hand, trapping her fingers. She let out a scream, ran out of the hall with tears running down her face (from pain, shock or both I'm not sure) never to be seen again. Music lessons were cancelled from then on, well at least for our class!

I try to think of the reasons why I had been a particularly badly behaved child in school, and I have come up with a reason (well at least part), that I can try and use as an excuse. While in St Pancras school I was moved up a year and then back down, twice, therefore had no stability. This sounds plausible, however my point falls apart because Robert Matuzczyk had gone through the same process and was accepted and eventually went to a public fee-paying school for his secondary education. The one benefit that I did have is that I had a damn sight more friends in school than anyone else because of this switching of classes and mixing with individuals from both of them.

My love of fishing and come to think of it, anything to do with water, started when I used to go crab fishing with a net off Felixstowe Pier while my older brother used a rod. However, this meant being accompanied by an adult and money for a bus, so I adapted and went closer to home. During the long hot summers of the 70's I spent a lot of time freshwater fishing. Riding on my push bike with my rod fastened by string to the frame, I would leave home in the early morning, get to the River Gipping and stay there all day, either on my own or with friends, I wasn't really bothered. Even during the winter, I would go. I had no fear of going on my own and the calm, peaceful, stillness of the early morning with its cool, fresh air and the almost motionless river water, looking like a mirror reflecting the blue sky above, all made me feel at peace.

In recent years I have told my wife about the different types of fish bait I used. Mostly it would be worms, dug out from one of my parents next door neighbours compost heaps, simply because they were free. If I could afford it, I would go to the local fishing tackle shop and buy a half pint of maggots. To delay them turning into inactive chrysalis and therefore no good as bait, I would slow down their metabolism by storing them in my parent's fridge. My wife was horrified, however not as much as when I told her how I used to revive them. I would take one maggot at a time out of my bait box and warm them up by putting them in my mouth, letting them stay there until they started crawling. My wife said she would never kiss me again! I'm glad I didn't use this story as a chat up line when we first met. Oh, by the way on our first date, one night in a drunken stupor, I fell asleep in my plate of uneaten curry at an Indian restaurant in Ipswich and when woken up I made Sharon pay half for the meal. I sure know how to show a girl a good time!

As a child, going on holiday to Felixstowe and staying on caravan sites, as we did nearly every year, two things of significance happened. The first was that I was employed selling donuts from a hut on the sea front. I didn't mind spending some of my holiday working, earning money, cash that later I could spend on slot machines or even playing bingo. Secondly, I was able to wander into the docks, right up to the water's edge and watch the ships as they arrived, docked and then sailed off. Today this would be impossible. Felixstowe Docks is the UK's largest container port. It has enlarged in size and capacity since the 1970's. Security has increased and each entrance now has static posts with their own Police and Custom and Excise officers, who patrol behind large fences.

On one occasion I walked the short distance from the caravan site to the docks with my brother and father. We got to the quay side and looked down on to a wooden pier. There were two Ridged Raiders tied up to it. We watched as two Royal Marines Commandos, wearing their distinctive green berets and dry suits, loaded up their boats with stores. They then untied their craft and set off out into the estuary and headed for the open sea. This was to be my first sight of Royal Marines Commandos. Back then Little did I know that I would grow up to be one.

The Dales Area.

The Dales area, unlike its namesake, the Yorkshire Dales, is not a vast wilderness but only fourteen and a half acres of old industrial land, in suburban Ipswich. It was where they used to excavate sand and clay to make bricks in furnaces. The site closed in 1959 and lay unused until the council bought it. Now it is a protected wildlife area for the local community. It has three access points on to the road, great for escaping when being chased, so I'm told! With two ponds and undulating terrain it made a fantastic location to play when I was young.

The top section of the Dales was sold for housing in the mid 1970's. While they were building there, Joe Tynan and myself used to climb up the scaffolding outside the half constructed houses and jump off into the sand mounds left next to the cement mixers. This building site was also a place to 'borrow' pieces of wood, nails and even rolls of insulation to build our dens with. We had ideas for grand designs but found them to be too difficult to build, so we kicked down what we had done, or for fun, set light to them.

The Dales had an abundance of natural resources. We would cut branches from trees where they had divided to form a Y shape. At about ten inches in length, we would wrap an old bicycle rubber innertube around the Y shape wood, leaving a length dangling in the middle, secure it with tape and there we had our home-made catapults. At weekends I would meet up with some local lads and play 'Attack the Hill'. We split into two groups, one was to protect the Hill, the other to attack it. The Hill was in the centre of the Dales, with steep sides, covered in foliage and only had one path to it, I spent hours attacking and defending that Hill. It was a bit like the 1987 American Film 'Hamburger Hill,' about an actual attack in Vietnam by USA Marines, but a lot less blood thirsty and thankfully in our action, no deaths. Although, I did end up with six stitches on my upper lip and a permanent scar because someone threw a stone in my direction, it landed on the ground in front of me. I thought it had missed and didn't bother to move. The stone had other ideas and decided to bounce up to head height and catch me right on the top lip, splitting it and sending, what seemed like pints of blood, gushing down onto my t- shirt. I wasn't mortally wounded but felt like a hero for 'taking one for the boys'.

One 'weapon' we used were long, thin, sticks, preferably from a Willow tree because they were very flexible and therefore had a good whipping action. With a knife we would make a spike at the thin end. On the spike we would load our ammunition, either a crab apple or a piece of clay dug from the hill side (the stuff they used to excavate to make bricks) termed 'Pug,' hence the sticks were named 'Pug Sticks'. With a Pug Stick I could launch the Pug or crab apple much further than just throwing them.

One time, we all stood on top of the Hill getting bored. Someone decided we should attack anyone travelling along a footpath that ran near the base of the Hill, about fifty metres away. To our delight an old man came along on his moped and we unleashed hell on him. Clay and crab apples rained down, some hitting his moped and one apple striking him directly on the helmet. We all cheered. At this point the old man had had enough. He turned his moped around and headed for the path that led straight up to the Hill where we were standing. Our joy turned to panic as we thought he might be in with a chance of catching one of us. I threw my stick away, thus getting rid of any evidence, ran as fast as I could through tiny, rarely used, overgrown footpaths, only passable on foot, making it impossible for a pursuing moped. Eventually making my escape on to the road via one of the three main exits. It wasn't until I got home and my adrenaline levels fell that I noticed that my hands and lower arms were covered in blood and a rash, To clear my way through the paths, I had grabbed hold of Hawthorn Bushes which tore through my flesh and Stinger Nettles that had caused the rash.

Castle Hill.

As I grew older, I spent a lot of time on a local recreation park called Castle Hill named after the council house estate nearby and an 19th Century house. I used to play football and hang around the playground which had a variety of different rides such as seesaws, swings and a witches hat. The witches hat was a cone shaped swing, with wooden seats at the bottom, on a central pole, which went in circles and wobbled unpredictably. The pinnacle of the central pole, for some reason, on every one of them including the one at Castle Hill Park, was painted red and it looked like a nipple. We named it 'The Witches Tit'. I believe the 'Elf and safety geeks,' as Terry Wogan used to call them, deemed them unsafe and removed them all in the mid 1980's, or was it because of the vulgar name we called them?

One summers day, straight after school, Steven Tinsley, Colin Gilbert, Robert Matuzczyk, and myself, went to the park to play football. We did this quite often and sometimes didn't go home until dusk. We were playing at the top end of Castle Hill park where a fence separated us from a road. Using trees as goal posts, I was enjoying the kick around when all of a sudden, a car screeched to a halt. Out jumps Steven's father, a tall man, with a moustache and who, like my maternal grandfather, always wore a suit. On foot, at some speed, he entered the park through a nearby gate, shouting at Steven with a slight hint of a Welsh accent, 'Where the hell have you been? You've missed your dinner and your mother was worried'. As he approached Steven, he grabbed him by the ears (remember my previous description of those) and dragged him back to the car. We couldn't stop laughing once they had both left. We were punished for using Steven's ears as a blank canvas, however for his father to use them as a form of punishment was okay, this we deemed unfair! You see, even his father recognised the potential of those large ears.

One more quick Story about Steven's father. He liked nothing more than, after a day at work, sitting in his armchair watching the television and having a smoke. One Thursday evening three of us went to Steven's house and sat on a settee in the same room as his father. Purchased from a joke shop, we planted an exploding cigarette in his father's packet of twenty Marlborough. We sat in total silence pretending to watch the telly and in great anticipation, trying not to giggle. When the joke cigarette exploded Steven's father exclaimed, 'Good god!' as his face was covered in black soot and his legs in tobacco. The only thing that had saved his face and lips from being burnt was the filter in the end of the cigarette. It was one of the funniest things I had ever seen and needless to say, we were banned from the house.

In Castle Hill park, the trees we used as goal posts produced red, plum shaped, inedible fruit once a year. We used these 'plums' as missiles to throw at each other in acting out war games. Not content with just throwing them at each other, we carried out an artillery attack on the park keeper's shed but got bored because we found out that he wasn't in there. Protected by the park's perimeter fence that separated us from a nearby road, we then decided to do a 'hit' on a passing cyclist. The cyclist was a middle-aged man, travelling uphill. Our first launch of plums just missed, landing in front of him, he turned his head and shouted in a deep voice 'fuck off'. Realising there were too many of us to confront he sped up and, at a safe distance and out of breath, finished off with a scowl 'you bunch off cunts!'

As per usual things progressed for the worse. One member of our group thought it would be a great laugh to ambush a passing bus, so we did. The first bus we attacked was a double decker and I will never forget the sight of the passengers jumping out of their seats as the plums hit the windows where they were sitting. The pièce de résistance was when one lad jumped over the fence ahead of the bus and launched several plums at the driver. The plums exploded on impact, their red juice, pips and skin slowly sliding down the front of the windscreen making it impossible for the driver to see out of it.

One other place I used to spend time was at Castle Hill Community Centre. Originally it was an eight bedroom 'Gentleman's residence', built in 1893 on the site of a Roman villa. It used to be surrounded by open fields, but now it is enclosed by a large white brick wall at the front, wire fences at the back and 1940/50's built houses on the sides. At the back of the house there was a level, grassed, open space about half the size of a football pitch, two fenced off, tarmacked, flood lit tennis courts/five a side football pitches and wooden huts reminiscent of military accommodation, used as changing rooms. When there were no organised games on the courts we used to play football on them. If they were being used, we would go onto the grassed area. During the summer instead of playing football we played cricket, both sports I grew to love. It was here at Castle Hill Community Centre, as a ten-year-old, I had my first experience of smoking. I was given a cigarette, one box of matches and under the influence of some 'older boys' encouraged to go on my own, hide under a bush and have a smoke. They watched from a distance under the pretence that they were keeping a look out. After several attempts with matches and draws on the cigarette I managed to get it going. I now thought I was a real grown up. One of the older boys came over and encouraged me to inhale the smoke. I did and immediately coughed, felt dizzy and was almost sick, much to the amusement of the big boys. I said to myself 'I am never in my life, doing that again' and I haven't!

Like all younger brothers, I too longed to be able to play with my older brother and his friends, who would often visit our house and play out in the back garden. Sometimes they would let me join in. My brother's interest in weapons started roughly at the same time as his interest in the military. At fourteen years old he acquired a 1.77 air rifle. One day he was in the back garden and I went out to see what he was doing with his friends. My brother told me that they were shooting each other with the rifle. He said it didn't hurt, especially if you got hit where your clothing was thick and loose, he promised. My brother volunteered me to his friends to be the target, told me to turn around and without any warning, shot me in the back. It hurt like hell and I ran off in shock and pain.

Several weeks later, in our back garden, I was playing darts with my brother and like all sibling's, we started to argue. With the 'shot in the back' incident still fresh in my mind and my temper rising, I threw a dart at him, as hard as I could. It struck him clean between the eyes. Shocked, he pulled it out and it had left a deep hole, with blood leaking out. My brother has never forgotten this incident with the dart and he often mentions it in conversation, especially when introducing me to people. I always counter this story with my account of how, at the age of fourteen, he shot his younger brother, in the back. Groups and individuals often look at both of us in disbelief, shake their heads and comment on what a pair of delinquents we must have been.

My Teens.

In my teenage years the fishing was dropped, and I became more involved in activities such as playing football, knock down ginger and scrumping during the summer. Knock down ginger was done mostly during the winter months when the nights were dark and the chances of getting seen and therefore caught, would be reduced. Normally this involved someone knocking on the front door of a house, then running away before it could be answered. We did it differently. You lost if you ran away first and would be ridiculed later by the rest. Inversely, to win you had to be the last to run. However, if you stayed and saw the occupants answer, you had a greater risk of being caught.

As winter went on our group grew in number and eventually swelled to approximately twenty, with most boys from the local secondary school. I didn't know some of the lads in the group, all I knew was they didn't care what they did, they appeared to have no morals or fear. Instead of knocking on doors they started to throw stones at them and windows as well. This escalated until one lad picked up a household brick and threw it at a front door. You could hear the thud and smash of glass as the brick made connection, then the sound of laughter and the running of twenty pairs of feet down the road. I sensibly, for a change, decided it was time to stop and left this group.

Recently, one of my childhood friends' father, that I hadn't seen for over forty years, stopped to have a chat with me as I was passing his house while he was pottering around in his front garden. He recalled my surname but not my first.. As soon as I told him he immediately said, 'Ah you're the one that made my mother in law scream when you put a condom (thankfully unused) through my letter box!' I always seemed to get the blame for everything even if it wasn't me.

A school friend had a love of motorbikes and somehow, he got hold of a working Honda 50cc moped. We would take it from his house, pushing it several miles along foot paths to where my school's cross-country route was. This allowed us to ride along fairly level public footpaths through the countryside. Once there, we would take turns at racing up and down the tracks, with no care in the world nor a helmet. I loved the experience of speeding along, feeling the wind in my face and the sense of freedom it gave me. The only fear I had was being caught by an irate farmer. Later, my same school friend sold this Honda moped and got another, second hand one, this time with a larger engine, gears and clutch, both operated from the handlebars. On my first ride of this motorbike, I hadn't a clue how to change gear and when I pulled the clutch in I expected it would act as a break. It didn't and to my horror I continued on, straight into a hedge. Luckily, neither I nor the motorbike received serious harm.

It was around this time that I heard one of my uncles was selling his Puch Maxi 50cc, two stroke, moped. The price he was asking was an astronomical £50.00. I was nearly sixteen and soon legally allowed to ride a moped on the road. I became very excited at the thought of being able to get my own. I had a newspaper round, earning £1.20 a week, and with some delight I thought that I could save up and get it. I tried raising money anyway I could. Just before bonfire night we did penny for the guy. It was too much of an effort to make a Guy Fawkes, so several friends and I got hold of an old wheelbarrow, 'borrowed' from a nearby front garden where it had been kindly left unattended by its owner. One of us laid in the wheelbarrow, covered his face over with a hood and pretended to be the Guy. Knocking on doors of random houses, our subterfuge worked in most cases, partly because we claimed that we couldn't wheel the Guy up to the front door due to their path being too narrow. Once when I was lying in the wheelbarrow, pretending to be the lifeless Guy, I got the giggles as a house owner with his three young kids approached. One friend prodded me to try and stop me from laughing, this just made me worse. I thought I had been rumbled so I jumped out of the wheelbarrow, ready to run and make an escape. The three kids went hysterical as they thought the Guy had come to life. The father got angry and gave chase after us as we abandoned the wheelbarrow and scarpered, unfortunately, this time without any money, not even a penny for the Guy.

I didn't see my uncle for a couple of weeks and regrettably he had sold his moped by the time we did meet up. However, I managed to get hold of an old 125cc trials bike, again a Honda. I tried on many occasions to try and get it to work but without any success.

A friend, that claimed he had some mechanical knowledge said it was a problem with the carburettor not sending enough fuel to the engine. We spent ages placing our mouths over the fuel tank cap hole and blowing down hard in an attempt to increase the fuel pressure. We then tried to start the motorbike by pushing it up and down my garden. It never worked and all I ever had at the end of the day was a nasty rash around my mouth and headaches from the fumes.

Up to now I was the youngest child in the family and some of my possessions were hand me downs. When I went to secondary school, I had to wear my brother's old blazer. It was so worn out that my father had to sew on leather patches at the elbows. I didn't care because I thought it made me look intellectual; so long to fashion! The first bike I had was passed down to me by my sister. The bike was designed for girls, red, with white tyres, no cross bar and too small for me. I had no choice, it was either that or walk. My dream bike was a Raleigh Chopper and my friend had one for sale. The asking price of £15.00 sadly was beyond my reach. Hardly any of my friends parents or mine had cars to ask for lifts to go to places and I couldn't afford bus fares, so cycling was the best option. The second bike I inherited was a ladies, with a black frame and a wicker basket tied to the front handlebars. I was happy that at least it was an adult size and later I managed to take the basket off and put on trendy 'cow horn' handlebars. These handlebars allowed me to do wheelies and take part in races on cycle speedway tracks. This was my favourite bike but had a short life. One day I was giving a friend a 'seatie' (two on a bike) and he accidently stuck his foot in the front wheel sending us head over heels and writing the bike off. My last hand me down bike was my brother's and it was a racer, on which I could go much faster and for longer distances than the previous ones. With Colin Gilbert my classmate, and his brother David, two years older than us, we used to go on epic rides. We cycled to many Suffolk countryside and coastal towns and villages such as Orford, Framlingham, (now famed for the home of singer/song writer Ed Sheeran) and Felixstowe, doing over forty miles in a day, some achievement for thirteen-year-olds. On one cycle to Felixstowe, we took a short cut on the wrong side of a dual carriage way. A policeman caught us and took our false names and addresses down. We never cycled so fast back to Ipswich or ever returned to that stretch of road.

Up to when my brother, Gavin joined the Royal Marines, we both had to share a bedroom on the first floor above the sitting room in our family's terraced house. The pair of us were sent to bed at the same time and often found it hard to get to sleep, especially during the summer nights. So we used to play games while our parents watched television downstairs. Somebody had given us two old carpet holders, (very similar to a carboard toilet roll centre but ten times the size). We messed about with them up in our bedroom playing a kind of Chinese whispers. One end to speak through the other to hold to your ear to listen. I can't remember how or why we started to fight but as I got very angry, to defend myself I used the carpet holder as a large battering ram and decided to throw it at my brother. He dodged and I totally missed him. The carpet holder smashed through one of our bedroom windows. Like a failed missile, it went flying on past the sitting room window below, where my parents were sitting. The tube came crashing to earth and ended up on the grass in the front garden, followed by broken glass cascading like a heavy down pour of rain drops. I heard my parents going ballistic, my dad's thundering footsteps coming up the stairs, along the landing and into our room. I shouted in desperation and self-preservation, 'It was him,' pointing to my older brother who subsequently was on the receiving end of most of the rebuke as I giggled from underneath my bed sheets!

When my brother eventually left to join up and thankfully for my independence and sanity, I inherited my own bedroom. The room faced north and barely ever got any sunshine. It was always dull and during the winter months ice formed, not on the outside, but inside, the one and only window. My kind brother Gavin left me an electric hot air fan blower to help make it just bearable. Inside the fan I could see red hot filaments which I used to set light to things. By poking incense sticks past the safety guard, I found it easy to get them lit. When a friend visited, rather than just setting light to one, I had several on the go and we used them as jousting sticks to fight against each other. The game was fun but during our duels sparks fell from the incense sticks on to my bed sheets and the carpet, resulting in large burn holes in both. I hadn't realised the amount of fire damage until we smelt something acrid and stopped. Yet again I was in trouble with my parents for what I saw as an innocently acted out game and this time I was unable to hide under my bedsheets or blame Gavin.

During the summer months along with my 'local' friends I went scrumping, mainly for apples and pears. It was just as risky a business as knock down Ginger and we were often chased out of gardens, which added to the excitement. Again, going into people's back gardens and looking for fruit, took a turn for the worse. Someone, I believe it to be Pecker, decided we would have a competition to see how many back gardens in a block you could run through in a straight line, parallel to the road, obviously without getting caught. The winner was the first person to have successfully climbed every obstacle in their way enroute without deviation and appear on the road, at the other end of the block of houses. This was called 'Garden Hopping'. We all lined up and started together, as many as ten lads at a time. Someone shouted go and off we went, climbing the first fence. I can remember never having so much fun, with the hint of danger, as I ran through vegetable patches, jumped over ponds and accidentally broke wooden panels on fencing as I climbed over them. At one point I almost wet myself as I heard a cry of 'Oh bollocks'. I turned and saw one of my friends, who, to his credit, was trying to stick to the rules of running straight, had climbed on a shed roof, the roof collapsed and his leg was stuck. Apart from laughing, I did think 'that must have hurt'. I climbed my final fence and reached the road only to see most of the group had finished. The lad who had fallen through the shed roof appeared with blood showing through his jeans but we had no time for sympathy, we could hear the police sirens heading our way. Unknowingly, this illegal Garden Hopping, a kind of Parkour training before its time, gave me an introduction to the skills used for negotiating obstacles on assault courses in the Royal Marines.

When I was fourteen years old my mother had a friend around to our house. I noticed that the woman was pregnant. A few days later in our living room lay a pile of new nappies and 'baby things' which my mother had bought when out shopping. I thought she was just keeping these for her expectant friend that had recently visited. Over the next couple of weeks, the pile of nappies turned into a mound; it just got bigger and bigger. One day I returned home from school and thought what the hell is happening with all this stuff? I put the question to my parents, 'Why are you buying all these baby things'? My mother looked at me and said, 'Oh I'm pregnant, didn't anyone tell you?' I was the youngest up until then, with only two years difference between me and my older sister and a four year gap with my older brother. I thought 'typical, no-body tells me anything'. Later on in the day I went to Castle Hill Park to play football, and when I broke the news to my friends all they said is 'Eww, we know what your mum and dad have been up to!'

Football.

I loved playing football and represented both primary and secondary schools for several years. While at secondary school I can remember going to Portman Road, Ipswich Town Football Club's (I.T.F.C.) ground with two other lads for trials, but unfortunately, I never heard anything. At one trial, with my first kick of the ball I scored and thought, 'That should have impressed them,' but yet again the scouts must have been looking somewhere else and missed it! It didn't deter me from continuing to play football and I also really enjoyed going to watch it.

In my younger years and teens, I followed I.T.F.C. with a passion, initially being taken by my parents to home matches. Back in the 1970's and early 80's Ipswich boasted one of the top teams in the country. Two Ipswich managers had directly gone on to become England's; Sir Alf Ramsey and Sir Bobby Robson. The club had won various English League titles, the FA 1978 and UEFA 1981 cups. The club had several British internationals playing for them, such as Mick Mills (England Captain), Kevin Beattie, John Wark, Terry Butcher and Paul Mariner.

Up to his death in the late 1970's my maternal grandfather, Victor (or Vic as everyone used to call him in his retirement) worked part time at the Portman Road ground. He served at a bar in the notorious North Stand where the two sets of rival supporters stood, separated by fencing, barbed wire and lines of police on the terrace and below on the pitch, facing towards the crowd. After a time, even the area of play was obscured from view by more fencing at the front of the stand put there to prevent any pitch invasion by fans.

From the age of twelve to fourteen, for every home match I would meet Vic at 12.00 and he would sneak me into the ground for nothing. I stood around for hours waiting for the game to start at 15.00 and watched as the ground started to fill up and the singing start from both groups of supporters. I always found it strange that these mainly young men wanted to display their masculinity by singing, why not dancing or knitting instead? Anyhow, there was always an atmosphere of excitement, fear hate and aggression. Various objects were thrown over the dividing fences from home to away supporters and vice versa. Empty beer cans, cups full of urine and coins were used as ammunition. Once I got hit on the top of my head by a coin and apart from it leaving a large bruise, it bloody well hurt!

It was standing only in the North Stand. Seating in the side stands was for the rich and not the unruly working class. On the terrace, the concrete steps sloping down to the pitch, were broken up by waist high metal barriers. At one match in a packed North Stand, during a crowd surge, I was pushed against one of these barriers and badly dislocated two fingers. To get medical attention from the St John's staff I had to get on to the pitch. They took me to the halfway line and through into a room to see the duty doctor. He asked me if I wanted to watch the match or go to hospital, I said I'll stay. So, he grabbed my hand and with no anaesthetic realigned my fingers (that bloody hurt too!) and told me to come back after the match. I didn't return, I went back to the North Stand and stood, in pain, watching the rest of the match, then walked home. I didn't want my parents to know about my accident because they might have found out that I had been in the North Stand and, with its bad reputation for violence, they might have stopped me from going again.

I witnessed some shocking spectacles of hostility outside the ground. Bricks thrown at away supporters' coaches as they left, all out punch ups inside pubs, spilling out on to the street and the cars of away supporters' who had chosen unwisely to park near to the ground, first rocked side to side, turned on their roofs and then the windows that already weren't broken smashed in. The police being outnumbered, just stood by helplessly and watched.

During the 1970's and early 80's violence for some young men was the main reason why they went to the grounds, the actual game of football was just a 'side-line act'. In those days there was no need for anybody to get prepaid tickets and the entry charge was relatively cheap compared to today's extortionate prices. You just paid in cash as you went through the turnstile and entered with no or very little security checks, just the occasional pat down by a police officer. Conditions in the ground were medieval. Toilets were full of human excrement, smoking allowed, and alcohol freely sold. The only food available was chocolate or sausage rolls and pies containing some form of gristle, passed off as meat. A lot of the fans in the North Stand started drinking in town as soon as the pubs opened at 11.00 and if they didn't arrive drunk at the game, they certainly left that way.

As I grew older, past the ripe old age of 14, and my grandfather couldn't work due to illness, I went to watch 'The Super Blues' play with some of my friends. They would call for me on their way and we walked from my house the 1.5 miles into town, spotting the other Ipswich supporters increasing in their numbers as we continued on our way towards the ground.

Sometimes I would meet up with friends from school and they would all be draped in their scarfs and flags. We often stood outside a notorious pub in town called the Balcony. Just fifteen minutes or so before kick-off, the Ipswich fans inside the pub would spill out on to the road blocking all the traffic, singing songs and walk the short distance to the ground. God help them if any away supporters were spotted. If they were they would get punched, kicked, their scarfs and flags taken as trophies. Once in the ground, sometimes the stolen scarfs were set alight just to 'wind up' the away supporters. The atmosphere in the ground was always intense and when the final whistle was blown by the referee, it continued outside. Police lines were formed across the road immediately outside the North Stand and after some singing and scuffles, the away supporters would disperse. Hordes of hardened Ipswich fans would go on what was locally called 'Chasing.' Basically looking for away supporters. Often groups would break down into the estates they came from within Ipswich, like Chantry, Whitehouse, or Whitton. The chasing sometimes meant running into coach parks, through the town centre or the railway station and playing cat and mouse with the police and of course, beating the hell out of the away supporters. It was violent, sometimes chaotic, but a sign of the times. When I left Ipswich to join the Royal Marines at the age of 16, so did my following of I.T.F.C.

Adventure Week.

At secondary school, my first impression of my new geography teacher, Mr Celerier, was that of a hard taskmaster, who took no messing around, gave us too much homework and with his blond hair and beard had the appearance of a ravaging Viking which terrified me. In my final two years at St Albans RC High, Mr Celerier became my form teacher, and I am eternally grateful that he did. To say that I was difficult to try and teach would be an understatement. I only went to school to see my friends, play football and because my parents made me. I hardly learnt anything in my last year except how to get out of most lessons. I didn't like any of the subjects, none of them interested me with the exception of geography. I really did try once in a maths lesson but within the first five minutes I couldn't understand what the hell the teacher was talking about, so I just lost focus and gave up. Subsequently, I refused to go to maths lessons. When I was supposed to be in maths, unbeknown to the other teaching staff, Mr Celerier gave me the key to his geography classroom so I could hide there. Time wasn't wasted though. He gave me books to read, one on judo so I could learn some self-defence techniques to assist me in preparation for my future career in the Royal Marines.

I would try any ploy to get out of class. During my final weeks at secondary school, my teachers decided that rather than keeping me in lessons and being disruptive, it would be better for me to do chores around the school. I was given the job of painting the walls of the boys cloakroom. I managed to complete this task in three days but thought hold on a minute, if I tell the teachers that I have finished they might send me back to class. So, just before last bell, when nobody was around, I took different coloured felt tip pens out of my pencil case and scrawled all over the newly painted walls. The next morning when I arrived at school, I reported the graffiti to a teacher, acting shocked and horrified at the damage. To confirm what I had said I then took the teacher, showed him the walls and said' I can't believe this, I will have to start all over again'. I repeated this ruse several times over, right up to my final day in education. If I had a final report from secondary school it would probably be finished off with 'Terry was taught beyond his academic ability, although his practical skills were outstanding!'

Mr Celerier and Mr Scott, the PE teacher, once a year took a select group of twelve boys on an adventure week up to North Norfolk. To be chosen for the adventure week you had to be deemed physically fit, have excellent attendance and good behaviour. Regrettably, I had frequently been on the receiving end of chastisement. Mr Marden, or Mad Man as we called him, the headmaster, had given me the 'slipper' on more than one occasion. In his office he had a metal locker and stored on the bottom shelf a variety of different sized plimsolls from adult male five up to twelve. The more severe your misconduct, the larger the plimsoll he chose. I once had a size 10 used on me for throwing books out of a first story window during a particularly boring English lesson. One narrowly missed Sister Monica (a Nun) as she was walking below and could be heard shouting 'Jesus, and Mary, Mother of God'. Sister Monica really deserves a book written about her to cover all of her exploits at St Albans. Just to say that her main physical punishment was slapping you across the face several times, with the cry of 'You wicked, wicked, child!'

If there were any breaches of health and safety rules in the school workshop, our woodwork teacher would hit us on the head with a piece of 'four by two'. Conversely he would happily wonder off into his storeroom for ten minutes to have a cup of tea, leaving us unsupervised working on industrial lathes! On the theme of health and safety I have to mention a despicable event and a very odd response to it by the headmaster of St Albans. One year at a time was led from their class to the boys toilet on the ground floor of the main education block. At the door to the toilet stood the caretaker who ushered us through, girls included. Inside we were greeted by Sister Monica who forced us to look at the spectacle in front of us. Someone had placed on top of a drinking water fountain a beautifully sculptured turd, perfectly balanced like a ballet dancer carrying out a pirouette.

Back to the adventure week and surprisingly, I was selected. I am sure it was because Mr Celerier wanted to give me a chance. Perhaps he saw some potential in me and thought the weeklong trip would help to put me on the straight and narrow. During the months leading up to the adventure week, to build up our fitness levels we had to stay after school to do circuit training in the sports hall. I really enjoyed it and learnt how to climb a rope properly. It was ideal preparation for what was to come in the Royal Marines. The trip involved staying in various Youth Hostels, taking our own food for the week, cooking it and then cleaning up afterwards. The accommodation and culture in the hostels were very much run along military lines. We all slept in one dormitory, sometimes on bunk beds and had to 'muck in' with the cleaning. The rooms were even inspected before we could depart.

On the day we left St Albans school, before we got to the youth hostel the adventures began. The canopy covering our ruck sacks flew off the roof of the minibus just outside Ipswich on a dual carriage way. The cause? Well possibly due to the fact that our teachers were having a competition to see who could get the top speed out of the old minibus! Two lads decided that they would sing and mimic the actions of Laurel and Hardy's song 'On the blue ridge mountains of Virginia' which was irritating, unmelodic and unfortunately for me, it became the adopted song sung throughout the whole week. I prayed that our initial journey would end but we had to, on more than one occasion, stop for a wee in

Thetford Forest or any convenient layby, which further delayed our arrival and prolonged my jarring, unmusical, agony.

The twelve of us did a lot of very demanding walks for a group of teenagers. The last being called the 'Long Walk' after the book and film of a true story by Slavomir Rawicz set during the second world war. Rawicz was a Polish officer who escaped from a Gulag and walked 4,000 miles to freedom. Our walk, all on a mixture of sand and shingle beach, took us along the North Norfolk Coast to Blakeney Point and was approximately twelve miles. Yes it was tiring but fun too. At one point someone discovered a dead Tope on the shore and held it up high as if it was some trophy until it slipped out of his grip and fell on his head!

I really enjoyed this adventure week and have been forever appreciative of Mr Celerier and Mr Scott for allowing me to go. In recent years I have been in contact with Mr Celerier, his wife and family and we have become very good friends. It's great to know that he still enjoys a nice, long walk in the countryside and plays an active role in conservation.

Going to my secondary school in the mornings, to maximise the amount of sleep I had, I would get up as late as possible to catch the 07.45 bus. The bus stop was only a two-minute walk away from my house. Often, I would jump out of my bed get dressed, rush out the front door without having a wash nor anything to eat! As a teenager my diet continued to be very poor. It consisted of anything that tasted sweet. When I got off the bus near St Albans school, I went straight to a news agent to buy sweets, either strawberry sherbets or bon bons that would serve for my breakfast and sometimes lunch. I didn't eat them all at once but slowly throughout the day. During lessons to hide the sweets from my teacher, and also so I didn't have to share them with my fellow pupils, I would surreptitiously unwrap them in my trouser pocket, then sneak them out, one at a time, and raising my hand to my mouth in pretence to cough, I would pop one in!

Because my family's income was below a certain threshold, I was allowed free school meals. I never liked the food at school and in the 1970's there were no choices, so I just didn't eat much. Once at home, for dinner I was quite content to eat a bag of toffee popcorn or chips from a takeaway. It was no wonder I was so thin and my brother used to call me matchstick; my body was not getting the correct nutrients and calories, that are so critical at that stage of growth. Today my teeth are in such a poor state and have cost me a fortune on dentist fees; there's a lesson for you Kids, 'Don't eat too many sweets and brush your teeth!' At the time I didn't care what I ate. However, in the very near future this insufficient diet resulted in my body's lack of development and growth, which ultimately affected my ability to perform to the high standards required by the Royal Marines. I was well below the physical size and muscular development of the rest of my fellow recruits.

Mid 1960's Felixstowe, Suffolk. L-R Mum, me, Gavin and Ruth.

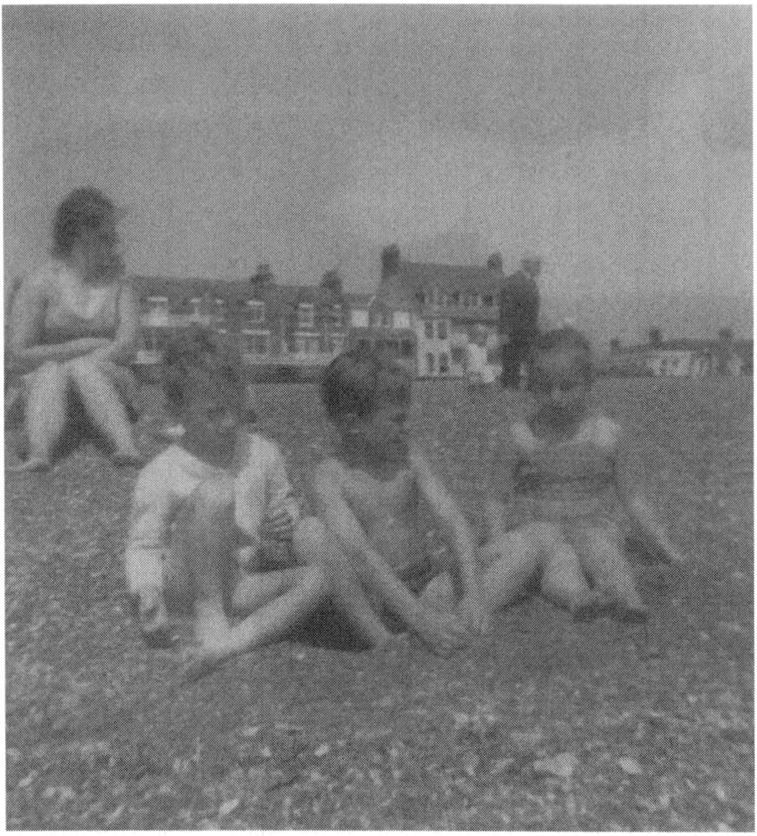

Late 1960's. My first fish caught with a rod and float; a 'massive' Perch!

On my way to support the 'Super Blues'. A shy and skinny me, second from the right

My secondary school football team 1976/77. Me, back row, 2nd left, next to Mr Scott our PE teacher.

Below; Rufus Celerier 1970's. My tutor, geography teacher and now a very close friend.

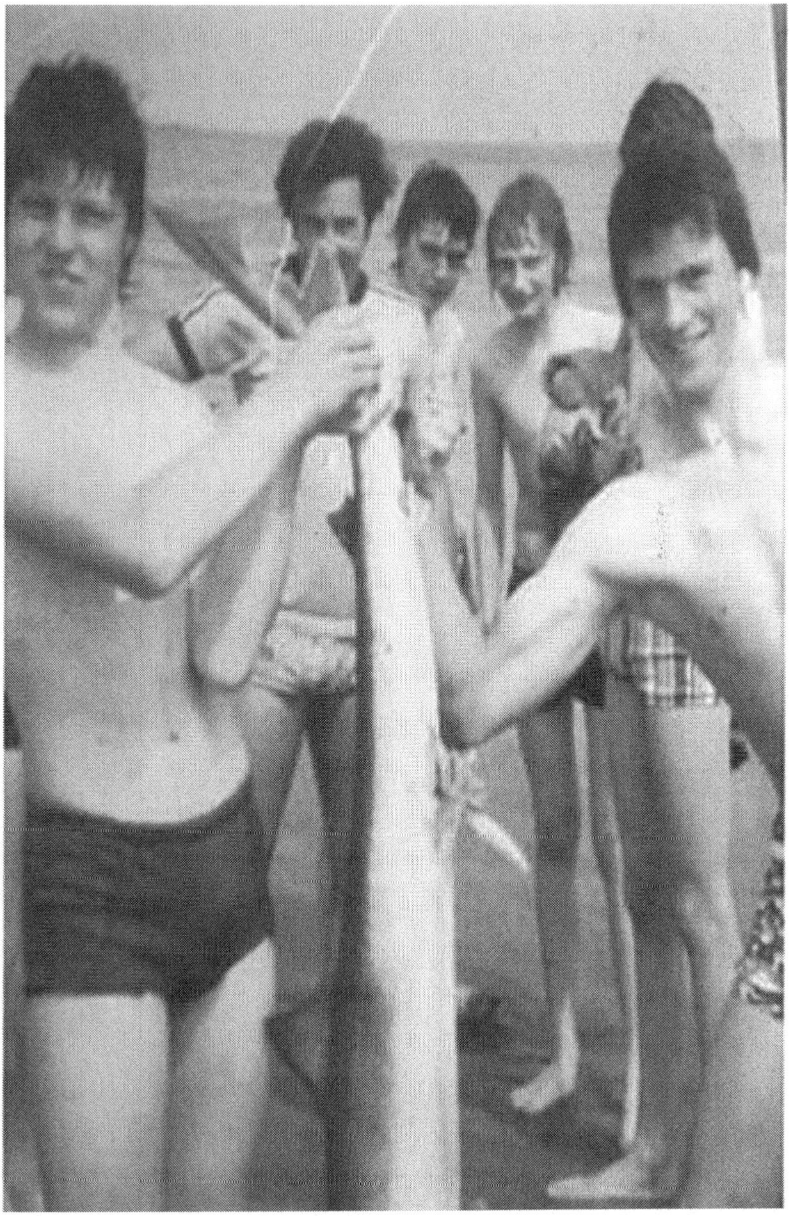

Adventure week 1978, me third from the right. The dead Tope we found on or near Blankney Point.

3. JOINING THE ROYAL MARINES.

The process of joining the Royal Marines for me was relatively simple compared to today's procedure. On the 17th of January 1979; a day that has been engrained in my memory ever since, I just walked in off the street and enquired at the career's office (now a trendy bar), at 53 Princess Street, in the centre of Ipswich. The building had two doorways, the left to the Royal Navy and Royal Marines, the right to the RAF. In the end I correctly turned left! Thank the Lord that the Army had their own premises on a different street or else, with three doorways to choose from, I would have been totally confused and probably ended up walking through the wrong door and signing up for the Army or RAF and failing at the first hurdle for pursuing my career in the Royal Marines.

As I entered the correct careers office, thus passing the first test, in front of me, his back to the window and the busy street, sat behind a teak-coloured desk, just like a headmaster, was Warrant Officer Second Class (W02) Beaton. Royal Marines. He was, surprisingly, less scary than my headmaster at school, and came across as being very friendly. He wrote down my personal details and then asked me if I knew anyone who had served or is currently in the Royal Marines. I talked to him about my older brother who had joined the Corps four years earlier and how I had been out to Malta for his wedding to Maria, while he was serving in 41 Commando RM (sadly due to MOD cuts, 41 Commando RM was finally disbanded in 1981). I said that out in Malta I had seen the comradeship of the Royal Marines and I wanted to be part of this elite organisation. I also told him that I had been to HMS Ganges, located just outside Ipswich, with my brother when he was interested in joining up.

HMS Ganges was The Royal Navy Training Establishment for boys from 1905 to its closure in 1976. From then on all new Navy recruits training was carried out at HMS Raleigh in Cornwall. As a child I can still remember seeing the young Navy recruits, in their clean, crisp, blue and white uniforms and polished boots, waiting to travel back to HMS Ganges at the Buttermarket Bus Station in Ipswich. There were rumours that 'Teddy Boys' carrying flick knives would get involved in fights with the Navy recruits particularly at weekends, so most law abiding people stayed away from the area.

Somehow, I must have impressed WO2 Beaton RM because he booked me in for a written test and medical examination in the near future. Approximately one month later I received a letter asking me to attend the careers office for a written aptitude test. I recall arriving early in the morning on the day of the test, after walking from home the two miles because I had no money for a bus. On entering the careers office I was taken to a small backroom and told to sit down at a desk. Sitting to my left there was another slightly older looking boy who was applying to go into the Royal Navy. On the desk in front of me were two pencils, a rubber and a test question/answer sheet. There was a quick verbal briefing given by WO2 Beaton RM and then we were told to start. After an hour the both of us were told to put down our pencils and go for a walk in town and return in an hour and a half to get our results. I was quite shy in those days and I didn't want to walk around with the other applicant, so I lied and told him I had to meet someone.

As I wandered around, looking in shop windows, time seemed to drag on. I remember feeling very anxious, it was pass or fail. What would I do if I bombed it? I was naïve. I had no second job lined up, it was make or break time. I needn't have been worried. Remarkably when I returned to the career's office, I was told that I had passed, even some of the mathematic and mechanical questions. What a shock! I returned home very happy.

Several weeks later the second phase of my assessment involved a thorough medical examination carried out by a local GP at the career's office, this time up on the first floor. I was deemed a healthy, albeit very skinny, sixteen-year-old. The only thing that caught me by surprise was the cough test!

On the 12th April 1979 I received through the post a certificate confirming that I had provisionally been accepted into the Royal Marines. Back then there was no Pre-joining Fitness Test (PJFT) carried out at a local gym. I am fairly confident that if I had had to take part in the PJFT and the one week selection process todays candidates have to endure, titled the Potential Royal Marines Course, (PRMC), I would never have passed.

On the back of the certificate were exercises, illustrated in the form of stick men that had to be carried out daily by myself until my joining day. They involved 7 stations titled 'Commando 7 Exercises', 10 per time. I never did stick to the plan however, I did start running on my own and when my brother came home on leave.

My detailed joining instructions arrived on 22nd of May. Enclosed was a travel warrant and precise details for the train times and connections. I was to eventually arrive at Lympstone Commando train station at 17.01 on 26th June 1979. There was also a kit list of what I was to take which included a razor and soap, even though I didn't need to shave yet. I still took one in the pretence of being a fully grown man.

The question I have to ask myself is why did I join the Royal Marines? Well, to be quite honest there is no one direct answer. As a child I had had no inclination to join any Sea, Army or Air Force Cadets. Before joining I had no or little military knowledge. Yes, my Father had been in the Army in the 1950's but he didn't speak of it and he never influenced me to joining up. Seeing my brother out in Malta and attending his 'Stag Do' gave me an insight into the comradeship and esprit de corps found in the Royal Marines and this made me think 'I want some of that!' Plus, Malta where my brother was based, was the perfect location; somewhere hot and sunny, with clear blue sea waters and skies. It just seemed to me like being on holiday with mates and at the same time getting paid for it too.

When my brother joined in 1974 the first ten or so weeks of basic training for the Royal Marines were carried out at Deal, Kent, then continued at Lympstone for phase two (the training depot in Deal closed in 1977). I had been to see my brother do his 'mini pass out' at Deal before he moved on to phase two, the Commando stage. My family and I watched part of this mini pass out from up on a balcony. It was an Initial Military Fitness (IMF) display by my brothers recruit troop, in one of the old wooden sprung flooring gyms on camp. I was amazed at the discipline shown by the recruits. I wondered how on earth they climbed ropes so easily and once up on top, do moves and holds, such as the crucifix, suspended with only their legs in contact with the rope. I wanted to be able to do this.

I did enjoy school, making friends and playing sports, however, academically I struggled, particularly in key subjects such as Maths and English. The first chance I was given to leave secondary school I took it. In the 1970s the leaving age was sixteen. You were given the option to leave early at the Easter break without taking any examinations, providing that you had a paid job to go to. I took that option. At the time, joining the Royal Marines gave me an excuse to say 'Bye, bye' to education and before I joined up, have time off to do what I wanted while others were still in school. It seemed to be an easy option. My naivety and lack of knowledge came back to haunt me in the future in two main ways. Initially while serving, I did not have the qualifications to get promoted. Secondly when I did eventually leave the Royal Marines, I had no academic qualifications. In the end with the support of my wife, a lot of financial hardship and study, I achieved a 2:1 (Hons), Degree. Oh, how I wish I had studied at school, (another life lesson for the kids!).

Why the hell did I choose the Royal Marines, why not some Army Regiment or The Royal Navy or RAF. Of all the services the Royal Marines Commando training is renowned for being one of the longest and most difficult basic modern infantry programme in the world. I must be a glutton for punishment.

As I have previously suggested, I was very far from being an 'A' star student when it came to studying. To think that as an adult I would be in education as a lecturer for twenty-three years, at the time seemed incomprehensible. At secondary school I was given, well in my opinion, far too much homework. Homework I thought, was a waste of time. I despised it. It took me away from important things. Why should I do it when I could be over the park playing football with my friends or fishing by the river. For the first few years at St Alban's I actually did complete geography homework all by myself, but asked my older sister, Ruth, to do the French for me. I received glowing comments from the French teacher in my exercise book for my written homework. However, this backfired in the class when once I was questioned in French by my teacher and didn't have a clue what to say in response. I sat there looking blankly ahead with twenty other students staring at me, my face turning as red as Rudolph's nose. Homework for all of the other subjects I left until the mornings and copied someone else's on the bus to school, or I just didn't bother to do it and made up some spur of the moment excuse for not handing it in on time.

Continuing on with the homework theme, at St Pancras primary I had a classmate that lived only two doors away from school, with both his parents and younger sister. You could see his house and the whole of the back garden from the playground, it was almost in touching distance. He only had to fall out of bed to get to school. As for submitting homework late or not at all, he had no excuses. If it snowed heavily he couldn't say he was stuck indoors or the buses weren't running, basically he was stuffed!

Before the Royal Marines, the only time I had tried to join anything remotely regimented was when I was about eight years old. My friend Robert Matuzczyk had endeavoured for some time to persuade me to join the Cubs. The Cubs were based in St Pancras RC church hall, near the centre of Ipswich and took place on a weekday, almost straight after school. One day Robert managed to get a lift from his mother in her Triumph Toledo, so I decided to give the Cubs a go. On the journey there I remember sitting in the back of the car feeling quite nervous. When we got into the church hall, I was taken to a side room and the first thing I had to do was to fill in a form including my personal details and then listen to a talk on behaviour standards expected whilst in the Cubs. After that I was allowed back into the hall to join in with the rest of the group. They were getting into teams to play indoor football, I thought great, I can't wait to get started. I was in one of the first teams playing so went straight on into the centre of the hall. As the whistle was blown for the start of the match by the referee, a Cub leader, the ball was thrown in. It landed right next to me, I drew back my right foot and went to 'toe punt' it as hard as I could towards the oppositions goal. Just as I let fly with my right foot, a boy from the other team fell over in front of me and instead of kicking the ball I kicked him, right in the head! He burst into tears, I was not only sent off by the referee, but also was told to go and wait outside in the corridor for the rest of the night. I tried to explain that it was an accident, but no one was listening. They were only concerned with dealing with the injured lad and getting the game restarted. At the end of the night a Cub leader came out and told me that they didn't want to see me again. So, there you have it, banned from the Cubs at the age of eight!

My last evening at home before joining up was spent messing around on the Dales with two friends, although my mind was completely distracted by what was going to be happening tomorrow and to be honest my heart was not fully into speaking or playing. I got home earlier than usual and my father, with as much empathy for my plight as a butchers knife, and a smirk on his face asked, 'Did you kiss your friend's goodbye?' That night was a sleepless one, my last at home. Going somewhere, alone, for a long period of time was alien and quite scary for me.

Leaving Home.

On the morning of 26th June 1979, I was up early. I checked all my belongings were packed in my suitcase and said goodbye to my two sisters. My older brother wasn't home on leave and to some degree I was glad because he would have given me some ribbing. Once, as a trained Royal Marine, I returned back to camp from leave at home, I opened up my Pussers suitcase and I saw on the inside of the top segment that my brother had written in big capital letters 'Sprog Barnes, by his old sweat brother!' He had also scrawled his personal issued number that indicated that he had joined up before me, just in case there was any doubt of me being the junior.

My father and Sister-in-law, Maria, escorted me up to London to make sure I didn't get lost, particularly on the underground from Liverpool street to Paddington. I took the train ride from Ipswich up to London, as I had in the past on shopping trips with my mother, full of excitement. As we were walking from the platform at Liverpool Street, I remembered going with my brother to his joining day at Deal in Kent. Underneath a stairwell in Liverpool street station, near some toilets, there had been a gent's barbers. On my brothers joining instructions it was stipulated that he must arrive with an appropriate hair style. In the 1970's for males, it was very fashionable to have long hair down to the shoulders, so when my father told the barber to give my brother a 'Short back and sides' I couldn't stop laughing.

It wasn't until I had boarded the 125 train to Exeter St David's and had said goodbye to my father and Maria, that my emotions got to me. I had a lump in my throat, and I felt sad. I stood on my own by a carriage door, my baggage at my feet, staring out of the window, thinking of my family. It was now 13.30 and since leaving Ipswich over three hours ago, I hadn't eaten. I just didn't feel hungry, the only thing to enter my stomach was nervous butterflies.

Suddenly I felt someone tap me on the shoulder, I turned around and looked at a face I didn't recognise. A lad asked, 'Would you like to go to the buffet and have a pint with me before we sign our lives away?' I didn't answer his question. I was in no mood for beer and besides, at sixteen and looking fresh faced, I feared that I would have been refused alcohol and that would have been embarrassing. I deflected the request by asking him where he was going; I was genuinely interested. I had a quick chat and found out that he was joining the Royal Navy and on his way to HMS Raleigh, in Cornwall, where their basic training took place. How my new acquaintance had guessed that I was going to join up I'll never know, with my long red hair and tall, skinny physique I hardly matched up to the preconceived image of a potential military recruit, especially for the Royal Marines. After a few minutes, the lad went off to the buffet to have his beer and I was left alone. Talking to this stranger and finding out that there was someone else in a similar situation too, gave me a bit of confidence. I moved, with my suitcase, from my position of standing in the corridor to taking a seat in a carriage, again next to a window. The journey seemed to go on forever. I never moved from my seat once, not even to go to the toilet.

There had been a slight delay of ten minutes, and even before we arrived at Exeter St David's I was panicking a bit, concerned that I would miss the connecting train. As the 125 arrived, I quickly disembarked, ran along the concourse and jumped two stairs at a time, up and then down a bridge connecting platforms where the 16.38 to Exmouth was waiting. Out of breath, I nervously asked a British Rail employee if it was the right train, and he informed me it was, but I'd better hurry because it was just about to leave. The local line train seemed antiquated compared to the modern one I had just left. The quality of seating had dropped and so had the speed, considerably. I boarded and again found a seat by the window. The train pulled away on what is now named the 'Avocet Line' and as we passed Exeter Central Station, I could see rows of terraced houses, similar to where I lived in Ipswich. I watched through their windows, as families were going about their business and I wondered what was going on at home at this time of the day. The train plodded along, stopping at small stations like St James and Newcourt, before following the River Exe Estuary to my right. More stations came and went; I was almost willing that Lympstone Commando would never appear. Feeling homesick I wished that the trip would go on forever, like Groundhog Day or bizarrely, the train would arrive back at Paddington, London.

All of a sudden there was a call from the train guard 'Lympstone Commando, alight here for the camp only'. To emphasise this, the message was repeated twice. I picked up my suitcase and noticed two or three other young men getting off too. I hadn't even been vaguely aware of them before. I had been in a world of my own.

We were greeted with no pleasantries, by a Corporal Mower who lined us up and called out our names. As he leaned over his clipboard and us, to me he appeared to be a 'Man mountain'. After the roll call the only instruction he gave was 'Follow me'. He went off at speed, running towards a steep inclined footpath, followed by several sets of steps eventually leading to the infamous, 1960's built, white painted accommodation blocks for recruits and junior Marines (Jnr Mnes). We obeyed his orders and tried to shadow his moves, bounding up the steps to try and keep up, but we all failed.

Block C was to be my home. I was totally knackered as I climbed the internal stairs up to the top floor and entered one of the six-man grots (sleeping rooms). I had been one of the last to arrive. There was a double bunk in the room on the far right hand side next to a window that over looked the river Exe, which I was allocated to. I was given the top bunk, someone else the bottom and all the lucky others had single beds.

I was one of over sixty under eighteen-year-olds ready to start our thirty-two-week basic training. Back then, there was no Induction Foundation Block for the first two weeks of recruit training. Nowadays this block is where new entries are housed, all together in a sixty persons dormitory, and carefully watched by their training team. The purpose is to help with the transition from civilian to military life and swiftly deal with any issues should they arise.

One recent message I received on social media was from a member of my troop in training, recalling his first day arriving by train at CTCRM. He was walking past the thirty-foot ropes on the bottom field and seeing recruits, in full fighting order, who were trying to climb to the top. As he heard a member of their training team shout at one recruit, 'If you want to piss, piss where you are on the rope you tosser'. My colleague thought, what the hell have I let myself in for!

Training to be a Royal Marines Commando.

As I have already alluded to, to be a Royal Marines Commando and earn the famous Green Beret, training is and has to be extremely demanding to pass, and only a few do. As an immature sixteen-year-old, the physical and psychological stresses were difficult for me to take on, to say the least,.

For today's candidates, you have to have a minimum height of 151.5cm (5 ft), that I would have easily passed, but I would have been well below the minimum weight of 65kg (10.24 Stone). I was skinny. My chest was only 30 inches on entry at the age of 16. I totally lacked any upper body strength, my arms were so weak that I could barely do one press up. In week two of basic training, at a weapon stance we were practising loading and unloading drills and taking apart then reassembling the SLR (Self Loading Rifle). It took all of my strength to pull back the cocking handle. Once, I thought the mechanism had jammed and couldn't, with all my might, cock the bloody thing. My section Commander, a fully trained RM Corporal and Personal Weapons Instructor, (PW), saw me struggling, grabbed the rifle from me, cocked it with ease and shouted, 'For fuck sake Barnes, get some muscles'. By the end of training my medical records show that my chest had grown to 36 inches.

The Naval Maths and English Tests (NAMET) were given to us in the first week of training. We didn't get the results until two weeks later and the training team were hit with a bomb shell. In the whole history of the tests being done, never had a recruit troop faired so badly. Of the sixty two, only two Jnr Mnes got enough marks to achieve the dizzy heights to the rank of corporal, the rest of us were doomed to stay as Marines, possibly for our entire careers. I have already mentioned my premature drop from education and was thinking that I would be, academically, well below all of the others, I needn't have worried! Our troop officer went berserk. He threw the results sheets in the bin and made us attend compulsory Maths and English lessons for the next few weeks. We retook the test and received the results on the 22nd September 1979. 0 – 0 was equivalent to an A in the old CSE's, if you scored 10-10, according to the training team you needed to check if you were a human or join the Paras. Luckily, some managed to get better grades, sparing us from yet another rebuff. Mine were 7-6 so I just scraped in as a homosapien, however, with the intellectual level of a nine-year-old. Later in my career I took the NAMET again and surprisingly, scored enough points to become a sergeant. Looking back, unlike todays recruits, I am so pleased we didn't have to learn verbatim the eight values, qualities, and the definitions of a Royal Marine. If so, I would probably still be there now trying to memorize them.

I walked around CTCRM believing that everyone knew my brother and was surprised to find out that this was not so. I would look at the trained ranks accommodation and often wonder if there were any of his friends there, particularly those that I had met in Malta. However, this was not the case. The only time I did meet another Royal Marine that had served with my brother was to be several years later, at Seaton Barracks in Plymouth when I was in 40 Commando RM.

The Royal Marines are unique in that both recruit and officer training are based at Lympstone, Devon, unlike the Army where officers are located at Sandhurst and other ranks at Pirbright. Also, CTCRM is used for selection to attend the PRMC and Potential Officers Course (POC) as well as specialist training. So, based at CTCRM a variety of different ranks and specialities (including 'Special Forces') can be met. I can recall on my second night I was wondering around camp and all of a sudden, I heard a loud voice directed at me shout, 'Who the hell are you'. I replied 'Terry Barnes, do you know my brother?' I saw him go bright red in the face and turn on his heel in disgust. I thought, 'What a very rude man'. I was to find out later that it was the adjutant of the camp.

One other story that has gone into Corps history which happened while I was in training, was that of Jnr Mne 'Bob' Mullin. Bob had joined the Royal Marines as a 'normal rank' and like all new recruits was anticipating a very abrupt welcome by his training team. After a long journey by train from home he disembarked at Lympstone Commando Station and found himself alone on the platform. He approached the guard on duty and was promptly sent to an accommodation block. When he arrived at the building, Bob was greeted by an attendant and was ushered to his own private, single bedroom. After unpacking he went down to dinner and was surprised at the manner in which he was treated. Everyone Bob met was calling him 'Sir' and dinner was eaten in what looked like a posh restaurant, served at the table by waiters in four stages. He wrote home informing his parents that they had been totally wrong and contrary to what they had said about a short, sharp, initial greeting, he had been treated well and that the hospitality was excellent. I believe it wasn't until a few days later during a conversation over breakfast between Bob and a high-ranking officer, it was discovered that Bob had been directed by the duty guard to the wrong building - the Officers Mess instead of the recruits accommodation!

The first few weeks of training opened me up to a whole new world of pain and distress. This was augmented with having to learn new military terminology. An example of the slang was 'Pongos' for anyone serving in the army. This was a dig at their perceived lower standards, particularly personal hygiene, 'Wherever the army goes, Pongos!' Some others included dhobi for washing yourself or kit, dhobi dust, washing powder (probably originating from the Indian word for washerwoman). Toilets were called heads, a term used on ships and 'Pussers' was anything that had been or was issued by the MOD, (possibly an adaption from the word Purser, an officer on ship who keeps the accounts for stores and money) or alternatively, a person sticking to the rule book. In training and also in Commando Units, Christian names were rarely used and I often never knew them, even of some of my closest colleagues. I had a very good oppo (friend) while serving in 40 Commando RM whose surname was Roden, but he was only known to me and others as 'Rod' or 'Rodders'. Five years after meeting Rod I went to his wedding in Somerset. I kept on hearing his family and civilian friends continuously talking about someone called Mark. I was just about to approach Rodders and ask who the hell Mark was when Sharon, my wife, looked at the front cover of the order of service sheet and there it was in black and white 'Welcome to the wedding of Mark Roden to.......

Back to 1979 and my Jnr Mne Troop was issued our Kit in week two. I would use the prefix 'new' but some of the equipment had been recycled. The previous owners had stamped their name and number on their kit. We all knew that this gear had been returned by recruits who had decided, with some help from the training teams, that the Royal Marines was not for them. It was a sombre reminder to me that hundreds of young men like me had tried but failed.

While the rest of the troop stood outside waiting, one section at a time was marched into the storeroom at CTCRM. Once inside, we had to line up facing a counter and stand behind a pile of clothing that had earlier been laid out, half on the floor, half on the counter. The storeman would then shout out an item of clothing and one at a time, we had to raise it high above our heads to show that we were in possession of it and then, as quickly as possible, try it on for size. The training team were getting frustrated at how long we were taking, so to avoid a bollocking, I didn't bother trying things on, I just stuffed most of my new belongings into either a green or beige kit bag.

By pure luck my boots did fit, however, the trousers were too big around my waist and too short in the leg length. This miscalculation was to cause me hell later on. I had to tighten my belt around my waist, which made it difficult for me to get my breath when exercising. Also, because of the shortness of the leg length, the bottom of my trousers would often come out from the top of my puttees. I would constantly get in trouble for this happening and more annoying for me was when it resulted in my puttees unravelling, when I ran or walked. This not only caused problems for the recruit behind me when marching, but I also had to stop to tie them up, meaning I had to fall out then catch up. It was an embarrassment, not only to me, but the training team too. When the troop had fallen in, I was often called to the front and found myself on the receiving end of more physical torture for everyone to witness.

Puttees were first issued way back in the 1890's. Originally, they were worn all the way up to the knees, thank goodness that for the first years of my service they only went up to the ankles. Wrapping them around the ankles and the top of your boot took ages and a specialist skill to get the small ends tucked way into a small square on the outside of the leg. In the 1980s and after the Falklands War, with the introduction of high-leg boots, these relics became superfluous. You Royal Marines today don't know how lucky you are!

Another artefact issued to us was the 1958-pattern webbing, first introduced in the 1960's. It was made of cotton and was a drab olive colour. The main body of the webbing consisted of a belt and attached to it, a yoke. At the front were two ammunition/magazine pouches, a water bottle carrier and to the rear, a pair of kidney pouches, a poncho roll and a large pack with straps that fell over the front and were fastened to eyelets. The webbing was not ergonomic, particularly when you had to attach the respirator case. When it was designed, comfort for the soldier was not a priority.

All of my webbing was second hand, possibly used by tens of recruits before me on their journey through CTCRM, but because of this, one blessing was that it didn't need wearing in. The canvas type material provided no water proofing to its contents. In fact, the webbing would absorb water itself and add to the weight you were carrying. Sleeping bags were just like a continental quilt with no water-resistant treatment. The stitching would undo, and feathers used to fall out. Often you would crawl out of the sleeping bag covered in feathers, looking like a half-plucked chicken. Sometimes they would smell of mouldy bread, or worse, the aroma of the last owner's body odour. Because the size of the backpacks was tiny compared to the bergens that are issued today, we could only just fit in our personal kit and rations. The sleeping bag had to be attached to the outside of the backpack, on top. To waterproof the sleeping bag we used to put it inside a bin liner. The bin liner was black and therefore tactical but it made a rustling noise and would split, so most of the time it was useless.

The webbing and backpack would tighten when wet and cause rubbing between the skin and fabric. This abrasive action mostly occurred on my lower back from the kidney pouches. Apart from the immediate pain, it also caused friction burns and eventually bleeding, as the grazes opened up. With no hiatus or sick note, this discomfort just had to be tolerated on a daily basis. Today, I still have scars on my back, and I have spoken to many Royal Marine veterans that served around the same time as me and found this to be quite a common legacy.

Before going out on exercise, my troop in training were often given two days' supply of ration packs, Hexamine stoves and spare Hexamine blocks (Hexi cooker and Hexi blocks). These would be replenished when needed, depending on the length of days we spent out in the field. For one day's rations the provisions came in a brown cardboard box, weighing approximately two kg. Amongst the sundries packets were tins of food e.g. steak & kidney pudding, chicken curry, baconburger and beef spread. Each box contained over four thousand calories. I would put most of the ration pack contents in the bin, simply because there was no space in my backpack, webbing or pockets. By the time 'Swift Sting', our final exercise in training arrived, the only items I took out of the ration box and carried were chocolate in the form of a Mars bar or Rolo's, sweets (hard boiled), a can of fruit salad (that was swimming in a refreshing juice) and my favourite, an oatmeal block. By now I was sick of eating the same old curried chicken, bacon burgers and biscuits AB (or 'Ard Bastards' as I used to call them). By reducing the number of tins or not carrying any, I not only saved space and weight, but it also meant that I didn't need to cook any hot meals. My thinking back then was that if I didn't fire up my Hexi cooker, to cook hot food, I would not have to use my mess tins. The Hexi blocks would leave a black residue on the bottom of the mess tin and it was very difficult to remove. Not using the cooker would save time and the mess tins would also be crystal clean for any inspections carried out by the training team. Putting on my sports science hat and looking back, this was not a good idea because I probably wasn't getting enough nutrients and calories to match the intense physical demands placed on me.

In week two of training, apart from being issued kit, we were eventually taken to the barbers situated in CTCRM and offered a haircut in one style only, crew cut. After I had had mine done, I felt like a real Marine, part of a team, with all of the troop having the same haircut, clothing, and marching together, we looked the part, hard men in appearance, if not in reality.

All of the troop had to stamp their own names and number on the issued kit to make sure that there was no mix up of what belonged to whom. This was especially important when you left clothing to dry in the troops allocated drying room, which was packed to the brim and consequently people might get confused and 'accidently' take your possessions instead of theirs.

The training team issued each Jnr Mne with a small, wooden block, about the size of a cigarette box, consisting of two rows. The top row had my surname and initials, the bottom my personal service number. Each letter and the whole wooden block were tenuously held together with white masking tape. Black, indelible ink in plastic containers was supplied for us to dip the block into and then, by pressing against your clothing, it was supposed to form a perfect, permanent print of your details. After using my wooden block several times, the tape holding the letters together became wet from the ink, lost its adhesiveness causing the wooden block to fall apart. I tried to hold the letters together by making a fist around them with both my hands and then dipping it in to the container. However, as I lifted the block up, ink went everywhere. It dribbled down onto my fingers and hands making holding the block as difficult as trying to grasp a wet bar of soap. This was made worse because, after several more submersions, the tape slowly gave up and eventually disintegrated. With nothing but my wet, slippery, and blackened hands to hold the letters straight and in the correct order, it made the task almost impossible. There was so much ink dripping off the block and my hands that my name became almost indecipherable and just appeared as a black smudge as I pressed it against material.

On the tail end of our shirts, we were told to clearly print our names on the inside. I had left my shirts to the end of the process because I thought that I would have had plenty of practice by then and make a good job of it. Unfortunately, when I stamped my shirts a familiar black smudge appeared, as it had on most of my clothes. My grey stone shirts seemed to absorb the ink more than the rest of my clothing. The black patch left from my attempts on the shirts expanded on the back, upwards, inside and out, as I helplessly watched it dry.

Several weeks later I had forgotten about this episode and one day we had PE, followed by Drill. The training team gave us the traditional and humanly impossible task to achieve; only two minutes to get to our grots and change into short sleeved order Lovats, the dress for drill. I put on my rig, including my stone shirt and fell in outside the accommodation block. We were then marched by our training team over to the drill square, to meet our drill instructor (DL). The DL did a quick inspection of the troop. I was in the centre row of three. He gave me a hasty look over at the front and then moved on to the back row. As he walked behind me, I felt his breath on my collar and he bellowed out ‘What the fuck is that spider doing crawling up the centre of your back Barnes?’ He then proceeded to poke me in the back with the pointed end of his pace stick, pretending to be scared of all Arachnida, much to the fun of the troop. It suddenly dawned on me that the black smudge from my ink stamping fiasco had crept up above my Corps belt line and this was what he had seen. My punishment was to stand with my face inches from a wall at the drill shed and proclaim at the top of my voice that I was a 'Waste of space'. This was followed by extra inspections for the next two nights while everyone else was at the Navy, Army and Air Force Institute (NAFFI).

While at CTCRM, time off in training was very rare. However, if you did have a gap in your training and were not on guard duties, for the first two weeks you weren't allowed to leave camp anyway. Once you were allowed off camp, the time allowed increased as you progressed through training, although no one was allowed to stay out overnight, well not until you eventually got to the Kings Squad (the last two weeks of training). If you had time off and you did want to go ashore, before leaving you had to go and present your pass and yourself to the duty JNCO at the guardroom, based at the top of the camp. Standing to attention, stating your service number, rank, and name, finishing off with 'Permission to go ashore Corporal' was the procedure we all had to go through. Sometimes you would get a relaxed JNCO on duty who would quickly look you over to make sure you were generally tidy. Others would just mess you around and this happened to me on one Saturday. The bastard JNCO on duty sent me away, twice to have a proper shave (as I have I already stated, at 16 I didn't need to shave yet), twice to iron a crease in the front of my jeans and finally he made me wait out in the rain. When he did eventually see me again he told me I looked like a bag of shit and needed to go and get changed. By this time, it was 18.00, getting dark and, I had to be back on camp by 21.00, so I just gave up!

Apart from having my teeth checked by a RN Dentist and various injections for Polio, Combined tetanus and enteric prophylactic

(T.A.B.T.) by the medical staff at CTCRM, I also had an interview with a member of the Women's Royal Navy Service (WRN, slang Wren). I believe this interview was carried out to assess how I was settling in, any issues I had ,and discuss feedback from the training team. To me It all seemed to go smoothly. Three years later while in 40 Commando RM I got hold of my personal records. The Wren had written a summary of our interview and the final comments were 'Although his brother passed out of training, I doubt very much that Jnr Mne Barnes T.V. will'. If I had seen this report at the time it would have seriously affected my confidence and therefore my chance of succeeding to be a Royal Marines Commando. I showed this report to some of my oppos (friends) in 9 Troop and they were uncontrollable with laughter, well Wren, who's laughing now!

Demonstrations were given in the accommodation blocks by the training team on how to shower, shave and iron the Royal Marines way. In the 1970's and 80's ordinary ranks of sixteen to eighteen-year-olds, mostly straight from education, were entered into training with men of the same age and were titled 'Jnr Mne Troops'. Those over eighteen were called recruits and generally had experience of employment in the outside world and they joined 'Recruit Troops'. In the pecking order at CTCRM, as Jnr Mnes we were deemed the lowest of the low, almost like children. We were still entitled to free milk and had designated 'milk monitors' from the troop whose daily assignment was to go to the galley at 06.30 and collect our quota. This soon ended when Margaret Thatcher came to power (remember the headline' Thatcher the milk snatcher?). Little did I know that three years later she would send me to war against Argentina.

Our troop numbered sixty-one at the start of training and although a few left early, within the first days and weeks, we were still classed by the training team as a numerically large troop. Because of this and the small or unavailable lecture theatres to accommodate us, some presentations had to be done in smaller groups using whatever rooms were free. One such session was carried out by our immaculately turned-out DL Sergeant (or spiderman as I used to call him, due to his fascination with threads hanging down from garments and my previous bollocking on the parade ground). Two sections of the troop were crammed into one grot (about twenty-five Jnr Mne's). Two beds were pushed to the side to make a space which we surrounded. In the centre of this gap was an ironing board, an iron and Spiderman. One at a time, Spiderman picked up every garment we had been issued and demonstrated exactly how they should be ironed. The Jnr Mne whose clothing he was using to iron had a smug expression on his face. He thought, like us all, that he was going to get away without having to do it himself (well, for the first time at least). The final piece of clothing we were shown to iron was the stone shirt. The DL was meticulous in his description, showing with precision exactly where the creases on the sleeves and back should go. After he had finished, Spiderman enquired if there were any questions and if not, explained that there would be no excuses for a poor turn out by anybody in the troop. The smug Jnr Mne, who had now had all his clothing ironed perfectly by our DL, raised his hand and asked, 'Once we have ironed and folded all our clothes, what should we do with them?' With a stare of despair and a shake of the head, Spiderman said, whilst carrying out his own instructions, 'You pick each piece up, rub it on the floor and throw it out of the window'. When the last piece disappeared out into the fresh Devonshire air, he turned to the now stunned owner and offender and said, 'What do you think you do with it you cunt?' The rest of us were rolling in fits of laughter which intensified as Spiderman slowly strolled out of the grot with a grin across his face; you see DL's can smile!

During this period we were being pushed physically and psychologically. I tried to hide any emotions, but it was difficult for me as a sixteen year old that lacked maturity. For some Jnr Mnes the strain showed and they broke down. During one 'beasting' (a term for intensive physical punishment, now politically incorrect and not used, oh dear!) I witnessed for the first time in my life, a person crying as he drove himself to his physical limits. Tears streamed down his face as he continued on. At first I wondered what was causing his discomfort, thinking it was just the amount of unachievable exercises we were instructed to do, but it wasn't because he continued on. He didn't speak at all. No swearing or complaining, just silence. I was mystified, wondering what the hell was going on in his mind. That evening I spoke to him and he told me that he had been close to throwing in the towel and going home, back to his parents' house in Bristol. It was when he thought of his family that he started to cry and this inspired him to fight on. All of the PT didn't bother him, it was the relentless feeling of being homesick that got to him.

Shooting.

Weapon drills and live firing, along with, funnily enough, first aid instruction, started early on in training. In week four the troop were taken to Straight Point Range, not far from CTCRM, situated to the east of Exmouth, bizarrely accessed through a holiday caravan site. The range safety zone goes out into the sea and shooting is often stopped because small fishing boats would stray into the arcs. When the lookout called a stop to the live firing, the training team had time to come up with some devilish method of torturing us. Once, the troop were subjected to an extra session of Physical Training (PT). During this PT, those that had 'messed up' in the eyes of the Corporals, were detailed off for even more punishment, this included me. The additional penalty was to clean up everything after scran (lunch) and I do mean clean up. Any leftover slops of food, we were told to eat and, because whole blocks of butter hadn't been touched, we were ordered to devour them too. One Jnr Mne was singled out to eat a 250g butter block in one go, but after a spirited attempt of two mouthfuls, he vomited. Witnessing this, one member of the training team walked up to the sick on the ground, picked it up in his bare hands and tried to force it back into the mouth of his victim, thus giving a new meaning to providing feedback!

The first time I fired a Self-Loading Rifle (SLR) on Straight Point Ranges I was shocked at the amount of recoil. By the end of the day of shooting my arms, shoulder and back ached, it felt as if someone had continuously punched me in the shoulder for a couple of hours. When I returned back to CTCRM and took my shirt off, I saw that the whole of my right shoulder was bright red and purple, bruising had already started to appear. A week later my troop were back at Straight Point Ranges, live firing again. From the firing point, using my arms to support me as I went down to lay in the prone position on the gravel, I was reminded of the pain I had suffered the previous week from the recoil. As we were ordered to make ready and I took off the safety catch ready to fire, I was anticipating the same discomfort as before in my shoulder from the kick. I pulled the trigger, inwards, very slowly and aiming in the general direction of the figure twelve target. In readiness for the pain, I closed my eyes at the same time as pulling the trigger fully home. This action was to be regrettable. A member of the training team saw me with my eyes shut. Instead of getting one kick I got two. The first was expected, from the weapon, the second was received after I had been ordered to make the weapon safe and came from a size ten DMS boot as it connected with my ribs. This was followed by an onslaught of verbal abuse and some running around with my rifle above my head, slightly different from other occasions. This time with my eyes shut. As I smashed into objects, tripped or just had close encounters, there was raucous laughter from my troop and the whole training team as they watched on. I was halfway through when the Corporal dishing out the punishment stopped me and said 'Do you know why you have eyes on the top of your head Barnes? To stop you hurting yourself, and others. If I was in front of you in a real fire fight, I'd half expect you to shoot an officer in the back but not your oppos, you arse!' He made me continue running around for a few minutes longer, then ordered me to stop, only to do press ups. It was a steep learning curve; don't close your eyes when firing a weapon, but more importantly never let a member of the training team see you doing it!

Changing Step, The Royal Navy Way!

Rivalry is renowned between the services. The Royal Marines and Royal Navy in a more friendly manner, possibly because of their close working relationship, than with the Army and RAF. The Royal Marines would pick on what was perceived to be the feminine side of the male matelots. While marching around CTCRM, if we ever passed a Royal Navy Officer the Troop was ordered to change step 'The Navy Way'. This involved the whole troop working in unison and had been practiced to perfection. At the order 'Royal Navy, change step,' en masse, our eyes were directed towards the Royal Naval Officer as in a pass by (saluting on the march). Each member of the troop placed both hands on their hips, the left foot was planted flat on the ground behind the body line to take your body weight. The right leg was swung forward placing the toe on the ground in front of the body. Like a pendulum the right leg was then swung back and forward of the body's line twice. As the right toe was placed on the forward and back swings we had to shout out 'Shall we, shan't we?' Followed by '...Yes we will'. On the 'Yes we will ' we launched ourselves into a high skip, clipped our heels together, changed step and carried on marching as normal as could be without our laughter interfering. Can you imagine fifty odd recruits, all together carrying out this bizarre drill with the sound of 'Shall we, shan't we? Yes we will,' booming across CTCRM. Civilians would stop and stare, trained ranks chuckle and you could even see a small grin appear on the face of the allegedly offended Royal Navy Officer. In recent times I have talked about this to my daughter. I gave her a demonstration and she has practiced it while out walking. After some failures and a lot of repetition, she has managed to master this action. If you ever visit Ipswich and see a young woman walking along the pavement carrying out this move, I do apologise, but don't stare, and please try not to laugh, but do think of me!

Going on Exercise.

In training, going out on exercise in the field was mainly carried out on Dartmoor or Woodbury Common. Both are in easy reach of CTCRM. The lesser-known Woodbury Common is classed as an area of outstanding natural beauty (AONB). On the Common there are some small, forested areas, but it is mainly open ground covered by rough moorland where heather and gorse grow. It is used and regarded by most civilians as a pleasurable place to perhaps take your dog for a walk, to burn off some fat or 'clear the air' after a large Sunday lunch and/or for the more active individual, orienteering or mountain biking. Near the Dalditch area of Woodbury Common, during the Second World War, there used to be a military camp with ranges where Royal Marines were based. This was abandoned many years ago and virtually nothing remains except partial walls and scars on the earth. Today, civilians are advised to avoid Woodbury Common at night because of loud bangs and bright flashes caused by recruits and trained ranks letting off munitions out on exercise. Even during the day civilians are warned that they might be startled by seeing strange bushes on the move! I must briefly mention here in my ramblings, that located on the common is where the infamous Endurance Course begins (I will give a description of the Endurance Course later when I go through the Commando tests).

When I heard other Jnr Mnes talking about going out in the 'Field', I couldn't comprehend what they were on about. I thought we were going to spend the night camping on the side of a playing field with football pitches and changing rooms. When I first experienced exactly what was meant by 'In the field', after going out on my first exercise which was perfectly named 'First Step', in week three of training, I initially despised it. Getting soaking wet boots, clothing and subsequently being cold for a three-day period on First Step, gave me absolutely no pleasure. To add to my torments, we were constantly inspected by the training team. Every morning we were checked. Our weapons were stripped down and barrels looked at, mess tins were wiped with clean fingers to make sure there was no food residue left, and inexplicably that we had polished our soaking wet boots, how ridiculous! On these field inspections the troop fell in, in three wide ranks with our kit laid out in front of us. A member of the training team would approach to scrutinise it and if any dirt or dust were found on any items, you would have failed. Offending articles would be flung off into the distance. Magazines, dirty razors and even toothbrushes suddenly sprouted wings and were seen flying through the air and landing in gorse bushes and puddles alike. The owners of this kit were instructed to crawl to retrieve it. Some of us committed a cardinal sin by neglecting to take our rifles with us and were swiftly punished with even more painful crawling.

After crawling around and, if you were lucky enough to find your possessions, you were then instructed to get your fighting order, weapon, steel helmet and stand on the flank away from the rest of the troop. When everyone had been inspected, those that survived by not being picked up during the inspection, breathed a sigh of relief, put their 'display' away, relaxed and made a wet (drink). While this happened, those unfortunate members of the troop on the flank, like me on successive occasions, were in for a beasting.

My first, but by far not my last, encounter with a beasting in the field was on First Step. This involved running through gorse bushes carrying my SLR above my head and sporting a steel helmet that had thin strands of painted hessian hanging down over my face. Wearing cam cream and the camouflaged helmet, I resembled an unkempt Rastafarian. The dangling strands of hessian combined with an ill-fitting helmet, which kept sliding down over my face, made it difficult for me to see in what direction I was running. At one point, with beads of sweat dripping down from my forehead and into my eyes making them sting, I had no idea where I was going. I lifted up my helmet, rubbed my eyes on the sleeve of my combat jacket and saw through blurred vision that I was going in the wrong direction to the rest of the group. For some inexplicable reason, this gave me the giggles. One of the training team heard me laughing and said, 'Oh so you think this is fucking funny Barnes?' 'No Corporal' was my swift reply but it was totally ignored. I was made to stand and watch as the rest were made to crawl through the prickly, painful gorse, making hissing noises and shouting 'I'm an adder'. At the time I was made to feel the most unpopular Jnr Mne in the troop, but I soon got over this because in the very near future I was not the only member of the troop to be singled out.

On exercise, one unfortunate thing I did pick up was the infamous 'Woodbury rash'. It was caused by frequently crawling through the thickets of gorse on the common which left cuts. The open wounds became infected, by what has now been identified as the Streptococcal Bacteria. Often, the pain of crawling through the gorse was intense and the only thing that eased the suffering was when we wore cold weather combat trousers, during the winter, which were lined, making them double the thickness of normal denims. I can remember, on returning back to Lympstone, pulling gorse needles out of my thighs with a pair of tweezers. I suffered terribly from cold sores and on one occasion the Woodbury Common rash had spread to my face, causing large fluid-filled blisters, with a red rash. I have some photographs taken at the time and I can honestly say I was not a pretty sight or even one that my parents would recognise!

PT Sessions – Initial Military Fitness (IMF).

To describe the rig Jnr Mne's wore for PT as laughable would be an understatement. We would not be out of place if we were seen on a cruise ship during the 1920's, walking around the promenade, perhaps playing quoits on the upper deck or even posing as extras in the film 'Carry on Cruising'. Shorts were made of cotton, with a string cord to tie off at the waist, very baggy and pristine white. They were a nightmare to keep clean and iron, as a crease, supposed to be 'sharp as a razor,' had to be made in the centre at the front and back of the legs. Socks were a navy blue, thin, tight and reached up to the knees, looking and feeling just like ladies' stockings, (so I have been informed!). On our tops we wore dark green long-sleeved, rugby style tops with a white, button up collar.

Why the collar was the only piece of the garment that was white I have no idea but, it was a pain in the backside to scrub clean. White canvas plimsolls, with a thin brown rubber sole and white laces were worn on the feet. These plimsolls had to be constantly whitened using Blanco, painted on with a small brush. If you had two sessions of PT in one day, this process had to be done twice. Sometimes the Blanco had not had enough time to dry before our next visit to the gym and I remember putting on damp plimsols. This was not too much of an inconvenience but what was, was the white stain left from the Blanco on the foot of your sock when trying to wash it out.

Marching as a troop to the gym at CTCRM in our ludicrous PT rig involved slapping our left foot down, hard on the ground. This was done to help keep us all in time. I remember sometimes getting pain in my legs and I am sure this has contributed to me having bad knees later in my life!

At CTCRM the PT, was mostly carried out in the main Sports hall, were very demanding and led by the Physical Training Instructors (PTI's) Wing. As Jnr Mnes we were not allowed to walk anywhere once we entered the holy ground of the sports hall. During the session it was constant running from start to finish. My troop was greeted by the sight of the lead PTI, a Cpl Murphy, high up on his box, like a preacher on an altar in a Church, barking his orders at us while his curates' (other PTI's) inspected our kit. Another duty for his curates was to swarm around us, like prostitutes around a £50 note, to make sure we carried out each exercise with the correct technique and completed the right amount. Throughout the sports hall there were black spots marked on the floor, in a grid, with about a metre between each. On the first session every member of the fifty plus troop (even more of the original sixty had dropped out of training by now), was given one black spot. This was your spot, if you finished exercises elsewhere in the sports hall, you had to run back to your spot without hesitation. If you forgot to return to your spot or went to an incorrect spot, then all hell was unleashed in the form of additional press ups. There was no compassion from the PTI's, only sarcastic comments like 'Who taught you to do press ups like that, a paedophile?' or 'Stop making girlie noises, I'm not shagging you'. I can remember when one lad only managed to get three quarters of the way up the 30-foot ropes in the gym. He was the last Jnr Mne down and the only one not to succeed, but we, the troop, all applauded him for his effort. The leading PTI was livid and said what a bunch of losers we were. Why? Well, we had rewarded failure!

Even though your body was yearning for more and more oxygen and struggling to achieve this, when you were back on your spot (if you managed to find the correct one), you had to carry on exercising by marking time (jogging), there was no respite. IMF, sometimes known as Swedish PT, uses a variety of exercises, drills, and rope climbing in a highly disciplined environment to turn raw recruits like us, from a civilian to a military way of thinking and fitness level. This process involves breaking you down and then rebuilding you in a regimented way so as to achieve a level of physical ability and discipline the ordinary person on the street would never dream of. To be honest, I didn't enjoy the IMF sessions, but I did find them a little less unpleasant than going out in the field. It was better for me to be beasted in a warm, clean environment than freezing my nuts off out on Dartmoor or Woodbury Common. In other words, IMF was the lesser of the two evils.

During the ten weeks or so of IMF I actually learnt how to vault over wooden boxes and thus only occasionally smashing my knees on the sides, leaving large bruises. I could climb 30-foot ropes and carryout the Crucifix (the method of securing yourself with your legs while releasing your arms at a height), with only minor rope burns on my hands and legs.

It was compulsory in training for us all to do a bit of pugilism. The whole troop, including training staff, watched as you were literally thrown in the ring, located in the main gym at CTCRM, with boxing gloves on and no head shield. Your opposition was another Jnr Mne from your troop, judged to be roughly the same height and weight as you. I was paired up against a lad that, by chance, had really got on my nerves since day one. I thought great, my chance to get you back, you swine. A PTI brought us into the middle of the ring and as soon as he said 'Box', as quickly as I could, I smashed the guy with a left and then right jab, both landing straight on his nose. I can still recall the shock on his face as his eyes watered and nose bled. And guess what? They put me in the troop boxing team!

A week later the troop was stood on the stairwell of our accommodation block getting a daily briefing from our troop sergeant. He announced the date of the inter CTCRM boxing competition and that our squad was to start training for it tomorrow (by the way, this training never happened). The list of names was called out and when he came to mine, he repeated it in almost a state of shock and said, 'Barnes what the fuck are they using you, for, the sponge?' Unfortunately the 'Sponge' became my nick name.

I was given a black slab, made of what, only god knows, to heat up in hot water and then mould to my teeth and use as a gum shield. Liquorish would have been more effective at protecting my teeth and at least wouldn't have tasted of rubber. I thought if I was going to take part then I had better get some guidance from others in the squad who had some experience of boxing. I asked one Jnr Mne what he did in preparation. He told me that in the morning of the fight he had something light to eat, like a pasty, but loaded with carbohydrates and protein in the weeks before to build up his energy stores and muscle. I thought about it for a moment then a simple plan unfolded in my mind; 'Eat loads'! I was skinny and needed to put some bulk on hence this phase of gluttony seemed sensible. An hour before my fight started, I had to go for a weigh in. When it was my turn, I got onto the scales and I was told by a PTI in charge that I was a staggering 4lbs over my category. The Troop PTI accompanying me said, 'Can't I take him for a run to try and lose it'? The PTI in charge replied, 'No chance'. With the poor advice I was given and all the extra food I had eaten in the days before, now stored as bodyfat, I returned back to my grot and troop to tell them my bad news!

The only other time I boxed in the Royal Marines was against a friend in 40 Commando RM, who I believe trained with or at least knew Terry Marsh, (an ex-Marine and undefeated World Champion in the Light Welterweight Division). Also my friend was later to be heavily involved in the Corps Boxing team. To put it bluntly 'Mike Tyson' beat the shit out of me and thankfully the contest was stopped early by a keen eyed SNCO. I would have liked to have said that a towel was thrown into the ring to save me from any more pain, but it looked like half of 40 Commando's laundry ended up on the canvas in haste.

Another Type of Adventure Training, The Recruit Way!

In week 15 of training the whole troop was taken up to Capel Curig in North Wales for what was called adventure training. It was a bleak place and on camp we had to sleep in our issued sleeping bags, on a concrete floor of an old building with no heating. At first I thought it was going to be a break from the normal harsh routine at CTCRM, a relaxing time like I had had up in North Norfolk while at secondary school; but how wrong I was to be.

The Mountain Leaders (ML's) beasted us at any opportunity. The whole troop was taken to Snowdon National Park by four ton lorries (four tonners). Carrying our loaded bergens, we were thrashed to the peak and then back down the Snowdon Mountain. I remember getting to the top and seeing an elderly woman, disembarking from the Snowdon mountain train, walking in her stilettoes, carrying her poodle under her arm and I was thinking what the hell? We had just slogged our guts out to get up here and there was this lady looking like she had just got off a bloody catwalk!

One morning half of the troop, including me, were taken canoeing on a lake somewhere in Snowdonia. Suddenly the weather took a turn for the worse and the rain and wind came in. In the middle of the lake I capsized and had to be rescued by a PTI who paddled in a canoe from the shore out to me, then towed me back into safety. I'm sure I would have drowned if he hadn't come along. Several others from the troop had to be rescued too. After five days, instead of returning back to CTCRM with new skills and feeling refreshed, I was the opposite, totally shattered and with a fear of all ML's!

Back At CTCRM and 'Death On Two Legs' (DOTL).

The water tank at CTCRM, sometimes known by recruits as the 'Septic Tank', looks like a concrete box which would be at home in an outdoor sewage treatment plant. Stating the obvious, the tank is full of water. It measures approximately ten metres in length and one and a half metres deep. Climbing nets spread across A frames at each end allow access to ropes suspended above the water for the 'Full Regain' to be performed in full fighting order. The water below is to cushion your fall should you drop from the ropes. The septic tank is located just below the shop (the old NAFFI) to the right of, and at the base of the steps, leading to the bottom field and close to what was our accommodation block.

In the Royal Marines Bible, falling in times were classed in the following categories: 10 minutes early is five minutes early; five minutes early is on time and on time is late. We were constantly late. As was normal, if one was guilty of a crime than the whole troop was deemed culpable by the training team and consequently a punishment must be suffered by all. Because of this constantly late appearance by our troop, just for the sheer hell of it, every day for one week, we were woken up at 04.30, ordered to get dressed and fall in by the water tank. We were greeted there by Corporal Peters, nick named 'Death On Two Legs' (DOTL), who later was to be a fellow colleague of mine and member of 9 Troop Charlie Company. We were to serve together in the Falklands War and South Armagh. During my time in training, I can only describe Cpl Peters as being fair, but 'A right bastard'. He wasn't particularly tall or muscular, with body builders biceps the 'size of Bournemouth!' His physical presence wasn't intimidating. What did scare me as a Jnr Mne was his ability to devise truly unique, quite painful punishments and dish them out ad hoc to anyone, he had no bias. His voice, with a distinct 'Geordie accent' added to his harshness and thank fully our ability to detect him even before we saw him. This was beneficial because we could take action by diving for cover behind walls or buildings, thus avoiding any encounter with him and the possibility of more unwanted penalties. I'm sure the only reason the troop had to endure this 04.30 awakening was because Corporal DOTL, was pissed off with having to stay on camp for the week as the duty JNCO. This duty meant staying awake for most of the night. Possibly adding to his frustration was the fact that he had to be away from his family for some time. As a means of letting off steam and maybe getting some sadistic pleasure too, he decided to make us suffer with him.

Back at the septic tank at 04.30, and my troop were told by DOTL to jump in from the side and make sure our heads went under the water. We then had to get out and fall in beside the tank. This process took about half an hour for all fifty of us to pass through. If you were first to go in, you would find yourself standing, soaking wet, in the freezing cold morning air, waiting for everyone to finish. Time seemed to stand still. Worse was to come. If one individual had failed to submerge themselves fully, then the whole troop had to go through the process again.

Often we didn't get back to our grots until 05.30 and by then it was too late to go back to sleep. Soaking wet clothes had to be washed, hung out in the drying room and we all had to shower. This messed up the heads, corridors and grots which had to be immaculate by 07.30 ready for our daily inspection. The floors in the accommodation were laminate and each day they had to be buffed up (polished) to a sparkling shine, with an orange-coloured wax, stored in large cylindrical 5 litre tins. We were supplied with a buffing tool which was oblong shaped, with a cloth on the bottom, about a foot in length and height with a broom handle attached. There was only one buffer available on our floor therefore it was in high demand by everyone. In my grot we often gave up waiting for it and used old towels and got down on our hands and knees to polish the floor with them. Slapping the wax on the floor with our bare hands, our skin would turn orange, particularly between the fingers, just like nicotine stains left by prolonged smoking. These chores all had to be redone after our morning dip.

Other tasks were expected to be completed on a daily basis too. Sheets, pillows and blankets had to be made into bed packs and placed at the top end of your mattress. Clothes had to be precisely folded to the specific size of the Globe and Laurel magazine. Boots polished and other equipment spotless, all stored in a pre-determined location in your locker, matching up to a diagram everyone was given.

Room inspections always gave me the giggles. Every time I heard the order being passed down the corridor, 'Stand by your beds,' I started to chuckle. Why? Well because I knew that most of the time someone in our grot would get picked up and then some or all of their kit would end up on the floor or worse, thrown out of the window. This I found hilarious, until of course it happened to me!

Once I returned from a lecture to find our whole grot had been thrashed. Lockers were pushed over on to their sides, their contents spread throughout the room and intermingled with other Jnr Mnes possessions. Beds had been turned upside down and one thrown out on to the landing. We stared in disbelief. Why was this done by the training team? The answer, because someone had quite simply forgotten to ditch the gash (empty the bin) before we left.

The term 'Nod,' the nickname for recruits and Jnr Mne's, stemmed from the observation that during training most of the time they were sleep deprived. Once out of the elements and sat in a warm classroom when they attended lectures or briefings, most of them would soon 'Nod off'. The lectures were carried out in or around 'Puzzle Palace', an education block at CTCRM so named because of the maze of corridors where it was so easy to get lost and arrive late thus, setting yourself up for another reprimand!

Lectures were a welcome break from the hard, physical sessions or going out in the field. During talks, outwardly I would give the impression that I was engrossed, listening to every word of the speaker, but inside my mind was 'Away with the fairies' and I would be willing for my eyes not to shut. Once I gave up the fight, I just couldn't resist the temptation of closing them. I was woken with a startle, followed by a bollocking, then told to do the 'Roman

Chair', (sometimes known as the Ski Sit') on a wall in the lecture theatre; in fact the same wall I was previously using as a pillow during my nap. The Roman Chair requires the subject to get into a squatting position with their back against a wall, feet shoulder width apart and flat on the ground, with a ninety degree angle at the hips and knees and hold for as long as humanly possible. It is used as a maximal test for muscular endurance and is torturous on the legs, especially for a very tired nod.

Another punishment imparted by DOTL is still vivid in my memory, while staying for a week at the transit camp, just above Oakhampton Village, on Dartmoor. This time the troop had to get up before sunrise, go shirtless, carrying our 'dhobi kit' (wash bag) and towel down to a stream just outside the camp, to have a wash and shave. It was winter, the water was freezing and icicles had formed on the edges of the stream. Not happy with our malingering, DOTL made us all stand in the stream, do press ups that submerged our whole bodies as we bent our arms on the way down, resulting in us gasping for air as we came up on the arm extension phase. It was a very, cold, blunt and rude awakening!

While at Oakhampton Camp one of the training team thought it would be a good idea to have a troop mascot to help build up team spirit. The object of our affection was to be a rock found by the roadside on the moor. The task of carrying and welfare for the rock, named Frank (I can't recall his exact name), was designated daily on a rota to a different member of the troop. Frank was taken everywhere we went while we were at Oakhampton Camp and also back at CTCRM. If you accidently dropped Frank or left him behind in the grots while he was under your responsibility, then you would find yourself in a heap of trouble. We even had a lead for Frank, had to take him for walks, to the galley for scran and even to the NAAFI for 'Stand easy'. He even had pride of place on top of a mound at the bottom field, where he 'stood' with the sick and maimed and watched over us as we were carrying out our PT. In the end Frank was unceremoniously tossed into the mud on the estuary of the river Exe where he rests, possibly with other rocks, for eternity

As Jnr Marines we had to wear black berets with a red patch and Corps Cap Badge, just above the left eye. The black berets were to signify that we were in training and distinguish us from the green of the Commando trained ranks. The cap badge was held in place on the inside of the beret by two protruding pins with eye-lets. These in turn were fixed in by a single pin, threaded through them like a brooch. These pins were used as a nasty, almost brutal, draconian form of punishment and feared by all Jnr Mnes at CTCRM. If you angered a training team member you might get 'Cap badged'. This was when the Jnr Mne, wearing his beret was struck on the front of the cap badge, sometimes with an object. The two protruding pins would be knocked into your forehead and immediately cause tremendous pain. At the very least an eye watering experience and the worst, bleeding, swelling and bruising the next day, with the possibility of concussion. It was a Nod's nightmare.

Your Dad's Dead!

One other Story I must tell, happened in training while I was staying on the first floor in the Normandy Block accommodation, and again it involved DOTL. One morning I was milling around in my grot when he came in and said, 'The Company Commander wants to speak to you'. I followed DOTL downstairs and to the Portsmouth Company Commanders office. I knocked on the door, was called to enter, marched in, saluted and reported correctly.

The Captain was sat behind a desk, he told me that he had some bad news and I might like to sit down. 'Your father has died' said the officer. I was initially shocked and thought that's strange. Last time I saw him merely a few weeks ago he looked okay and I had only spoken to him the night before on the phone when all seemed well. A visit by the Grim Reaper to my father was the last thing I, or he, had expected! I could feel myself getting upset and thought of my future and that my father would want me to carry on training, finish and get the famous Green Beret.

The Captain told me in a kind manner, sympathetic to the situation 'I will give you some time on your own in here to speak to your mother on the phone'. He dialled a number and after passing me the handset, stood up and walked out of the room. I could hear ringing then a click as someone answered. Before the other person spoke, I asked, 'Mum are you alright?' She said she was obviously upset but didn't seem too distraught to me, almost as if she had been expecting it; strange!. After a few sentences, I thought 'I don't recognise that voice'. I said, 'Mum, it's Terry.' The woman replied, 'I don't know a Terry, I want my Peter'. Shocked I stood up, put the receiver on the desk, walked to the office door, opened it and saw the Company Commander standing there. I explained to him that the woman on the other end of the phone was not my mother. He asked, 'Is your name not Peter Barber'? I replied 'No', and then he pushed past me to get to the phone saying, 'You better get back to your grot', without even an apology. Back at my grot I found the appropriately named DOTL standing by the doorway. He said, 'Don't worry son, take your time'. I told him that it wasn't my dad that had died. He swore at the top of his voice, 'For fuck sake, you've got to be joking'. I think he could tell from the frown on my forehead that I wasn't. Later in the day, DOTL and my troop sergeant came to see me to explain that they had been told by the hierarchy that a Nod who's surname began with the letter B, father had died. They came to the first person on their troop register whose surname started with that letter. Great I thought, what a bunch of twats! To this day I'm still not sure whether it was a genuine administrative mistake or just some prank to see how I would react. Surely, they couldn't have been that depraved and cruel; could they?

<u>Life As A Junior Marine Continues.</u>

Apart from the early morning septic tank plunge, mud runs on the River Exe were another form of punishment. As a troop, we were marched down to the bottom field, taken across the railway line, and onto the mud flats of the estuary. Once there we were physically 'thrashed' by carrying out a variety of exercises and sprints. During training at CTCRM I ended up in the mud three times. Again, it wasn't so much the exercise that bothered me, (although I probably wouldn't have agreed with this statement at the time), it was the cleaning of my clothing, and sometimes, if we were wearing it, webbing, which stressed me out the most. It was very difficult to remove the mud from the crooks and crannies and the unpleasant, lingering smell if you washed your clothes by hand.

Scrubbing items with a brush did very little to entirely remove both. With a total of only four washing machines and driers on camp for all recruits to use, it was an impossible task to get every item washed thoroughly and dried for the next day.

Below I have given a tongue in cheek description of a mud run; the Ornithologists among you might enjoy this!

Mud, Glorious Mud!

CTCRM looks down and across the striking vista of the River Exe. The river at this point during low tide, leaves extensive mud flats; a playground for a variety and sometimes unique flora and fauna. Particularly in the early mornings, under the vague description of fauna, you might come across the elusive Royal Marines Recruit. This occasional spectacle can be observed throughout the year, even during the dark depths of winter, with the cold ambient temperature having no effect on their behaviour. These creatures can be seen, in some numbers, leaving the relative safety of Lympstone, crossing the railway track and entering into the estuary. By their actions the recruits appear to be at home, jumping, diving and generally running around in the mud. To the casual observer one might think they are seeing the protagonists on a feeding frenzy and in fact it has been known for some individuals to accidentally swallow quantities of mud. Why? Well we are not sure, but quite possibly, it could be to gain extra nutrients to supplement their meagre diet from the galley.

Out front, alone and in pristine condition, standing on two skinny legs is the dominant one. 'Mother Duck' can just be made out to be strutting around, gesturing with his unfeathered bare wings, and making a deep honking noise from within, indecipherable, but sounds like 'go, go, go'. After only a few minutes the recruits are almost totally camouflaged with mud, the only thing visible is the whites of their eyes and the beads of sweat running down their foreheads, glistening from the early morning sun rays as it starts to rise above the embankment at CTCRM.

Amongst the calls of the Avocets and Curlews the recruits give their positions away by the frequent sounds of whimpering and wailing and the occasional cry of what could be interpreted as 'Oh no, not again!' When stood erect no webbed feet are observable because the depth of mud is up to their knees, perhaps the elusive SBS (Special Boat Service) frog might be amongst them?

On completion (approximately after one hour), the recruits, looking totally exhausted, leave the quagmire and re-enter CTCRM. The disorganised flock are led by Mother Duck, who can now be seen close up and is sporting a white singlet top, embossed with what looks like two small pieces of red coloured wood in the centre of his chest and something green on his head, (we will come to the significance of that in the future). Displaying its puffed-out chest, this inflated individual appears to gain control and after some cackling, gets the recruits into single file. He then sends freezing cold water over the cohort from what can only be described as a long red appendage emerging from his hip. The recruits scream, what this represents, ecstasy, pain, or some unusual mating ritual I'm not sure. The result is that some of the group's original plumage and colour is returned. Back out in the estuary, what is left in the mud are strange patterns and if viewed from above sometimes they can resemble numbers or perhaps letters.

This strange wildlife phenomenon can be witnessed in week two or thirty of Royal Marines recruit's training (dates are published to their parents who arrive in flocks). The latter is recommended because the recruits leave a more decipherable message in the mud. This can be ideally viewed from up on the embankment, outside the old NAAFI or on the JNCO's balcony. If you do not have access into the camp, I would suggest taking a stroll along the new public footpath that now passes close by CTCRM. During inclement weather, it might be worth risking a quick glimpse of this phenomenon by catching the regular train from Exeter to Exmouth and hopefully it will briefly stop at Lympstone Commando Station – good luck!

Rock Climbing.

Let me introduce to you, the reader, two methods of how to put a Jnr Mne off rock climbing for life. The first, while he is attempting to climb, is to release the only rope attached to him at about five foot from the ground as he is descending. He falls flat on his back, straight onto the granite below, feels like he has been hit by a bus, winds himself, simply so you, as the person in charge, can finish early and go and have a wet with your oppos.

The second method is carried out when a run up (this is the technique used to ascend up a cliff face as opposed to an abseil down). is being performed. As he reaches the summit of the cliff the people on top are ordered to carry on pulling the rope, which is fastened to the Jnr Mne, and instead of landing safely and stopping, he gets dragged along the ground, smashes his knee against a boulder and ends up in hospital. Well, this is exactly what happened to me in March 1980, while adventure training in North Wales and on Dartmoor. Ever since if anyone asked me if I would like to go climbing, they get an abrupt 'No'. The strange thing is after these painful incidents, I used to love abseiling, especially out of helicopters. Nowadays, I would once again like to have a go but I think that my body would definitely let me down, rather than, as in the past, a halfwit with a rope.

After leaving hospital at CTCRM, I was, and I am not ashamed to say this, back trooped (put back in training). Also, my maternal grandfather had died, and I was given a long weekend off to attend his funeral. This meant joining a new troop in week 24 of training on my return from leave. 'Back troopers' are often frowned upon by the original recruits or Jnr Mne members of the troop they join. This is possibly because they are looked at as being weak, a failure, and also that they have not been in the cohort since the start and therefore not shared the same trials and experiences. However, I didn't find this with my new troop, they all seemed quite friendly and I was left to get on. Also, my training team had changed from a brutal, to a more supportive mentor role, led by Lt Byford and Sgt McIntyre.

Week 24 .

Programmed in week 24 of the Nods training schedule is the field exercise 'Holdfast'. As the title suggests, it means holding defensive positions against an enemy. This exercise was carried out to create a scenario that had been feared by the West during the cold war years. If the USSR and the Warsaw Pack went to war with the rest of Europe and sent divisions of units, especially tanks such as the T54, flooding in we would have to hold defensive positions. It was planned and no secret that the British Army was to defend central Europe and the Royal Marines the northern flank. What did it mean for us on Exercise Holdfast? Well, it meant spending hours in pairs, digging, with a small sized shovel and pickaxe, a six foot deep and long (or there abouts), two foot wide trench on Woodbury Common

It was difficult digging in the dark. Not being able to see what you were trying to remove and constantly watching out for your partner as they swung their shovel or pickaxe seemed a recipe for disaster. The trench would be half covered by a tarpaulin, topped with soil and turf for camouflage and was supposed to be able to take the weight of a tank going over it. The other half of the trench was exposed to the elements.

Our two-man teams would do a buddy, buddy system, whereby one would sleep or cook while the other stood guard and then after a time, swop roles. It always seemed to rain on exercise and Holdfast was no exception. Often, the sheltered part of the trench would let in water, either from the roof or just drain in from the open section, making all of your kit soaking wet and, after digging and lying in dirt, your possessions absolutely filthy. While trying to sleep in the sheltered section it would be tight if the sides hadn't been dug wide enough, or even painful if rocks were sticking out. With shoulders and hips crushed up against the walls I felt enclosed and, possibly with the fear of being buried alive, claustrophobic.

A bonus while on Exercise Holdfast was that we had to wear Nuclear, Biological and Chemical (NBC) suits. These were made of nylon with a second, charcoal impregnated, felt layer. These kept us warm but also protected our legs and arms when we crawled through the gorse. On Holdfast we not only suffered from a lack of sleep, but after four days and nights we also had to yomp back to camp in our NBC suits. The first mile with our respirators on. I felt like I was in a sauna, my mask filled up with snot and phlegm and the eye pieces had misted up so I could hardly see where I was marching and I kept bumping into the guy in front. It certainly was the worst exercise in training and I had to do it twice due to me being back trooped! Little was I to know that only just over two years later I would be digging in on an Island and living in the same filthy conditions, at a location over 8,000 miles from the UK, the Falkland Islands!

<u>The Commando Tests.</u>

Moving on from exercise Holdfast the final big tests began. Because we were in the Commando phase of training we no longer wore black berets but cap comforters. This headgear distinguished us from other Nods. To keep our fitness levels up, we had to run everywhere we went on camp, outside of our accommodation block, whether in uniform or civilian clothes. This was a pain in the backside when we had to do personal administration jobs such as taking our dhobi to the laundrette, or in other situations, like returning back to our grots from the galley with full stomachs.

In the last few weeks with my newfound troop I began to progress.

I seemed to be left on my own by the training team and not negatively criticised all of the time. I felt more confident and this seemed to show by my progress. I was no longer the whipping boy. For example after some tuition and encouragement I could now do a full regain over the septic tank. Do not let me fool you and make you think that things had become easier, they hadn't. The Commando tests had started in earnest, (a full list can be seen in Appendix A).

The time limits, obstacles and routes for the Commando tests have not been changed before, during and after my attempt in 1980. The only difference now is the new equipment, clothing and faces. The one exception being an extra minute for the Endurance Course because of a slight change in the route. At reunions or memorial parades, I can look at anyone that has a green lid on their head and smile, knowing exactly what they have gone through. They are part of the Royal Marines Commando family and mine too!

I had successfully completed all of the previous assessments throughout training. These ongoing, progressive and demanding tests don't often get mentioned. Things like passing the assault course, before it is combined with the Tarzan, the 200 metre fireman's carry, climbing the 30-foot ropes and a full regain over the septic tank wearing full fighting order, personal weapon tests on the SLR, GPMG (General Purpose Machine Gun) and the SMG (Sub Machine Gun) to name but a few. Also, one that is completed after being out on the final exercise for four days and nights, when you are already sleep deprived, filthy and wet from the constant Dartmoor drizzle, is the 10-mile load carry back to

CTCRM. There is the personal administration of cleaning and preparing clothing, footwear, weapons and accommodation to a high standard ready for inspection by the training team, all adding to the physical and psychological challenges throughout.

The bottom field at CTCRM can be seen from the train as it passes, on its way back and forth between Exmouth and Exeter, occasionally stopping at Lympstone Commando Station. This image can strike fear into any recruit. Today I still get butterflies as I arrive at CTCRM by train and the assault course first comes into view, followed by the white accommodation blocks. The bottom field is not only home to the assault course, but it also houses a small 25 metre live firing range, where you can sometimes witness recruits returning from just completing the Endurance Course, getting ready or taking part in their shooting test. About halfway up from the station, the bottom field has a well-worn circle forever imprinted on the grass, where hundreds of recruits and trained ranks on selection courses (e.g. PTI 2's) have walked, run, warmed up, cooled down or thrown up once they have finished their exercise sessions or the Tarzan Assault Course. I mention the bottom field because often this is the first place you see as a recruit and possibly the last as you leave the camp at CTCRM, as a trained rank or a disappointed civilian.

After training I only returned to CTCRM once as a trained rank while I was in the Corps, in a Land Rover to pick up some ammunition, with colleagues from 40 Commando. Although the buildings were familiar, the environment seemed far too Pussers for me (strict) and alien to the more relaxed atmosphere in a Commando Unit.

The 9 Mile Speed March.

This is as it 'Says on the tin'. A nine mile speed march, carrying full fighting order and rifle, to be completed in 90 minutes as a troop.

On the day of my 9 Miler, I can remember leaving CTCRM in a convoy of four tonners, then being dropped somewhere on or near Woodbury common. The run back to CTCRM was mainly on narrow country roads, finishing along 'Heart Break Lane' and finally into camp. Today I believe recruits are drummed in by the Royal Marines Band, back through CTCRM as they finish their last few hundred metres. Running along the roads and lanes at some points felt quite oppressive. These were mostly small single track width, enclosed by hawthorn bushes, with steep banks on either side, letting little or no breeze through to help cool me down. With thirty one Jnr Mnes' gasping more and more for air as the distance and stress increased, it was not pleasant, especially if you were in the middle of the troop. To make things worse, I had someone in front (who I won't name), whose feet were 'Ten to two' and kept on putting me out of step and therefore also everyone else behind. If you, unluckily, have ever experienced this I'm sure you'll know that it can be extremely frustrating and can slowly wear your patience down. If you haven't, well it's like being in a hurry to catch a bus, you're in a shop at the checkout and in front of you is someone, holding up the queue, who's decided to empty their piggy bank and is counting out their copper coins to pay a massive bill.

The whole troop managed to complete the 9 Mile Speed March

and yes, it was tiring, but at this final stage of training we were exceptionally fit and expected to pass. The purpose of this test was to simulate being tasked to move long distances quickly, on foot, in war. If you couldn't pass this test and still be able to stand on your own two feet, in reality this meant that you would not be able to fight in a battle. Thus being a liability to yourself and your comrades.

The Endurance Course.

The Endurance Course is a six-mile (9.65 km) run with obstacles. It starts with a two mile section on undulating footpaths, through a moorland landscape and includes pitch dark tunnels, the sheep dip (two tunnels that are totally covered by water), parallel pipes, one called the 'Smartie tube', and wading pools, including Peters Pool. Then there is a four mile (6 km) run back to CTCRM. Thrown in at the end is a shooting test, where the recruit must hit 6 out of 10 shots at a 25m target. If you fail the shooting you fail the whole test. This had to be finished in 72 minutes, I believe due to route changes, this has increased by one minute.

As already mentioned the Endurance Course is located on Woodbury Common. Before my syndicate started, we had to get there on our own two feet, ready at the start line for an inspection. All Endurance Course attempts were carried out in the morning. The start line was about three and a half miles away, so we had to leave CTCRM very early to get there on time, often in the dark, especially if you were one of the first three man syndicates. These syndicates were chosen alphabetically and, of course, Barnes was right at the top of the list. Once at the start line the inspection was carried out by the training team. This involved checking our fighting order had all of the equipment in it, our water bottles were full and even that our boots were polished.

As we set off at a run, the first obstacle was a zig zag shaped tunnel followed by a downhill into Peters Pool. It was winter when I did the Endurance Course and there was ice on the top surface of the water. Being the first syndicate of the troop through, I could hear the cracks opening up as the ice smashed when my lower half entered. It felt like glass slicing through my shins. If I was lucky and Peters Pool was low due to a lack of rain, then I would only get wet up to my midriff. However if it had been raining the water would sometimes reach my neck or higher. If you were short in stature then you really were at a disadvantage. After Peters Pool, the route took me up and down a steep path that led to the Sheep Dip. Going underwater at the Sheep Dip never bothered me. The only thing with this was that it was near the start of the course and you got saturated by water. The water would seep into every piece of clothing and crevice of your body and it made the subsequent obstacles, and run back, even more demanding because of the added weight of wet clothes, kit and sometimes painful chafing between the legs.

As soon as you were through the Sheep Dip, you could leave your syndicate and complete the rest of the Endurance Course and the run back to CTCRM on your own. Some of the other tunnels further on were in complete darkness, contained water and were graced with large pebbles on the ground. Often with the SLR slung across my back, the barrel would get stuck in the roof of tunnels as I crawled along. I found this very frustrating because of the delay it caused and sometimes I would end up cracking my head on the ceiling or with the rifle barrel, as I tried to dislodge it. As my legs were numb from the cold, most of the time I couldn't feel the bumps and scrapes to my shins and knees. There were rumours going around CTCRM that some civilians would throw bottles down the tunnels so that we had to literally crawl over broken glass. Luckily, I never saw nor experienced this. Today, to prevent any misuse and for health and safety reasons, most of the tunnels have locked gates on them.

Once all of the obstacles were finished, the route to Lympstone from Woodbury Common, took us on to tarmacked road. The sad thing is, I quite enjoyed (if that is the correct term) the run back. I was on my own, I could go off into my own little mind set or stare at the countryside thinking of nothing. It was almost a stress release. This mind numbness was only matched by the cold numbness felt in the extremities of my toes and fingers!

As I ran down Heart Break Lane and glanced up to my right, pinned to an oak tree I could see the legendary caricature of a Bootneck with the caption reading 'It's only pain and below, 500m to go'. When I got to the top of the stairs of the foot bridge which crosses over the main road between Exmouth and Exeter, my legs burnt. Once, I was accompanied some of the way back by my section commander Cpl Watts (KIA 1982 Falklands War). As I got to the main gate at CTCRM his words of encouragement really helped me for the final push (I shall continue with this story later in the book). At the range my SLR even though wet and dirty, fired and although I was tired I passed the shooting. As I was walking back through camp to my grot I noticed blood on my denims, just below my shins. When I took them off my lower legs were covered in grazes that looked like they had been slashed with a knife, it must have been the ice on the surface of Peters Pool.

The Tarzan Assault Course.

To get to the start of the Tarzan Assault Course you have to climb up a 30 metre ladder, carrying your rifle, full fighting order and holding in one hand, a toggle that you have previously dipped in water to help prevent friction as you slide downwards. At the top you are greeted by a PTI. On his command you had to put the toggle over the downward rope, then loop both of your hands through. On the word 'Go,' from the PTI you push off from the platform and at the same time raise your feet for the first few metres to avoid the safety net just below. On the slide down as you gather speed, then eventually approach the earth, a safety rope stops you from smashing into the climbing net, metal uprights and/or the ground. Your momentum continues as you swing forward then back. By untwisting one hand from the toggle, you fall to the ground, landing on two feet. Then you release the other hand, fling the toggle to the floor and run as fast as possible to the first obstacle of seven.

During one go on the Tarzan Assault Course, any fears that I had about how high I was off the ground, were reinforced by what happened next. At the top of the death slide the lad in front of me was almost halfway down and somehow prematurely, managed to slip one hand out off the toggle and fall to the ground. In a cry of pain he lay there and you could see by the angle of his legs, at least one was broken. Back then the sick bay entrance was based in the pre-war buildings, (that still stand today and are used by the All-Arms Commando Course) located only a few feet away from where the lad lay. The doors swung open, the injured Jnr Mne was quickly thrown on to a stretcher, the two bearers almost jogging back into sickbay with their load and no expression on their faces. To make the situation worse it was a Friday and pass out day. It was traditional for the parents, families and friends visiting for the pass out, to have a tour around CTCRM. One such party just happened to be having a quick look at the Tarzan Course at the same time as the incident. Just before the lad in front of me went, from the top of the tower I could hear below the RM officer leading the tour saying, 'Yes, this is the famous Tarzan Course, the start of which you see in front of you and it is called the 'Death Slide'. Just after that, the lad landed on the ground next to the visiting and stunned civilian group, who stared in disbelieve at the medical staff's lack of empathy as they took him away. I thought that because of this accident we would be stopped from continuing. But the PTI standing next to me, who also had observed the same event, had different ideas. He casually said, 'Check your toggle so you don't do what that twat just did' and told me to go!

After the final obstacle on the Tarzan Course, you then have to run as fast as you can past the FIBUA (fighting in built-up areas) house, static training buildings and the range. As your lungs are gasping for air you are greeted by the smell rising from the nearby sewage plant, then it's on to the bottom field. Once on there you continue to complete the twelve obstacles of the Assault Course, such as the monkey bars, six-foot wall and a half regain.

The combined Tarzan and Assault course was all to be completed in thirteen minutes. For me it was absolutely gut busting, almost a sprint from start to finish, every hurdle had to be attacked and cleared at full effort, there was no let up. During the cold, the metal bars on the obstacles would numb my fingers and there was always the fear of falling off into the freezing water below or on to the gravel. This could cause a delay in your time, resulting in a failure, or worse, an injury.

The final task, using a rope, was to scale up the near vertical thirty foot wall. Once at the top of the wall and safety, with what air was left in your lungs, you had to shout out your name to a PTI who was recording your time. I can remember as I reached the pinnacle of the wall, feeling like my lungs were just about to burst, shouting my name out and almost throwing up. The PTI saw that I was just about to puke and had the wisdom to turn me away from where I had come just in case my vomit went cascading down the thirty-foot wall onto some other poor Jnr Mne making his way up.

The Thirty Miler.

Out of all of the Commando tests, the last, and by far not the least, was the Thirty Miler. This was done carrying your fighting order and rifle, and had to be completed in under eight hours. It was a mixture of running and walking, starting across moorland, followed by tarmac roads. I found this the most challenging, both physically and psychologically of all of the Commando tests. Walking around CTCRM you could always tell the lads who had just completed the course. Most looked absolutely knackered and quite a few were hobbling while trying to hide the pain, but all showing stiffness in their legs. They were allowed by their training team to wear flip flops on their feet for the next few days as they went about their business in CTCRM, showing their blisters off, almost like a badge of honour. The thing is that the Thirty Miler must not be looked at as a single test, carried out in isolation. It comes at the end of an enduring week of other extremely demanding tasks, thus demonstrating exceptional 'Spirit' and a physical fitness achieved only by top performing athletes in sport. But unlike the situation in top sport, particularly football, where you have everything laid on a plate, such as very large financial packages, huge houses and fame, in the Royal Marines your incentive and reward is your coveted Green Beret.

On the day of my Thirty Miler, I remember getting up at some ridiculous hour of the morning, while it was dark, having a dhobi and going to the galley for a 'specially prepared' breakfast (the scran wasn't any different from normal). After a quick inspection by our training team, the troop were loaded on to the back of the four tonners and driven from CTCRM to a location on Dartmoor. When we arrived at our destination it was still dark. The troop had a final inspection of our fighting orders and a briefing.

As we set off in our section of ten, the sun started to rise against the background of a clear sky. The first path led us up to a Tor, the one of many to come. We stopped off at various check points on the Moor, where wet's and words of encouragement were given by members of the training team. At one check point, close to lunch time, I can remember being handed a Pussers pasty and devouring it, and at the same time knocking back a cold wet made from a glucose powder, tasting something close to oranges. Because the concoction hadn't been mixed properly, some of the powder used to make the drink hit the back of my throat and rather than quenching my thirst, it made me feel like someone had rubbed the back of my gullet with coarse sandpaper.

The first fifteen miles or so seemed to pass quickly, we all managed to stick together, the difficulty was not the general incline and decline but the uneven ground of the moorland. Your gait had to change nearly every step as you went up and down on sods of grass, sometimes missing your footing and falling over. With aching legs and back It was then a struggle to get back up. For the unlucky ones like me, our feet would end up in a puddle of brown, stinking water. The DMS boot offering no or little protection from water, caused the sock and foot to get wet, this would have dire and painful consequences later on in the yomp for me.

Just over halfway through the Thirty Miler the terrain changed from moorland to track and finally asphalt road, which made the going slightly easier. Regrettably, on our last quarter of the yomp my section took the wrong route due to a map reading error by another Nod who in my eyes, rightly to some degree, received a lot of verbal abuse. We ended up doing approximately an extra one and half miles. This may not sound far but after you have already completed twenty miles plus, it can be soul destroying.

Just after this incident, psychologically it was the most difficult part for me. I suddenly felt stressed and panicked because I thought I was going to fail. I started to go into my shell, not speaking to anyone and before I knew it, I was dropping back from the rest of the section but thankfully only by a few metres. I looked up, Sgt McIntyre turned to me and said quietly, so nobody else heard, in a calm manner, and characterised by his Scottish accent, 'Barnes, you've not caused me a single problem since you have been in my troop, don't you dare start now'! His face was serious but deep down I knew he only wanted to motivate me to pass.

By the time my section approached the finish line I had caught up. The last few hundred metres was downhill and instead of helping, it ended up making it more painful because my toes were being pushed further to the front of my boots, making them throb. As we passed the finish line I was almost in tears, well I admit my eyes did water! Where I stood I felt like collapsing in a heap. Listening to instructions, I was told to lay on my back and rest my legs on a grass bank to raise them up. As I lay there, I thought 'Fuck, that was the hardest thing I have ever done'. I can't remember the journey back to Lympstone, only the stiffness and soreness as I dismounted off the back of the four tonner when we arrived. It seemed to take an eternity for me to walk back to my grot. However a final challenge awaited. Climbing up the stairs to the top floor in our accommodation block was a nightmare. Eventually arriving back in my bed space I flung my rifle and fighting order down on the floor. After many painful attempts, I managed to get my puttees, boots and socks off. My left foot was covered in blisters on the bottom and top, worse was to come. My right foot had suffered little damage on top, only a small blister on the big toe, underneath was very different. My whole sole was one large blood blister from heel to toe. As I pressed the skin, fluid moved up and down, like oil on water. I pushed too hard and the substance gushed out, on to the nicely polished floor we had spent so long last night preparing for inspection. I didn't feel any pain at this stage but thought I had better put some TCP on my foot to stop it getting infected. I was so pleased that I had watered down the antiseptic because the pain was just bearable. If I had put the TCP on undiluted or worse Dettol, like some other members of my troop, you would have heard me scream in unison with them.

Getting up the day after the Thirty Miler was truly an agonising trial. My body ached all over and as for my legs, I seriously wanted to have them amputated to stop the pain. After a shower and check by the training team we were allowed to relax for the rest of the day. So I went off over to the NAFFI to get a drink wearing sports rig and flip flops, knowing that no one would bollock me for being inappropriately dressed and if they did, I could say 'Kings Squad,' (well almost). It was with a smug expression that I walked into the Nods bar at the NAAFI and watched as eyes turned to me, they knew and so did I, that I had finished the Thirty Miler. I ordered a Cider and Black (blackcurrant), a popular drink at the time and sat down contented. I was seventeen, a Royal Marines Commando, yet in the eyes of the law I was not yet an adult or legally allowed to vote or drink alcohol. Still the weekend was near and 'The Gronks Ball' in the River Exe Club would soon be here. All that was left of training was a week of rehearsal for my pass out parade.

Early July 1979, 16 year old Junior Mne Barnes showing off my first crew cut!

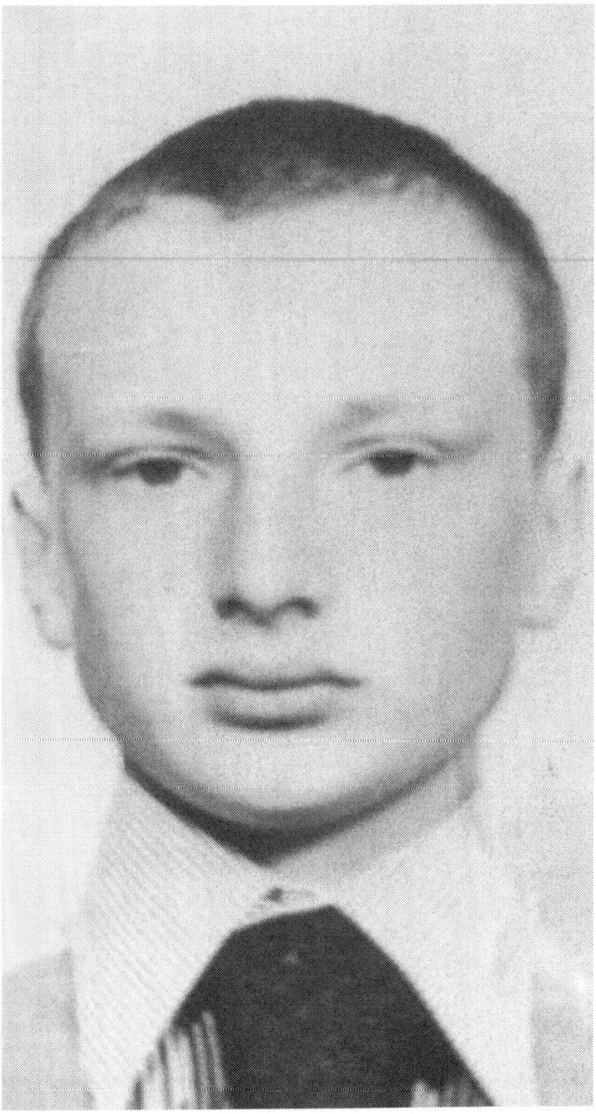

My Pass Out Troop at Commando Training Centre Royal Marines, 1980.

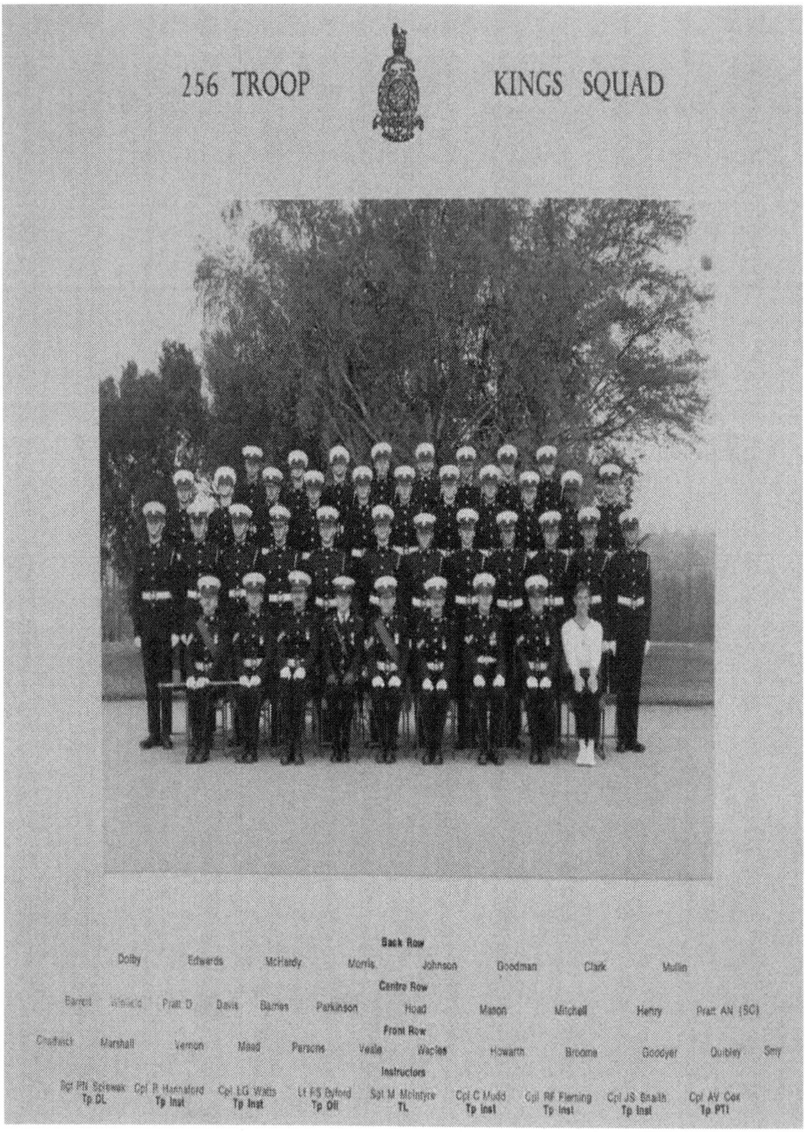

4. PASSING OUT AND MY FIRST DRAFT.

My pass out day parade was on 2nd May, 1980. The troop didn't have the prestige of a member of the Royal Family attend the drill. Instead we had a Commodore from the Royal Navy, who just gave us a glancing inspection with a few words of encouragement, took the march past and hurriedly disappeared into the Officers Mess for drinks and scran. My close family came down in a minibus from Ipswich, to spend the day at CTCRM and take me home for a long weekend leave before I was to join, with nine others from my troop, 40 Commando Royal Marines (RM) based at Seaton Barracks, Crownhill, Plymouth. My mother only remembers how good the food was in the galley, particularly the Cornish pasty, and not our well-rehearsed drill and presentation of berets! I could not wait to get out of CTCRM and never to go back, the day I had dreamed of since joining had actually arrived. Yes, I was a bit anxious about joining my new unit, but it couldn't be worse than training, could it? It was moving to receive my Green Beret in a ceremony that my parents were able to celebrate with me. We were given our Green Berets days before passing out so we could shape them properly for the ceremony. It was like receiving the best present ever, twice; the second time in front of my family, where at least I managed to control my emotions.

After my short break at home, I travelled by train, then taxi and arrived at Seaton Barracks, Plymouth at approximately 05.00 on a Tuesday. As I nervously walked into the guardroom before I could get a word in the duty Corporal behind a desk asked, 'Just drafted here'? Followed by 'You can get your head down in one of the cells if you want mate'. I was going to reply with, 'Yes Corporal' but because he had called me mate, I just replied 'Yes, cheers mate' and he didn't even blink an eye.

I completed my joining routine and was allocated to a Company and troop. Unknown to me at the time, the Company I was sent to was where I was to spend a large part of my military career, my beloved 9 Troop, Charlie Company, 40 Commando RM. This was unusual because in the Royal Marines, unlike some parts of the armed forces, you are drafted to a different unit, ship or establishment every eighteen months.

However, all did not start off rosy. 40 Commando RM had just returned from leave after being on a yearlong tour in NI. The Marines on that tour were obviously closely bonded and although some had been drafted, many remained and I felt as if I was an outsider, a persona non grata. Being so young too, I was often picked on to do extra things such as cleaning the heads, emptying the gash and my name came up for guard duties more often than it should. Being the 'sprog' of the group, you could expect this to happen to some degree in any organisation,.

I was put into a section of the troop whose commander had been returned to unit (RTUd) from the SBS. His service within the SBS accredited him respect and in fact some fear by others. This led to Marines, even by some of the same rank or above, being scared to question and confront him. He held an arrogance and coldness in his eyes which said, 'I'm better than you' and he had a particular dislike for the new lads, which was bad news for me. He treated those of us in his section like raw recruits and thought that we needed to do extra PT sessions, often while the rest of the troop went home. My section commander was quite frankly a nasty piece of work, a bully. I felt trapped. I was part of a captive audience and forced to carry out his orders. I despised this period in the Corps and the section commander too. It wasn't until years later that I heard from my oppo's in 40 Commando RM that my then section commander while he was in the SBS, was detested. In fact he had been RTUd because he upset everyone and was 'dropped' (punched) by someone else in his section. I also learnt that he was only ever in it for himself, not a team player. I wasn't at all surprised! He was the type of guy that wouldn't even piss on you if you were on fire unless he was desperate to relieve himself or could benefit in some other way.

Anyway, it was a terrible way to start my career off in 40 Commando RM. It knocked the confidence out of me, and as a result, I isolated myself from others and went into my own personal shell. I didn't connect with anyone in my troop for months. In my spare time I would just go for walks to Mutley Plain, a suburb in Plymouth with shops, just to get away from camp and people.

Like anywhere, there were the occasions of high jinks which sometimes went over the top and one incident comes to mind. A Marine that had joined 40 Commando RM just after me and was straight out of training, had a girlfriend living in Exeter. She was pregnant by him and every opportunity he got, and rightly so, he would travel back from Plymouth to see her. Because of this, his standards slipped, he would get picked up on parades, he rarely helped out cleaning, and didn't mix; his heart just wasn't in it. One day some 'Old sweats' took it upon themselves to break into his locker where they found dirty dhobi and mouldy pieces of food. They filled a bath full of cold water, washing powder, and any type of disinfectant they could find, then threw all of his possessions in it. One at a time, the sprogs of Charlie Company, were taken to go and see what would happen if you didn't keep up with the standards of the Royal Marines. This unfortunate lad now had the added stress of cleaning this up and getting everything back in order. Later in the year this poor soul was to die in a horrific road accident.

Out On Exercise With 40 Commando RM.

During my first year in 40 Commando RM I went on several exercises. The first one was on Salisbury Plain, titled 'Rough Diamond' and it was almost no different from my nemesis in training, Exercise Holdfast. It rained constantly, filling up our trenches with water before we had even finished them. Compared to Woodbury Common the only blessing was the chalk was easier to get through when digging. On one occasion and being a sprog, I was detailed off for a working party to help dig in a Land Rover. It was a mammoth hole and once finished, feeling exhausted I had to return back to complete my own trench.

On Rough Diamond, during a company advance to contact with the enemy, I was deemed a casualty by an umpire and sent back to the medical tents to spend one luxurious night under cover, while the rest of my company were out in the elements. That night as I lay on a camp bed I could hear the heavy rain hitting the canvas of the ten man tent I was in. Feeling so pleased I wasn't out in the trenches, I fell asleep.

The next day, in bright sunshine, I was released as a casualty and told that I had to make my own way back to my Company. Fortunately, I managed to find our Charlie Company Technical Quarter Master (TQ). The TQ said that he would be taking a four tonner out to the troops tomorrow for a resupply. In the meantime, he put me on sentry duty, in a field about half a mile away from their temporary location. He gave me my arcs of fire and then left and unbelievably, forgot about me. I lay in this field for over half the day and to be honest I was quite happy daydreaming. It was only by luck that I was eventually relieved. When a fellow Marine happened to be passing my position I asked him the time and he replied, ' Bloody hell, how long have you been out here'? I said, 'Oh about 5 hours'. He told me to come in and have some scran at HQ, then he would find a four tonner to take me back to 9 Troop.

On my return to my troop, it looked as if they had had a very rough night. I found out that one lad had had enough of the exercise, left his trench, walked to the nearest road, hitched a lift with a civilian and eventually got on a train back to Plymouth to see his girlfriend.

While on Rough Diamond I had my first experience outside of training, for carrying and firing the 84mm Carl Gustav Mk 2. Weighing almost 32 lbs it was a struggle keeping pace with the rest of the troop while doing a speed march. However, the compensation for me was being able to fire from it a high explosive anti-tank (HEAT) round at an old burnt out vehicle and watching the devastation it caused.

On another exercise, worse was to come. 40 Commando RM embarked on HMS Bulwark in preparation for 'Exercise Teamwork 80'. Before we left for Norway where the exercise was to be carried out, the ship sat off Plymouth Sound. Someone in the hierarchy decided it would be a good idea to do a practice disembarking on to Dartmoor, then for us to do a yomp overnight and afterwards return back onto the ship by helicopter. 9 Troop were flown off HMS Bulwark by Wessex helicopters just as bad weather closed in and it became dark. I can remember looking forward towards the cockpit and seeing through a gap the pilot's lower legs and feet, pushing up and down on the two anti-torque peddles like two pistons on a steam locomotive, in an effort to try and control the aircraft. Once on Dartmoor, the wind picked up and the rain came down heavily and persistently. It was an awful night, one of the worst experienced in Devon for years. In fact it was so bad that some lads succumbed to hypothermia and had to be evacuated by four tonners, ironically brought in from our base, Seaton Barracks, only a few miles away. It was deemed too dangerous for the helicopters to fly due to the exceptional high winds, so the rest of 40 Commando RM had to survive until daybreak and hope the weather improved. It was a hellish night, and in the morning I was relieved to get into the warmth of a helicopter and back on-board HMS Bulwark; what a farse!

The ship then sailed to Brest, the port city in Brittany, where we spent a day with the French Commandos before embarking and sailing to Norway. On board was no luxury. HMS Bulwark was old and only a year later she was to be retired from military service. Charlie Company stayed in a cramped mess deck that had very little ventilation, slept in bunks that were stacked three high and on mattresses that were wafer thin and allowed the loose and broken springs to poke through. Inspection 'rounds' on all mess decks were done every morning and night. On board the monotony was intense. The only things to break the boredom were slipping away to the tiny NAFFI shop (it was a hatch), scran or when we were taken onto the flight deck for circuit training.

'Exercise Teamwork 80' was a NATO organised exercise that took place in the southern area of Norway. The exercise was from 18th to 24th September 1980 and it consisted of approximately 18,000

Marines and soldiers from mainly UK, USA, The Netherlands and Norway with a smaller contingent from Belgium, Canada, Denmark, France and Portugal. The forces were spilt into two opposing groups, Blue and Orange. 40/42/45 Commandos RM were assigned to Blue landing forces with the 4th Marine Amphibious Brigade (USA), and The Amphibious Combat Group, Royal Netherlands Marine Corps. 40 Commando RM were to be landed by helicopter in the Kirstiansund/Halsa area and based there throughout the exercise.

Near Kirstiansund where we landed by helicopter, a local farmer had allowed Charlie Company to pitch up our two-man tents in one of his fields. He even gave permission for some of us to sleep in his straw filled barn, what luxury! We were not tactical while staying in the tents therefore at night we had large bonfires and somehow, someone obtained beer. I can remember Martin James, another man mountain, drinking cans of beer, sitting by an open fire, singing and telling stories for two days solid. 9 Troop were taken into a nearby village to look at the shops and bars and I even had the chance to go fishing in a fjord. This was a new experience for me, and I had wished that going out in the field was always like this.

I can only remember doing one meaningful military exercise in Norway. At one point, Charlie Company had gained the high ground and we were attacking an enemy position below. My section, heavily loaded with ammunition and weapons, followed our section commander as he jumped over a fence and into a field of low cut grass. Unknowingly and unluckily for us, the field was occupied by a very large and hormonal bull. On seeing this intrusion to his manor, the bull put his head down, directed his horns at our leader and charged towards him. I have never before seen, defenders of the Realm, 'Roughfty toughfty' Royal Marines, panic so much. In fear and desperation, we sprinted towards the nearest gate, fence, or hedge. What made it more amusing was seeing some Marines getting tangled in barbed wire during their attempt to escape!

After Exercise Teamwork 80 and back on HMS Bulwark, for the return journey to Plymouth, the ship stopped off in Hamburg and 40 Commando RM were allowed ashore. Just like the bull we were full of hormones and naturally in an attempt to release these we all headed for The Reeperbahn, the main street in the city's famous red-light district. On one run ashore a Marine who was with us, thought he was in luck when a 'woman' took him to a bar and paid for his wets. We sat at a table opposite the couple and watched, with smiles on our faces, trying not to laugh. They kissed and the Marine started fondling with her breasts, and as his excitement grew his hands moved downwards to the 'woman's' crotch only to find an erect penis. He turned his head, looked at us and shouted 'You bastards, she's got a meat and two veg'. It was a transvestite bar, the rest of us had known, our colleague hadn't.

The Reeperbahn was quite a rough area of Hamburg. One night I was in a bar with a couple of other Marines, we went to leave and for some unknown reason a guy standing by the exit lifted up his jacket and pulled a knife out on us. Luckily, my Marine training kicked in, so I, with the others, ran like hell! I can always remember in training at CTCRM, the first thing we were taught in an unarmed combat lesson. If you have a civilian pull a weapon out on you in a pub, get the hell out of there to live another day, you're not Superman or Bruce Lee. Of course, in a combat situation this would require a very different offensive response.

Back from Hamburg, 40 Commando RM spent a few weeks at Seaton Barracks, before we were on the move again. This time, we left Plymouth and went adventure training up in Scotland, staying at the Cameron Barracks, just outside Inverness. Every day for a week Charlie Company were taken to Aviemore to learn and take part in downhill skiing. After just an hour of instruction on how to do the plough, about twenty Royal Marines, all novice skiers, were let loose on the slopes. I can remember getting the lift to the top of the mountain, literally falling off and then skiing as fast as I could with no way of stopping, except for either falling over or hitting something or someone. Classes for civilian beginners were happening at the same time as we were skiing (well at least attempting to). Listening to their instructor out front, these classes would stand in lines and were often used, deliberately, as soft, stopping mechanisms for Marines because they were the spongy option compared to hitting fences or trees. Sometimes this stopping technique was done in vain, resulting in only slowing down the momentum of some Marines. As they smashed into civilians, they carried on down the slope, continuing this process of attempting to stop, until they arrived at the bottom of the mountain, leaving chaos in their wake. I had one go at skiing the black run, the steepest grade. It took me over 45 minutes to get to the end, most of the time was spent on my arse!

Although Inverness was a small place, we managed to find some decent pubs to drink in at night, when the notorious fearsome

Scottish women were out in their numbers. A few of them latched on to us and followed as we left one drinking establishment to go to another. Out on the street one of these fine Scottish ladies said, 'I need a shit', pulled down her knickers and defecated in the middle of the road. Nice!

Up until now I had felt like a 'Prole' from G. Orwell's book 1984; on my personal island of Oceania, being constantly monitored by 'big brother,' with no empowerment. Adventure training in Scotland was the first time that I really experienced fun and laughter in the Corps. Likewise on the brighter side of things, as time went on I started to open up and made some friends, in fact lifelong ones. People like Ged Herd, Ricky Miller, Chris Pretty, Glenn Thompson, Joe Goff, Rod Roden, Jock Hepburn and Andy Gaunt to name a few (apologies if I missed you out!), joined 9 Troop. Also, I met Micky Chin, later to be my brother-in-law!

During the riots that took place across England in 1981 we were put on standby to support the Fire Service. 40 Commando RM received several antiquated Bedford Green Goddess fire engines that had been brought in from god knows where, possibly the 1950's by a time machine! We continually practiced rolling hoses out and back, fixing them to sand pipes or outlets on the side of the vehicle. Also offloading ladders from the roof, putting them up against walls and then, you've guessed it, putting them back on the fire engine! Thank goodness that in the end we were never called upon to demonstrate our new skills of fire fighting in the public arena, or else the fires would still be burning. If not physically, then metaphorically in the hearts and minds of people, manifesting as rage at our inadequacies .

Runs Ashore In Plymouth.

In the early 1980's the New Wave fashion and music arrived. We would often go ashore from Seaton Barracks as wannabe Simon Le Bon, Adam Ant or Tony Hadley. Nearly every night we ended up in what can only be described as a saloon punch up, with who, I have no idea or why it was initiated. Just like in the wild west films, during one fight I saw two Marines on the first floor of a pub uproot a piano and then, with some effort, throw it down a set of stairs!

I once found myself spending the night at Charles Street Police Station, wrongly accused of punching and knocking out a matelot in a night club, how ridiculous! The runs ashore and battles were many, perhaps a prelude to what was to come in 1982. One story I must include is about my brother-in-law to be, Micky. It was reported in the local and national papers, but regrettably I have no reference or date. The article reads: 'Plymouth still has its fair share of hard men, to judge by a report in a Plymouth Local newspaper. A police panda car driver had to be cut free from his extensively damaged vehicle on Saturday night after being in collision with a Royal Marine riding a bicycle. Further, the Royal Marine was unhurt!'. At the same time in the local newspaper there were reports of clothes, particularly women's underwear, being stolen off washing lines from peoples back gardens in and around Crownhill. Several days later in Seaton Barracks a Marine was caught in his pit masturbating while wearing a pair of woman's knickers!

A typical run ashore for 9 Troop in Plymouth on either a Friday or

Saturday evening, would start off with one of the lads ordering taxis for us. From the main gate at Seaton Barracks, we would often get dropped off at a pub called the Good Companions', or by us, 'Dodgy Oppo's'. Other alternative starting places were the Mount Pleasant (a coincidence that it shares the same name as the mountain and airfield in The Falklands), close to Union street or the Three Crowns or a wine bar down at the Barbican. The options were endless. The decorum of some pranks sank below the depths of hell's gates. While standing at the bar in the Mount Pleasant I watched with interest as Spud Murphy left the heads and returned to the packed bar with an ice bucket under his arm. He then went up to several punters asking them if they wanted ice with their drinks. Spud approached two ladies who took up the offer of what they deemed to be a kind act. As one woman used the tongs to pick up a block of ice, the other let out a scream. Instead of ice between the prongs there was a single half frozen turd! On the start of another run ashore, some anonymous Marine threw a thunder flash under a car. The resulting noise boomed out across the Barbican and many people thought it was a terrorist car bomb going off, especially when they saw sparks under the vehicle. The Devon and Somerset Police arrived, cordoned the area off because contrary to a bomb, they believed a gas main had exploded. The other thing that went off was most of 9 Troop, running at great speed, in fear of being caught. The funny thing was that during this time period I got pinged with a chit to go on a Royal Marines Military Police Training Course. I was threaders. I went to the admin block, spoke to a Marine there and somehow managed to waffle my way out of the draft!

Normally on runs ashore, 9 Troop's second port of call was the Long Bar situated on Union street. As you entered the pub from Union street, as the name suggests, there was a long bar to your left, taking up most of the space on that side of the building. There was a dance floor in the centre, and toilets with a small rear entrance cum exit. For some unknown, historical reason, Royal Marines have a custom of frequently stripping off their clothes when drunk on runs ashore. One lad from Charlie Company, early on in the evening, took it upon himself to shine in this tradition and be the first one to run through the Long Bar, naked. Phil's plan was to strip in the toilet, leave his clothes with another Marine who would exit through the back, walk around the outside of the building and meet Phil, with his clothes by the front door, where he could get redressed. So off Phil's accomplice went or at least that's what Phil thought. Phil now completely naked, darted from the toilet, ran at break neck speed through the packed crowd in the Long Bar, followed by cheers from other Marines, shock and disgust from some civilians. He got to the front door only to find no oppo nor his clothing. Phil had to face boisterous comments, laughter, personal embarrassment, and beer poured over him as he went back and forth through the pub to try and find his so called oppo and clothes. Before he was arrested by the police for indecent exposure, thankfully someone took pity on him and reunited him with his belongings.

Sometime in 1981 Micky Chin brought his sister, Sharon, down to Plymouth for a run ashore and to meet some of his oppo's. She stood in the Long bar, the only female, with a collection of Marines hovering around her. I heard comments like, wow she's beautiful and I'm going to try and trap her. I was only interested in intoxicating my brain with a liberal amount of alcoholic drinks and was a bit offended that she had drawn attention away from what I wanted to do. Not being one to go with the flow, I said to the lads I was standing with, 'She's a gronk'. I turned my back and carried on drinking. Five years later Sharon and I were married!

After the Long Bar, and at this stage being very drunk, most of 9 Troop would head further into the dark, seedy depths of Union street to find and enter a night club. Union street was a hive of activity during the weekends in the 1980's. Most of the pubs and all of the night clubs had bouncers at their doorways. Civilian Police along with Military (MP's), patrolled up and down the street, in vehicles and on foot, even during the day. Once an American Ship was docked in Devonport and their Navy and Marines could be seen wandering around Plymouth on shore leave. To prevent any trouble, the Americans deployed their MP's too. The American MP's wondered around the city, particularly Union street, with wooden batons the size of baseball bats as a psychological and physical warning to any potential troublemakers.

In 1981, Union street was the first place in the world that I had ever seen with female bouncers. One particular female bouncer who frequently stood on the entrance to a night club, scared me, not so much from her appearance but by her reputation. She dressed like a skin head, wearing Doctor Martin boots, tight blue jeans with braces, white short sleeved shirt and had a shaven head. This female bouncer was also covered in tattoos, evident on her forearms and neck, but to be quite honest, she was slim and had an attractive face. You did not trap her, she trapped you and if she wasn't happy with your sexual performance, she would let you know. Once, dissatisfied with a poor Marine who wasn't up to standard because he had the dreaded drunken droop, she decided to show her contempt by swamping over his pit, then stealing his wallet as she left. I also found out, through word of mouth, that she had a concealed tattoo on the inside of her upper leg, it had the word 'Twat' in bold and an arrow pointing up to her vagina!

The night clubs on Union street had a pecking order of class. Diamond Lil's was one of the smallest in size and the dingiest, on a par with the nearby Ace of Spades. Lighting was purposely dimmed to hide the condition of the interior décor and possibly the women that frequented the place. Diamond Lil's was hardly the most elegant of places to enter when sober, with its wall paper partially falling off the walls and carpets that were damp, sticky and encrusted with stains from old beer and vomit, which stuck to the soles of your shoes. I rarely went into Diamond Lil's because on my first visit, I was banned for vomiting over a woman at the bar, it was an accident, honest! All I can remember of the event is hearing a female screaming and her male partner threatening to punch my lights out.

Cascades night club, sometimes known as the Royal Marines school of dancing, was only a slight improvement on the previous two, simply because it played, what we thought, was decent music. 9 Troop frequently ended up in the largest and most trendy club on Union street, called Castaways. In Castaways the Royal Navy recruits from HMS Raleigh, probably on their first run ashore since joining, would stack their No 1 caps on tables, and sometimes leave them unattended. We couldn't resist the temptation of either just knocking the caps over, sitting on them or pouring drinks over the top so it looked like a champagne fountain. With behaviour like that it's not surprising that by the end of the night out we ended up in fights, with either other servicemen or civilians or a combination of the two at the same time.

One time I was quite happy dancing the night away in Castaways when suddenly I saw one of the lads from Charlie Company join me. Only a few feet away and facing me, he produced a smoke grenade. Holding it in his right hand and carrying out the correct procedure, he pulled the pin, shouted grenade, and rolled the thing into the centre of the night club's dance floor. Orange smoke wafted up to the ceiling like a mushroom shaped cloud caused by an atomic explosion. The whole dance floor and main bar were engulfed with thick smoke, making it very difficult to even see your own hand in front of your face let alone dance. The management and bouncers had no option but to evacuate the night club. Before the Police arrived, I stood outside the main door watching as people were escorted out by friends and bouncers alike. Their eyes were streaming with orange tears, snot running down from their noses and clothes stained the same colour. But the funniest thing was seeing Marines exiting still holding their pints of beer!

If I survived the night unscathed, after leaving Castaways I would often buy, from the cheapest food outlet still open, a kebab topped with chilli sauce. Though as soon as I ingested it, I would immediately regret doing so because it would slowly slither down my oesophagus and painfully destroy the lining of my stomach causing cramps and eventually resulting in diarrhoea the next day.

Later I would go to the taxi rank and share a car back to Seaton Barracks. If we didn't have any method of paying, we did the obvious thing for a fit bunch of Marines, 'a runner'. I even chanced it a couple of times on my own. One ploy I used in my drunken discussion with the driver, was to try and convince him that I was part of 59 Independent Commando Royal Engineers who were based in Crownhill Fort and therefore get dropped off there. The Fort was close to, but just out of view from Seaton Barracks' main gate. It was a simple, short run over a grass hill that had a small dirt foot path along it, then across a dual carriageway and into the safety of Seaton Barracks. Most of the time the taxi drivers had no chance of catching us in a foot race and by time they had reversed their taxi and were back on the dual carriageway, we were well out of sight.

Once I did a runner with a couple of other Marines but this time the taxi driver gave chase on foot. He ran over the hill and saw we were heading for the main gate of Seaton Barracks, thus giving away our final destination. This put the Marines on main gate duty who were watching in a difficult situation. Did they let us through, stop the taxi driver, with the fear of him making a complaint and then them being reported to the duty officer? Or stop us, their fellow Marines and get a lot of stick from the lads the next day? In the end it was a dilemma that they didn't have to face. Rather than heading for the front gate we ran down hill, turned left at a cul de sac off the dual carriage way, past the officers married quarters and swimming pool, where we could enter the rear of Seaton Barracks that was unmanned, by jumping over a fence. Unfortunately, this new route increased the distance we had to run. I had been at the front of the chase and got the giggles as I looked back and saw my fellow Marines struggling, but not as badly as the taxi driver. He had stopped running, was leaning with one hand on a garden wall and throwing up. He never got his money, only an empty stomach, the bitter taste of bile and defeat!

Once safely back on camp, if I hadn't succumbed to a Chilli Kebab from Union street and my stomach was empty, just like the taxi drivers was, 'Duchy's' was always open, until god knows what hour in the morning. Duchy's was located within Seaton Barracks, in a prefab hut behind the main guardroom and provided to takeaway, anything a greasy spoon café did. Burgers, hot dogs and chicken were on offer, but my favourite was the full fry up consisting of burgers (without the roll), bacon, sausages, mushrooms, onions, baked beans topped off with a slice of cheese and finally swimming in tomato ketchup. This was served in an aluminium foil tray with plastic cutlery to eat with. I used to buy several cans of fizzy goffers to wash down the cholesterol filled food. If I didn't manage to eat it all that night, I could have the remainder cold, in the morning for breakfast, providing my hangover would allow me to do so.

On some drinking sessions in Plymouth we dressed up in a predetermined style; these were called 'Silly rig runs ashore'. The most commonly used dress was the toga. It was simple to put together. All that was required was for you to use an issued single white bedsheet as the toga and put any shoes on your feet. Sometimes we wore boots and puttees just to add to the glamour! It was a rig that all of us had so no one had an excuse for not getting dressed up, or should that say dressed down? The only problem was where to keep your money. I just stuffed mine down my pants, some lads didn't wear any so god knows where they kept theirs, especially their loose change. On one silly rig run ashore with 9 Troop, Sam Sampson trapped a gronk and spent the night with her in her flat. He woke up the next morning, looked at the woman next to him, thought oh my god what have I done and subsequently escaped, silently, without her knowing. Sam couldn't get a taxi or bus back to Seaton Barracks because he was penniless from the night before. Wearing a wig (until he got a sweat on), boots, ladies skirt, blouse, his face covered in smeared make up and a hangover from hell, he had to walk back to camp. To make matters worse, because of the time of day, as he made his way through the city centre, up through Mutley Plain, Crownhill and eventually Seaton Barracks, he had to take on the glare of nearly every commuter on his or her way to work. Poor Sam, the embarrassment must have been immense, but we found it very funny!

The one occasion the troop didn't' go ashore, well, at least not straight away, was when the Company Commander decided to have a 'party' on the first floor of the NAAFI in Seaton Barracks. The function room was oblong in shape, had a wooden floor, a dance area in the centre surrounded by tables and chairs, with a bar at one end and a stage at the other. The entertainment arrived late. It was three strippers and their bouncer was the husband of one of them. There was some resentment from the lads because of the delay and when the strippers performance was seen as lacking, some verbal abuse started. I shan't go into too much detail, but the insults grew worse and some objects were thrown towards the stage. It ended up with one Marine taking a red fire extinguisher off the wall, placing it in the centre of the stage, like some phallic monolith. Shouts of encouragement to the ladies were given and along with advice on how to use the fire extinguisher to improve their act. The strippers and the husband left in a hurry to catch the next rain back to London.

To celebrate the marriage of Prince Charles to Lady Diana Spencer, one day in July 1981, we had a 'Splice the main brace'. At Seaton Barracks we had to fall in at Charlie Company lines, early in the afternoon, in sports rig, carrying our Pussers black mugs. These mugs went on top of the issued water bottle and held approximately half a litre of fluid. After a formal briefing about administration, we had to line up with our mugs, walk up to a collapsible wooden table and receive our ration of rum out of a bottle from our Company Commander. Our first 'round' was enough to fill a quarter of the mug. After everyone had had one ration it was found that there was a substantial amount of Pussers rum left. Some Marines and JNCO's went up for a second, third and even fourth time. A few didn't bother queuing up they just asked to have their mugs filled to the top and then tried to 'down' them in one. It was possibly the most bizarre sports afternoon I had ever seen. At the end of the splice the main brace we were dismissed for the rest of the day. It was a contest for some to walk, let alone to get back to their grots or in a few cases. their married quarters.

5. OPERATION CORPORATE (FALKLANDS WAR 1982).

Introduction.

During the Falklands War, for me, all sense of time was lost, as days no longer had names and seemed to blur into one. Hours might have been minutes and minutes, hours. When the lives of you and that of your Oppo's are at risk, time does not matter, it is the events, actions and outcomes that do, and we may recall them in vivid memories. In this section of the book, I will describe what I witnessed and my emotions at the time. It covers my urgent return from live firing at ranges in the North West of England, sailing on the Canberra, landing at San Carlos. Then progressing to my actions on land, which include being stranded in a minefield at night, and a map reading error which led to a helicopter drop in the direct line of fire, and a rarely recorded firefight by 9 Troop Charlie Company

40 Commando RM. Finally, the return voyage and back home in England.

There were situations that deserve mentioning which were almost as frightening as my 'final days' on the front line in action. Occasions such as leaping across from the SS Canberra to landing craft during a large swell in the South Atlantic or spotting sharks while swimming in English Bay at our stop off on the Ascension Islands on the way down. Also the more emotional aspect of carrying injured personnel from helicopters at Ajax Bay, entering The Red and Green Life Machine with a colleague, Mne Ged Herd and seeing medical operations on the go as well as carrying body bags, via the captured Argentine prisoner's enclosure, to a temporary grave site. These scenarios I have described later and hope I have done them some justice.

In the 'fog of war' soldiers will become confused and possibly separated from others. People that have been in the same location at the same time, may have different views. Both can be correct from the protagonist's perspective, similar to the ambiguous images portrayed in the famous My Wife and My Mother In Law, the rabbit or duck illusion and Rubin's Vase. This is my personal account.

As an unassuming, physically fit, nineteen-year-old Royal Marines Commando, marching or 'Yomping' came as second nature. Carrying large rucksacks or bergens laden with an array of personal equipment, ammunition and rations was part of my job description. The G10 58 webbing and directly moulded sole (DMS) boots with puttees were a throwback to the 1960's and really not sufficient for the Falklands environment. This topic has been the centre of many a discussion and not the main aim of my discourse.

However because of the substandard, non-waterproof, DMS boots, I must state that I suffered from trench foot caused by having wet feet as a consequence of our initial landing at Blue Beach, in San Carlos Water. This pain in both feet was ended by a visit from a medic on Wreck Point, East Island, who offered me some magical purple tablets and told me to get them down my neck with anything drinkable. So, I did, with a can of Guinness that someone had brought in with a resupply. For a while at least, I was in a state of euphoria! Eventually each and every Marine was reunited with their pair of dry Hawkins Cairngorm boots and wait for it, they were made of leather, completely waterproof (well up to the top of your ankles) and unlike the DMS boot, required no puttees. These boots helped to relieve my trench foot. However, the Cairngorm boots were far from perfect as Vince Combe a member of 9 Troop at the time recalled, 'I remember standing in the sinks full of hot water on the Canberra trying to soften them up a bit and then dubbing them. I ended up with a big hole at the back of my ankle and wore blue Adidas trainers whilst above Ajax Bay, protecting the Rapier site, because I refused to seek treatment. My trainers are probably still buried up there'.

I did witness some exceptional soldiering, such as Lance Corporal Chris Pretty taking his gun section, made up of Ged Herd and one other to the furthest right flank of 9 Troop while under enemy fire with no cover and facing away from the main enemy's position therefor being unable to see the deadly rounds coming in on his position. Captain Andy Pillars (Charlie Company Commander) walking through a minefield in the pitch black to check the injured were being dealt with and that the path was clear. I know that there is a great deal of other examples witnessed by members of 9 Troop and the rest of Charlie Company. I apologise for not recalling them all, but I must mention one other before I get to the main event. I am afraid it was a certain Lance Corporal Pretty (again). During one yomp even though Chris had his own particular problems, he offered aid to a struggling Welsh Guardsman on a particular hard going rock run when advancing in the dark hours, near Mount Harriet, who was crying out 'I can't go on!' Later, when daylight came Chris took his shirt off to reveal abrasions, still bleeding on his shoulders from the extreme weight of carrying his own bergen that was full to the brim with spare 7.62 link rounds for the GPMG.

We relieved members of 45 Commando RM from guarding a Rapier site at Wreck Point on or around the 2/06/82. This is where our section of 9 Troop, call sign 3.3.C was to be based for the foreseeable future. At this location we completed, with local rocks and turf, the building of our infamous 'Sangar'. The Sangar, used by us as a central sentry position, was surrounded by our newly arrived Artic Two-man Tents for sleeping in. After taking my 'medicine' of purple tablets and Guinness to relieve the pain of trench foot during the day, in my tent, I woke in the middle of the night with stomach cramps. I had no option but to run outside in the pitch black and relieve myself as quickly and quietly as possible of what I can only call a large amount of diarrhoea. I then returned back to my tent, a satisfied Marine, fell asleep contented and forgot about the event. The next recollection I have was being woken up for stand to, just before dawn. We went to our given positions for approximately 30 minutes, until daylight arrived – standard military procedure. On returning back to our two-man tents to prepare some 'wets and scran' all that could be heard was a flurry of expletives from Cpl Dee Irving (our section commander), 'What the fuck' and then 'who the fuck' continued with 'which one of you cunts took a dump right outside my tent'. I recall loud laughter, especially from Big Ged, who has never stopped retelling the story of who defecated outside the section commanders' tent. At the time of Dee's investigations and vicious allegations regarding who the culprit was, I had completely forgotten about my previous night's events and I was, and still am, in complete denial of the charge, and therefore fingers are still wagging as to 'who took a shit outside Dee's tent!'

Where Are The Falkland Islands?

The Falklands Islands are situated on the coordinates of 51° S, 59° W, some 300 miles off the coast of South America, approximately 750 miles North of the Antarctic and just over 8,000 miles from the UK. There is a land area of 4,700sq miles and a coastline of 800 miles (1,288 km), the Islands highest point is Mt. Usborne at 2,312 ft. (705 m).

Consistently high westerly winds average 19 miles (31 km) per hour, while the mean annual average temperature is about 42 °F (5 °C), with an average maximum of 49 °F (9 °C) and an average minimum of 37 °F (3 °C). Precipitation averages 25 inches (635 mm) annually, (2020 Encyclopædia Britannica).

The Falkland Islands are in the southern hemisphere, winter is during our summer period. In 1982 it was essential that the British land forces achieved their objectives as quickly as possible before the onset of winter and the deteriorating weather conditions, that normally started in late June.

Geography.

Although there are over 700 Islands in the archipelago, the two main ones are the West and East Falkland Islands, bisected by the Falklands Sound. Lafonia, on the East Island, is the only major flat land with the rest being mountainous and hilly. Stone rock runs made of hard quartz blocks cascade down from the tops of these features, spreading out into the valleys below, making it very difficult (if not impossible) for vehicles and walking.

Flora And Fauna.

The vegetation mainly consists of white grass, diddle-dee and some tussock grass, these are low growing and wind resistant. There is no natural tree growth on the Islands because of the constant and high winds and also poor soil conditions. The earth, where bare rock is not exposed, consists of peat and boggy wetlands.

There are no land mammals indigenous to the Falklands but an abundance of sheep and a few cows. Numbering in their several hundreds of thousands, five different species of penguins inhabit the Islands, including the large King Penguin. Various seals can be seen throughout. Numerous birds visit and live around the archipelago ranging from the Albatross to the more inland loving, famous Upland Goose.

The Falklands is one of the fourteen British self-governing overseas territories. The Falklands government also looks after the British overseas territories of South Georgia and the South Sandwich Islands. In 1982 most of the 1,820-population lived in the capital, Port Stanley, others lived in farmsteads called 'Camps' spread throughout the Islands.

A small Royal Marines Commando garrison (NP8901) had been stationed in the Falklands since 1966, based at Moody Brook barracks, close to Port Stanley.

The volcanic Ascension Islands, another overseas British Territory, some 4,000 miles from the UK (halfway to the Falkland Islands), with an American built runway, was the obvious choice for a logistical staging post during the Falklands War.

Altcar Ranges; The Call Back To Plymouth.

I can recall getting the news that we were to travel back down to Plymouth from Altcar Ranges on or about the 1st April, yes, I too thought it was an April fools! To me, being at the ranges meant nothing more than just a rubbish run ashore in Southport the nearest town or travelling further to Liverpool. I would have preferred to stay in Plymouth. On a run ashore, one of our lads decided to 're-arrange' a flower bed in Liverpool's city centre. The local constabulary took no messing around, with truncheons drawn they lined us up against a wall for interrogation – thank god no one cracked and owned up to this misdemeanour or else we would have ended up in Police cells.

Going out on the ranges and shooting my SLR for five days was necessary but sometimes boring and by day three, secondary to going ashore and having a laugh with the lads. As for the recall, at least it got us out of the monotony of one of the most 'mind numbing' jobs up there, butt duties. In the butts, behind the safety of an earth embankment, the task involved endlessly lifting and pulling down Figure 12 targets on wooden frames. When each shooting session had finished we had to indicate, with a large white pointer at the end of a broom handle, to the shooter where his shots had hit. Then lowering the target, gluing paper squares over the holes on the figure 12, raising it back up and repeating this process all day long; it was dreary. I can remember while down in the butts with DOTL, saying that this was as close as we would ever get to being shot at. How wrong he was to be!

There were only two enjoyable memories from Altcar Ranges. The first sitting in the NAFFI (shared with Pongo's who were the target for many a wind up). The bar was a godsend, a place where we could get out of the persistent rain. Secondly, I really used to love playing football with others from Charlie company on an ad hoc, uneven grass pitch, near the main gate. Sadly, due to the recall, these had to abruptly end.

While travelling back to Plymouth from Altcar Ranges there were lots of rumours going around Charlie Company, especially the one about it being an April fool's. The seriousness of our journey back had not been voiced. All I was aware of was that we were not going to get any Easter leave and having the feeling of disappointment that my two weeks of drinking back home in Ipswich had to be put on hold. We had the luxury of civilian coaches for our journey back down the M6, listening to the music on BBC Radio 1. Jokes were made about our previous attempts at mimicking the marching as seen in the film Stripes, starring Bill Murray and somehow it led on to a conversation about Monty Pythons 'Ministry of funny walks'. Within minutes of our conversation finishing, we pulled into a service station. As we were still sitting on the coach Lance Corporal Jock Hepburn pointed towards a man walking from the carpark to the services, saying 'Hey lads look at that!' We all looked out through the coach's dirt covered windows, some from the other side of the coach standing up to see what Jock had identified. It was a man dressed in a suit and for some reason this poor person had a very strange, if not awkward, gait, combined with his head bobbing up and down, seemingly uncontrollably as he went along. For a moment I thought he must have heard us talking and was taking the piss, but this was impossible. It looked like he was doing an extremely good impression of one of John Cleese' funny walks. We were in tears of laughter as we stared in disbelief – trust Jock to see this unfortunate individual!

Back At Seaton Barracks, 3rd April 1982.

I still thought we were going to go on Easter leave when we eventually arrived back at Seaton Barracks from the Altcar Ranges. I believed it was just another training exercise to keep 40 Commando RM on our toes, a similar regime to the recent spearhead routine that we had just completed. This spearhead procedure involved standing to at any time of the day or night and after collecting our kit bags, suitcase, weapon and as quickly as possible falling in with the rest of the unit. Once on parade, we would empty our kit bags and lay out all our belongings on the ground. The lid of our suitcases had to be left open for its contents to be looked at too. Then there was the inevitable waiting. After what seemed like hours, an inspection was carried out by an officer. After the inspection we were ordered to put everything back into our kit bags, close our suitcases, and shoulder our weapons, just to be told it was only a drill not once, but several times. What a pain in the arse that was!

If we ever needed to replace any of our personal kit we had to go to the company TQ. The TQ was normally a SNCO. One particular Charlie Company TQ treated all of his stores as his own and all ranks below him with contempt. During the day he would rarely open up therefore we had to knock on a door to try and get his attention. Even though we could hear him inside he rarely answered. On the odd occasion when he did, the effort of unlocking a door was too much for him so he would just open a small peep hole. Like a ferret poking its nose out off a rabbit hole he would nearly always shout the immortal words 'Fuck off, we're closed'!

Charlie Company were formally told about the Falklands invasion by our troop officers as we paraded at the Company lines in Seaton Barracks, although previously we had seen reports on the television and in the newspapers, so had an idea of what was happening. The only thing I previously knew about the Falklands was that it was a draft for 18 months long that few Marines wanted, miles from anywhere and cold. In contrast it was said that one of the best posts you could get was being sent to Diego Garcia in the Indian Ocean. I originally thought that the Falkland Islands and Diego Garcia were, geographically close together!

I can recall packing some of my kit, just as I had done while on spearhead, into my green canvas kit bag and was feeling pleased with myself on two accounts. One that I had managed to crush everything into my kit bag and two, I had already completed the very time consuming task of painting my name, service number and the number 6 (6 representing 40 commando RM) on the base of the kit bag, unlike some Marines who had just been drafted to the unit.

While I was 'fell in' on the Motor Transport (MT) vehicle park cum parade ground at Seaton Barracks and getting my kit inspected, I got 'bollocked' because I had packed an American crime novel paperback, much to the disgust of one inspecting, non-commissioned officer. I was not sure whether this revulsion was because the book was non-essential and I had wasted space in my kit bag or because the author was an American.

A Young lieutenant asked me how I would deal with the heat and sun due to my fair complexion. First of all, I thought great, it's going to be suntan time down in the Falklands. Secondly, I told the officer because I was named the 'Ginger darkie' by a member of 9 Troop (himself of Afro Caribbean descent), I would go brown in the sun'. The officer just snorted at me and said 'I'd like to see that,' then turned to the next man. It was obvious that the young officer had, just like me, no idea what climatic conditions were like in the Falklands.

Interestingly, since writing the piece above I have recently had my DNA tested to try to give me some tangible facts to help me look back objectively at my family history in order to clarify or dispatch claims. The results of my test arrived through the post and, as suspected, I was mainly from Northern European ancestry. However just over twenty two percent was Indian. My older sister Ruth has also had her DNA analysed by a different laboratory than the one I used and her results were very similar for India. To help put my mind at ease, I asked a paternal uncle if he would share his DNA results with me. He was obliging and his came back at forty nine percent Indian. I always thought that there was some gene in me that caused my sun tanning; these DNA results confirmed my beliefs. Also, wait for it, remember what I mentioned earlier about the possibility of some German roots on my paternal grandfathers side, well, the gossip could be correct as twenty percent of my DNA is from the Germanic region.

While on standby for the Falklands, 40 Commando RM were given three days leave. I did not bother going home to Ipswich, it would have taken too long to travel there and back. I can remember feeling sorry for the married lads with kids that lived elsewhere in the country and like me, it was too far for them to visit in such a short time. For most of us, the single Marines, it was just another long weekend run ashore in Plymouth, a total alcoholic blank in my memory I am afraid. I can only recall standing outside the Three Crowns pub in the barbican, lobbing empty pint pots into the docks and shouting ‘grenade!’.

I had trivial worries compared to others, particularly the Marines with children, but they seemed important to me at the time. One was, while I was away, where the hell was I going to leave my motorbike and bright orange helmet, that according to some, matched the colour of my hair! (for which I received a lot of banter). The helmet had been given to me for free by an uncle and forgetting about the colour, at least it did its job of keeping me safe on the roads! My saviour for this dilemma came in the guise of a girlfriend's Dad. He offered to look after my motorbike and orange helmet. Did I trust him? Did I hell, but that was the only option I had at the time and another advantage was they lived close to camp. The girlfriends name was Bernadette and I believe I kissed her once!

I had, as many young men do, too much testosterone floating around my veins, and as one consequence, had a sexual fantasy for the group 'Blondies' lead singer, Debbie Harry. I had a poster of her on the wall above my bedside space in Seaton Barracks. I was extremely worried that this poster might get 'borrowed' while I was away or wrecked by someone returning from a run ashore down Union street during our three days of enforced leave. So, I neatly folded away this treasured possession of mine, stored it in my Pussers suitcase and in my memory, as a vivid, and pleasurable picture of Debbie Harry.

Travel Down To Southampton And Embarking On The Canberra 7th April – 21st May 1982.

By now the world had heard about the details of the Falklands invasion or as it was named by the Argentines, Operation Rosario. While waiting at Seaton Barracks, we knew, for a change, that this was for real, not an exercise. What made it even more personal for us was that it had been sixty-eight fellow Royal Marines led by Major Norman RM, who had put in a tremendous effort to repel the attackers. The Royal Marines did this without any casualties to themselves but had inflicted a lot on the enemy. Eventually, the Royal Marines were ordered to surrender to save further bloodshed and because of the overwhelming numbers of Argentine Forces on the ground, sea and in the air.

The ocean liner, SS Canberra was built at the Harland and Wolff shipyard in Belfast and launched on 16 March 1960 at a cost of £17,000,000. The ship was named on 17 March 1958, after the federal capital of Australia, Canberra. Her maiden voyage was in June 1961 and she sailed in the P&O fleet from 1961 to 1997. When Argentina invaded the Falkland Islands in April 1982, the Canberra was cruising in the Mediterranean. The Ministry of Defence requisitioned the Canberra for use as a troopship. Before she reached Southampton, an advance party had been flown from the UK on to the ship at Gibraltar, to look at the adaptations required for her new military role. She was quickly refitted, then sailed from Southampton on 9 April 1982 for the South Atlantic with most of 3 Commando Brigade on board, including myself and the rest of 9 Troop. The Canberra was soon to be given the nickname the 'Great White Whale', due to her size and colour. Many years after the Falklands War, it was very sad news to me when I heard that on 10 October 1997 SS Canberra was removed from the P&O fleet and sold for scrap. I had always hoped to return on board as a civilian with my wife during our retirement years for a final cruise.

On Thursday the 8th of April 1982, Charlie Company had a police escort as our convoy of coaches travelled to Southampton from Plymouth to meet up with the Canberra. The number of escorts increased as we approached the docks in Southampton. I saw police outriders on motorbikes stopping traffic ahead and civvies looking at us as we passed. I suddenly felt important, like a celebrity or royalty – maybe a story to tell friends back home?

On seeing Canberra for the first time, I had a feeling of excitement and nostalgia. As I have already stated my Dad, as a boy on his own, had sailed from India to England to live and this replayed through my mind, time and time again. I was just 19, and thinking how on earth did he manage as a 14-year-old? What concerns and worries did my father have, as for the first time he approached the ship he was about to embark on from India. Did he experience the same nervous butterflies I was now getting?

When the coaches came to a stop and we debussed, I remember off-loading our kit from the coach and walking past all the military and civilian stores of equipment, vehicles and large chicon's in sheds, stockpiled on the dockside at Southampton.

With the rest of 9 Troop, I joined the queue of Marines, in single file, concertinaing back and forth as one along this human line, up to the entrance of the ship. As I was walking on to the Canberra, halfway up the gangway and looking over the edge, I remember thinking 'this ship is enormous and that's a long way down to the water'. At the top of the gangway I entered into the Canberra through her main doorway and tried to find my way to my cabin along with many other Marines, all of us heavily laden with kit. I headed downwards on the ship and through what seemed to be a maze of narrow corridors and stairs, smashing my bergen against obstacles in the way. Everything inanimate and human was hit; walls, ceilings, fixtures and fittings, nothing escaped, including P&O staff. As I passed the Canberra's Bursars central office, I felt comforted at seeing six or seven civilian staff there and wondered if they were going to stay on board. Watching them go about their work and hearing their voices, with their British accents made me feel relaxed. I thought that the civilian staff on the ship might offer a welcome break in conversation with other Marines and possibly have a more sympathetic ear, rather than the sometimes abrupt military manner and banter. The P&O staff, for better or worse, would be a reminder of home, of England and what we, if we had to, were going to fight for; the freedom and dignity that the Falklanders had had so ruthlessly taken away.

I for one was glad to be on a civilian ship and not a military one. On board the Canberra I could see that there was so much more space, and even luxury compared to the latter. I was pleasantly surprised with our accommodation on board. A four-man cabin, although designed for thin, petite adults, at least it came with its own sink. I shared this room with Ged Herd, physically large and a kind heart, Simon Poole, great 'dits' and pranks, and Gaz Pinchers, who had an extremely deep voice and big ears to flick at from behind. I had no problem with any of these guys, all were good lads, ready for a laugh but professional soldiers at the same time.

As I walked into the cabin for the first time and what was to be my home for the next few weeks, I put my kit down, and slid it under one of the bottom bunks and then sat on it. I couldn't believe it, we had fresh, white, crisp and clean sheets laid on top of a comfortable mattress. My previous perceptions on the coach had been correct, it was like going on holiday!

Within minutes of arriving on the ship most of 9 Troop, including my cabin, were called forward to be part of a working party to load stores on to the Canberra from the dockside. I thought here we bloody well go again, we'll be there for hours, slugging our guts out and at the same time getting fed up with the process. We were given the task of loading, in a human chain, some 'nutty' boxes on to the ship from the dockside along a gang plank, and eventually to one of the many storerooms on board. One of the lads from 9 Troop, grabbed a 'spare box' and ran back down to his cabin before the MP's and civilian staff noticed he and the box of chocolates were missing. True Royal Marines style, 'proffing' anything that's plentiful and available! Once A Marine Always A Marine (OARMAARM!).

Early evening on 9th April 1982 (Good Friday), everyone aboard the Canberra was told over the tannoy system that the ship was about to slip its moorings and leave Southampton docks. Most of 9 Troop made our way up top, to see England for what was for some servicemen, the last time. As I passed through the ship, I can remember seeing cardboard that had been laid on the floor to protect the carpets, it had already been dislodged due to the large amount of footfall and I was thinking what's the point of that, it will disintegrate once it gets wet.

As the Canberra set sail, I went for a view outside, ending up on the bow, port side. By now it was already dark. I stood, watching crowds of people that had gathered on the quay to wish us well as we left the safety of home. I could hear the Parachute Band Service playing on the dockside. One song took me back to my childhood. Hearing Rod Stewart's 'We are Sailing' reminded me of being at home with my family watching the documentary series called 'Sailor' about HMS Ark Royal and its service men on board, that were away from home for several months at a time. 'We are Sailing' was the theme tune to the programme and when it was first launched in the 1970's, I was still at school, and my brother had just joined the Royal Marines. Every time my mother watched 'Sailor' and heard this song, she would burst into tears, no doubt thinking about her oldest son. Back on the Canberra, before I had heard that song, I had had no thoughts about my family.

As the Ship moved off along the Southampton Water towards the open sea, she passed an embankment to the port side, where I could see people standing, shouting and cheering. These were members of the public who were flashing lights from torches, cars and high up in tower blocks, owners flicking light switches on and off in their flats, to acknowledge our departure.

Part of me was thinking this is surreal. I was feeling slightly anxious but at the same time thrilled at going off with a group of friends on a voyage to the unknown. I did not sleep much that first night on board the Canberra. Ignoring shouts from my cabin mates, to turn the 'fucking light off!', I tried reading late and into the early morning, the first chapters of my fictional American crime novel, but that did not help much with my insomnia.

Scran in the galley on ship was good compared to the compo rations I was expecting. The diet was varied and the environment plush. At first the ships stewards even published the daily menu on an A4 sheet and posted it on the walls outside the Atlantic Restaurant where we ate. This soon stopped. In the first few days, it was nice to see civilian staff cooking and serving. However, we were soon brought down to earth. Royal Marine Chefs moved in and they soon got to turn the atmosphere from civilian to military, for example giving a rap on the knuckles to any Marine for taking an extra sausage or any other additional food. Also, at the start of the voyage we were eating out of China plates, but this changed to well used, metal cafeteria trays, the ones that are split into sections for mains, dessert and a cup holder. Apparently, the lower ranks were not grown up enough to have plates!

The Officers on board were given the 'Crow's Nest Bar', situated just below the ship's bridge. I only once briefly visited there, what for I cannot recall. The place reeked of opulence and was used on civilian cruises as an area for the first-class passengers, where they could order exotic drinks and speciality food. It was a home from home for some of the officers. A reflection of the standards found in an officer's mess and well out of bounds for other lowly ranks like me. Also, on the upper floor, still open for a while and being manned by P&O staff, were the shops selling the ship's souvenirs, clothing and some chocolates. This was a reminder of civilian life. Some members of 9 Troop would go to the shops, spending twenty minutes inside, an achievement in what was a relatively small retail space. Then leaving the shop without a single purchase, but at least with a glimpse and lascivious thoughts of one of the females who worked there.

As we sailed out of the English Channel and into the Atlantic Ocean, each unit on the Canberra produced their own T shirts and sweatshirts. How these were designed, manufactured and posted to get to us while we were sailing south, I have no idea. I still have two, one is in its original plastic wrapper. I wish they would still fit!

40 Commando RM junior ranks were given the William Fawcett Room to relax in, have lectures, briefings and entertainment. There was a bar, piano and large glass windows that looked out on to the promenade deck giving great vistas of the sea and distant horizon. As we sailed on PT increased in number and intensity, as did the warnings of being put on a charge for various infringements which were posted on notice boards in the daily orders, e.g. wandering into civilian bars, or for being sunburnt! During the day, the William Fawcett Room became a great place to observe and count the laps around the ship completed by other poor souls from different units running past doing their PT. Of course, this spectating was fine until it was your turn to run and suffer, while others watched and possibly laughed.

At first, all Marines trained and ran in just sports kit and training shoes. As we sailed further on south we slowly replaced sports rig with fighting orders, carried weapons and, on our feet, it was back to wearing DMS boots. At the same time the temperature rose and as a result from sweat and footwear, blisters and chaffing befell to many Marines and Paras. After constant running on the promenade deck, I managed to get some fairly large blood blisters on one foot, so I went down to sick bay to have them checked. I remember lining up, waiting to see a medic and comparing the size of my blood blisters to others. Meanwhile behind a curtain we could hear cries of pain as the treatment was being administered to a patient. We couldn't stop laughing at the shrills caused by the discomfort being carried out on our colleagues ahead. When my turn arrived, I was told to lay face down on a bed, bend my leg at the knee and place my foot up in the air. I have no idea what happened next, but it felt like someone had whacked the sole of my foot with a cricket bat. I turned my head around and saw the medic with a needle in his hand and a sadistic smile on his face. 'Bastard' I said aloud. What chemical 'Doctor fucking Jekyll' had in the syringe and just injected me with I was guessing (perhaps some iodine?), but if I were a captured Argentine soldier and being tortured, I would have said anything! Thank the lord I only had one foot to be treated. My only other visit to see the medical misfits (staff) was in the beginning of May to give blood after a call came out across the ship for donors. At the time I felt relaxed, I had no fear at giving my blood, however today, put a needle anywhere near me and a grey mist descends and I know passing out is not far off.

While making my way up to the flight deck on the Canberra for circuit training, I saw the newly built ramps designed to transfer the injured from the flight deck down to the hospital, situated one floor below. I had quite a sobering thought that if we did actually go to war, one day I could be lowered down this route. I quickly dismissed this notion, at nineteen years old I believed, like many of that age, that I was invincible.

The BBC World Service was broadcast throughout the ship with hourly news summaries. This helped us keep up with what was happening in the world and back home. Also on board, specific announcements were made to the troops over a tannoy system. To broadcast a message, you simply had to fill in a form and take it to the main communications office situated in the centre of the ship. There was no vetting. This office was manned by civilians and they had no idea what military terms and jargon were and meant. L/Cpl Hepburn sent up a spoof message and told us to 'wait out'. Commander Yarker RN (Executive Officer) was one of the top military men on the Canberra. The message L/Cpl Hepburn had left was announced over the tannoy not once, but several times during the day and night; 'Commander Yarker your baked beans are ready!'

One day I just happened to be on deck, looking out of the stern, observing what was happening on board and catching some sun rays. As the boat was cruising along I felt a slight shudder and thought nothing of it. Someone near me shouted we've hit something, I thought it was a prank. Regrettably for one particular whale, happily swimming past it was far from a joke. I looked out to sea, portside of the stern and could see the blue and white of the wake being churned up by the propellers, turn to a deep red hue. A live whale versus the Great White Whale was no contest.

Below; one of the sweatshirts motifs, designed and purchased on the Canberra, sailing south.

Most of 9 Troop on board the Canberra sailing south.

Ricky Miller – Marathon Man And Male Model.

Sailing south on the SS Canberra was such an illustrious experience for me. In fact, a family affair, from the past to present. Unknown to me, exactly twenty years previous to my departure, some of my close family had sailed from Southampton to Sydney Australia as £10 POM's. In 1982 also onboard the Canberra, I had a cousin 'Woody' of the same age, from the same town (Ipswich), embarked with 42 Commando Royal Marines, happily sailing south too. Regrettably, we did not see each other on ship neither on the way down or on the return voyage to the UK. Once on land I did get within touching distance of him on Mount Harriet, but fate was to be cruel as I will explain later.

For me life on board the 45,000-ton vessel was an event that brought back perceptions of the British Empire at its height during the Victorian period. An idealistic time for some when British Troops visited far flung locations such as India during the Raj or the African Continent. This nostalgia was especially prominent in my thoughts when temperatures increased, and as we sailed off the West African coast near Sierra Leone.

During this stage of the passage, life was comfortable, almost luxurious, especially compared to other units such as 45 Commando Royal Marines in cramped Military and RFA ships. The Canberra was spacious and without difficulty accommodated the 1400 Royal Marines Commandos from 40 and 42 Commando RM, 600 Paratroopers and other attached units, making a total of 4300 military personnel on board. (Ref: Van Der Biji. N (2007) Victory in The Falklands).

Some higher ranks thought that this mixture of different troops and past rivalries could end up with disastrous consequences and battles being waged on board ship, even before we reached the Ascension Islands, let alone the Falklands. Yes, rivalry between the Marines and Paras is renowned, however during my time on the Canberra I never personally experienced or witnessed any issues between the two groups. I feel there was a mutual, hidden from public, respect for each other from both Marines and Paratroopers. Very strenuous PT and concerts by The Band of Her Majesty's Royal Marines helped to reduce any signs of antagonism. The 'Cherry Berries 'seemed to get on with their work and so did we, both groups in a very professional and intense manner. I remember frequently seeing the Paras running on the promenade deck, circuit training, walking up stair wells and in the galley, doing similar activities as us. I just ignored them. Yes jibes and jokes were made and one particular slur comes to mind; 'There's only two things that accidentally fall out of the sky, bird shit and Paras and they're both crap'!

Civilian staff from P&O on the Canberra was slimmed down to fifteen women and approximately three hundred and ninety-eight males. These employees had a variety of jobs and backgrounds. Roles such as cooking, carpentry and laundry had to be done, even some bedroom stewards were kept on in the officers mess.

For 9 Troop as already implied, when it came to fitness, running was core, but it was interspersed with circuit training sessions on the recently built midships flight deck. The circuits involved many newly devised exercises by PTI's, one requiring teams of five men to lift a heavy wooden beam above our heads, doing shoulder press and squats while relying on others not to let go!

Other classes were a regression to basic training at CTCRM. Some familiar IMF exercises had to be relearnt. The workouts mainly consisted of constantly bouncing up and down on both feet, like a person on a pogo stick, feet together or apart, forwards, backwords, side to side and combined with arm swings. The pogo jumps were all well and good on terra firma, in a gymnasium with lovely, even, wooden flooring and designated spots marked out for each person to focus on. Try doing them on a rolling ship during heavy weather, with a strong wind, in a limited space, on an unlevel surface, with over one hundred other participants! We must have looked like a raft of penguins on an ice pack lacking any sense of balance, who are being pushed in unison by the wave action of the sea to the edge of the ice and back. It reminded me of being at primary school and running around in the confined space of a playground, pretending to be Spitfires, with our arms outstretched, and trying to avoid hitting each other.

Some exercises became too difficult to control and hilarious to watch as well as dangerous. The whole of Charlie Company looked like they were being pulled in harmony by an invisible thread one way then the other, with the Marines on the outer edges of the deck almost falling into the sea. This became even more hazardous when weapons were introduced. We were instructed to do various exercises with our SLR's by swinging them up and down, around and around, sometimes just missing the heads of our nearby Oppos. Some static arm drills were carried out by holding the weapon in front or at the side of your body for as long as possible. These isometric muscular workouts were particularly painful but done to help deal with the long hours of carrying or holding still while firing a rifle.

Running around the SS Canberra promenade deck early on, on the voyage south, as already mentioned, was limited to wearing comfortable T-shirts, shorts and training shoes. Boots were banned because of the concern over the damage they might cause on the surfaces and structure of the deck in the long term. As the days progressed and the heat increased, on runs 9 Troop now carried all the weapons it would have to manhandle on land but gratefully kept the PT rig. This included the 84mm weighing 33lbs making it virtually impossible for one man to carry the whole time at a running pace. I can remember the No1 and No 2 for the 84mm constantly having to pass the weapon over to each other for a rest and then eventually both exhausted, swapping with other members of the troop.

A Royal Marine PTI discovered that one lap of the promenade equalled a quarter of a mile, so a simple equation was fifty-two laps totalled thirteen miles, a half marathon. So, to keep up spirits a half marathon was organised. However this was downgraded to ten thousand metres, (approximately six miles) because of the heat and high humidity conditions. Each military unit and civilian staff were asked for representatives to run.

On the day of the race many people on board, both civilian and military, watched from the side-lines. Some of the civilian crew had befriended service personnel and 'came out' (an appropriate term for our times), to support their old and new chums. A few of the P&O male Stewards were not heterosexual and appeared on the promenade deck (or from wherever they could see) to cheer on participants. Some not only wore t shirts and badges representing their preferred military units, but also lipstick and mascara.

Nine troop, Charlie company's representative in the race was a young 19-year-old Marine, Ricky Miller, who unknowingly had previously caught the eye of several of the male stewards that were now watching. From the start Ricky was focused, not only on finishing but winning. He also had to try to ignore the pain he was suffering after borrowing a pair of training shoes from another Marine in 9 Troop, Andy Gaunt, that were too big, well past their sell by date and had a pungent aroma.

During the run, every time Ricky passed near the stewards that were supporting him, he was met by a cacophony of strange, male, high pitched cat calls of encouragement, promises of one-to-one invites to their cabins if he wins and a deluge of other innuendos. I had always wondered why Ricky had a contorted expression on his face as he passed by: was it the ill-fitting training shoes or was it the lewd comments from the Stewards? You decide.

Several days after the race I was approached by a male steward and asked if I had seen Ricky, questioned if he had recovered and generally, how he was. I declined to answer. Later on in the day, while relaxing with some of 9 Troop near the Alice Springs Pool on the Arena Deck, I noticed the same Steward trying to catch a glimpse of our young Marine Ricky, who was dressed in only his speedo swimming trunks. Oh to be thought of as a male model and a marathon runner to boot!

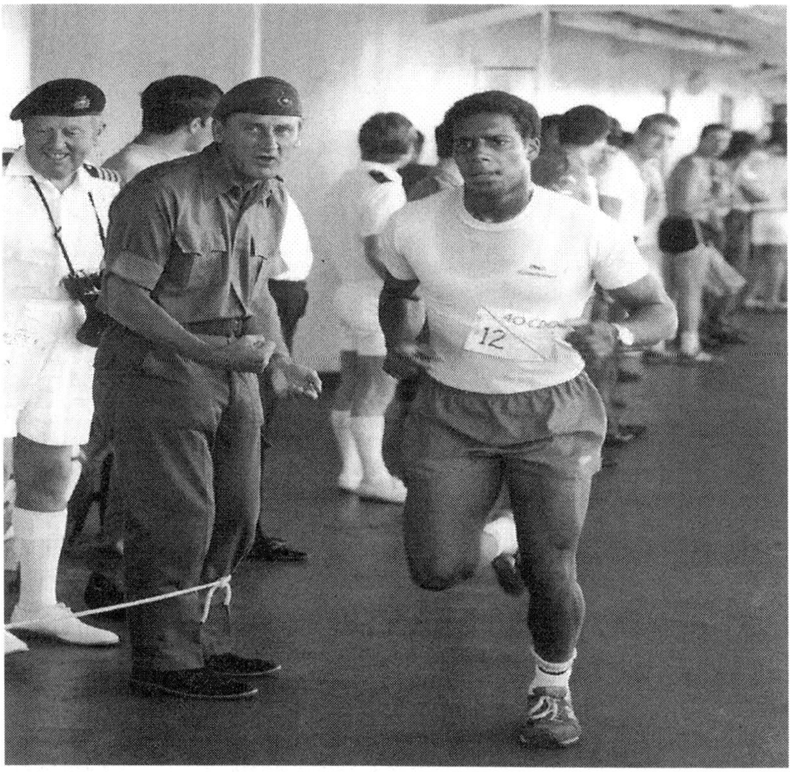

Picture: Heading south, close to the equator, on the Canberra promenade deck, Ricky Miller, 'Marathon Man and Model, being encouraged by Lieutenant Colonel Malcom Hunt, 40 Commando Royal Marines Commanding Officer. Note Ricky showing on his face, none of the suffering caused by wearing Mr Gaunt's training shoes or the lewd comments.

West Africa And On.

Sierra Leone is situated on the West African coast of the Atlantic and is approximately halfway between the UK and the Falkland Islands, (4,000 miles). The country achieved independence from Britain on 27th April 1961. Freetown is the capital and a major port on the Atlantic Ocean. On the 17th April 1982, the Canberra stopped there for supplies.

The night before we reached Sierra Leone, I left the William Fawcett Room and took a stroll around the promenade deck. It was just before sunset and off in the distance I could see land. One noticeable difference was the increase, not only of temperature, but in the humidity too. Walking in the open air on the promenade deck seemed surreal, again I was taken back to the days when Great Britain really did rule the waves and Africa, just like India, was part of the Empire.

As the Canberra approached its mooring, a jetty just outside Freetown, on the morning of 17th April, I, along with most others on board, went out on deck to have a look, while some troops were still carrying out fitness training. For most of us on board this was our first glimpse of Africa.

The water had turned from a clear blue colour at sea, to a silty dark brown as we had approached Freetown. Looking over the edge of the Canberra I could see locals on land and some in wooden dugouts paddling at speed against the current to come along side to take a look at us. A few of the people in the dugouts were trying to sell us souvenirs. The pedlars, with great accuracy, would launch up to the first deck, a 'gift', tied to a rope, the other end anchored to their canoe. The idea being that the potential buyer could untie and examine the goods and hopefully, well at least in the seller's mind, send the money back down to the canoe tied to the rope.

It was announced over the tannoy system on the Canberra, that on no account were we to buy anything, especially local produce and live or dead animals! At some stage, the hierarchy on the Canberra had had enough of the local pedlars in their canoes, and a fire party was ordered to turn the water hoses on the dug outs. However before this decisive action took place some of the 'buyers,' rather than returning the rope, decided to try and haul the vendor, dugout and his goods up on to the Canberra. I can recall a group of three to five Marines in a line, seizing a rope and having a tug of war contest with the poor local. The owner eventually losing and seeing his livelihood disappearing in front of his eyes as it spilled out and fell into the dark brown water below, his now vertical canoe dangling precariously on the side of the ship. The dismayed owner, having given up the ghost and struggling against the tide, gradually swam back to land, shaking his head. Anything and everything was thrown down onto the dugouts to try and dissuade them. I even saw an old broken chair go over the side, just missing the intended recipient, and then for him to dive in and recover it. The man was 'chuffed to bits' because now he could sell the plastic chair on for recycling and make some money! Regrettably by the end of the day for some owners of the dug outs, small bits of plastic and splinters of wood in their hands were all they had left of their livelihood's.

As well as the locals on land, a family with British connections had arrived to cheer us on, with only good will in their hearts. I can remember that they were easily distinguishable for several reasons, the most obvious being that they were the only white people. In this group there was a young lady, in a white dress, who received so much foul abuse, mainly sexual, that even I was embarrassed.

The whole family were welcomed with a chorus of insults and as a result, I fear, were scarred for life.

No one was allowed ashore at Freetown, for fear of contracting diseases, particularly malaria. I was one of the very lucky few who can say that I actually set foot on land in Africa. At night, under the supervision of L/Cpl Chris Pretty, about four of us from 9 Troop were detailed to go on a working party. After several attempts some locals had failed to load onboard the Canberra, oil barrels through a side entrance. We climbed on to a rickety pier, jumped off on to the dockside and rolled the barrels on board, using a makeshift ramp made of wood. Several times I crossed my fingers in hope that the ramp, severely bending under the weight of the barrels and me, didn't snap. Apparently, the Sierra Leonean's had been trying to do this for the last three to four hours. It took us about twenty minutes. Thank goodness there were no health and safety officers watching because if rules were enforced, as stringent as they are nowadays, we would have had all hell to answer for.

Below; a troop from 40 Commando Royal Marines circuit training on board the Canberra as she entered Freetown, Sierra Leone.

Above; a few of the ill-advised owners in their dugouts, being encouraged to move away by jets of water from the fire hoses off the Canberra.

Just before midnight, after our working party had finished, the Canberra slipped her moorings and continued off into the Atlantic Ocean heading south, leaving Sierra Leone and the rest of West Africa behind. The humidity soon decreased as we left land, but the intensity of the heat and PT sessions did not. I had always shown an interest and taken part in sports and fitness, probably because I was encouraged early at primary school to do athletics and play football, so I didn't mind the extra PT. Out at sea again, with the cloudless blue skies and clear ocean water we could see, from the bow of the ship, flying fish and porpoises in the wake. Further on, the ship went through the doldrums, where the water was almost transparent and perfectly still. I can remember wishing there was a call of 'hands to bathe' (this is when a ship stops and the troops on board can take a swim in the open sea, normally off the stern). Without the luxuries we have today, such as refrigerated fresh food and water, I wondered how on earth sailors coped in the days when they relied purely on the wind to sail. Being stuck in the doldrums must have been horrific.

Running around the promenade deck on the Canberra continued relentlessly, sometimes in different directions to help stop the boredom. After each run, we would almost sprint down to our cabin to be the first of four to reach the small sink and the desperately needed cold drinking water. Mne Simon Poole had come up with a novel idea, apparently told to him by one of his aunties. If you submerged your hands fully in water and held them there, you would cool off quickly. Yes, it did seem logical but the arguments it caused at the single basin were endless. Accusations of others taking more time were rife and counterproductive because of the increased body heat caused by tempers rising. I think that Mne Poole just did it as a ruse and once to help confirm my suspicions, I saw a glint of a smile on his face.

At some stage the Canberra crossed the equator. Unlike on other ships in the Task Force, there were no ceremonies held on board. As we approached Ascension Island, there was an attempt to try and blacken out the ship. Pussers black masking tape was put to two uses. First, it was put on windows in the shape of a cross to stop glass shattering on to the floor or personnel and causing injury, should it break as a result of an explosion. The second use was for the tape to hold up large sheets of paper or cloth over windows of the ship to try and stop any light at night from escaping and potentially giving our position away to Argentinian aircraft and ships. In the heat the stickiness of the tape gave up. At first slowly the ends curled up and eventually it just fell off so was totally useless at holding up anything.

My first glimpse of Ascension Island on the morning of 20th April (Tuesday), was the sight of a volcanic landscape, with no flora. Isolated in the middle of the ocean, it's topography looked lifeless like a vision of Mars or Dante's inferno. I was later to find out that the Royal Marines had a history in the Ascension Islands, apparently a garrison of Bootnecks was based there in 1823.

The Canberra anchored on the western side of the Island, close to Pyramid Point. Moored nearby were various military and requisitioned civilian ships. Amongst these various ships, RFA, frigates, destroyers, roll on roll off etc, there was an exceptionally large tugboat, one of the largest in the world. I believe it was the Salvage-man, although someone did say that they thought it had been lent by the Americans.

With several other members of 9 Troop, I spent most of my spare time during the day fishing off the stern of the Canberra, while she was stationary. We used handlines, simple hooks without barbs and a piece of meat as bait. I caught plenty of Black Trigger fish. If you threw in anything edible and sometimes inedible, they would destroy it in a mobbed frenzied attack. Waste put overboard was devoured therefore the Black Trigger fish soon became known as 'the Shit Fish'. If we tossed an injured Trigger fish back into the Ocean, its previous acquaintances would smell the blood, and as cannibals, devour it. When we ran out of bait, we just cut up some of our catch. By looking overboard and the water being crystal clear, amongst the shoals of Trigger fish we saw a wide variety of different sea life including a turtle and a lone Hammerhead shark that was casually swimming passed, (what an odd looking creature!).

One day Charlie Company disembarked from the Canberra onto landing craft, wearing bright orange life vests. It was to practice live firing and landing craft drills on to Ascension Island. This was my first sight of the Green Mountain. In contrast to the desert appearance of the surrounding lowland that reached all the way down to the sea, the Mountain was a microclimate of green vegetation, situated right in the centre of the island. It looked like the peak on the fantasy setting for Beach Sports on Wii games.

We were put ashore at English Bay. Most of 9 Troop, except for the gun teams, spent the day on the beach. We watched landing craft arrive and depart and saw light armoured tanks rev up their engines as they sat idle on the beach. I enjoyed getting off the Canberra, walking barefoot through the white sand and swimming in the crystal-clear and warm water. We were not allowed to go deeper than shoulder height into the ocean for one good reason, sharks! While swimming I had one eye on the water the other on the armed guard that had been stationed at each end of the bay in case a shark with the taste for human flesh ventured too close for comfort. One thing that did put my mind at ease, and aroused other thoughts, was the appearance of a woman in a bikini carrying a snorkel and flippers but sadly, accompanied by her male partner. They were both Americans based at the Wideawake Airfield and had come down to the bay for a dive. I thought, why can't I get a draft to a place like this!

I should also mention that we did get one other chance to get off the Canberra, albeit for a very short time and not onto dry land, but by flying in circles around the ship in a sea king. This then hovered off the main landing platform as 9 Troop practised descending roping drills.

Below top; a view from the Canberra looking onto the Volcanic landscape of Ascension Island and the military ships moored close by. Bottom; two Light Tanks at English Bay, Ascension Island.

The Canberra (The Great White Whale) taken from a landing craft as I approached and then reembarked from Ascension Island.

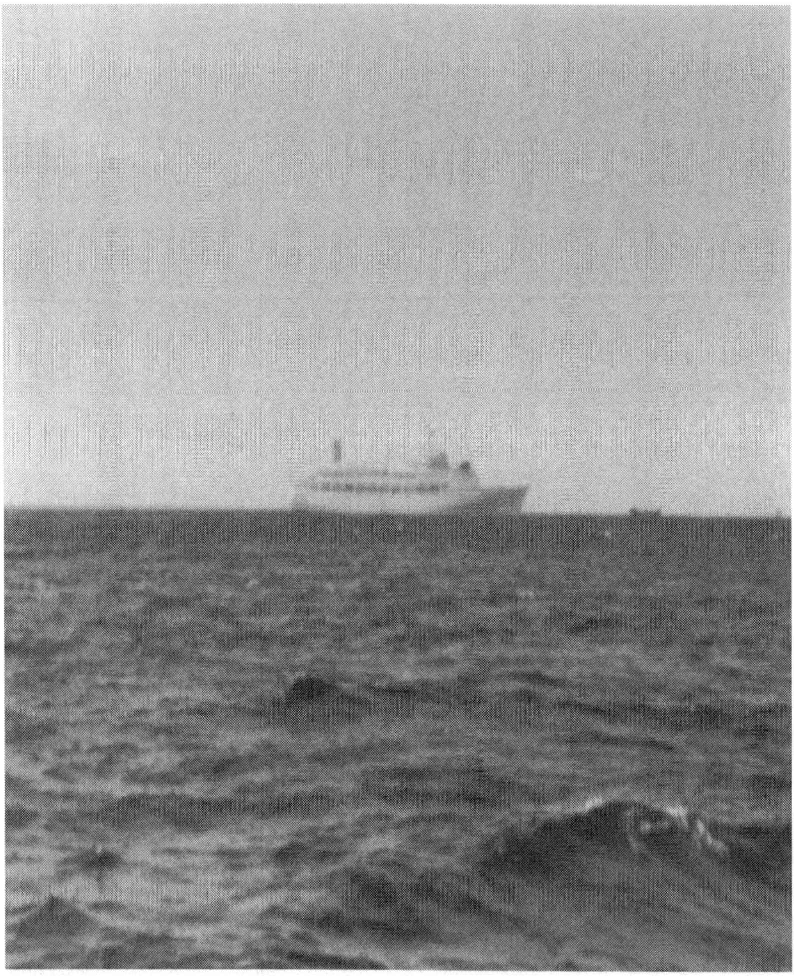

Next Page; Charlie Company, 40 Commando Royal Marines. This picture was taken on the Canberra just off Pyramid Point, Ascension Island.

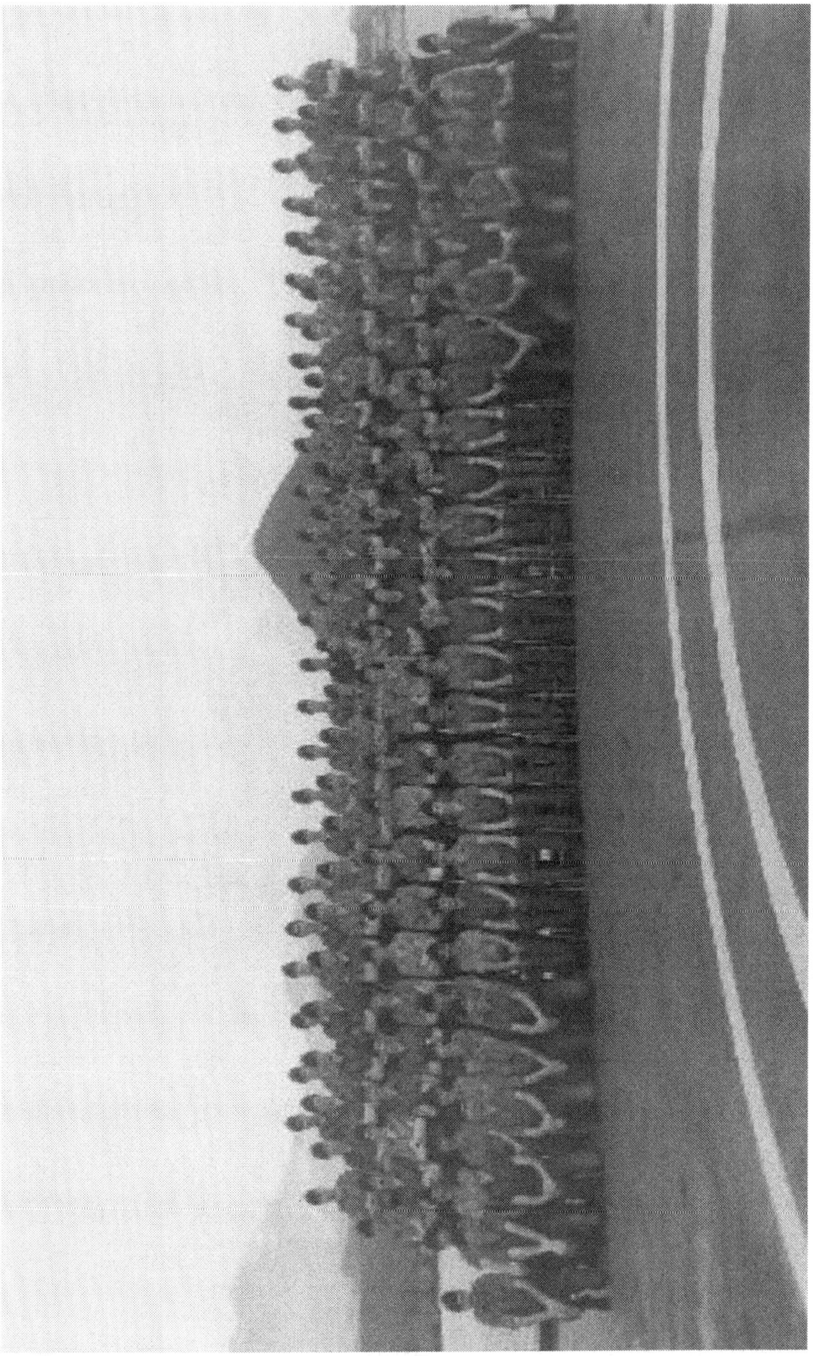

As we left the Ascension Island and headed back to the Canberra on the Landing craft, I was pleased to be going back to the comforts of a civilian ship, after so many weeks on board it started to become our home.

A few days after the Canberra left the Ascension Island was the last time that I saw Cpl Watts (K Company 42 Commando Royal Marines) on a run, dragging a 'tail ender' by the scruff of his neck around the promenade deck. I must explain (and/or remind you) that Cpl Watts was in my training team, as my section commander at CTCRM in the late 1979 – early 1980's. Once I was struggling at the end of the infamous Royal Marines Endurance Course and rather than yell and swear at me, Cpl Watts spoke calmly and gave me words of encouragement. I dug in deep and really pushed myself as hard as I had ever done and, as a result, was successful at achieving the allotted time. After I had got my breath back, Cpl Watts turned to the other Jnr Mne's and said, 'This is the type of effort I expect from all of you, excellent Barnes, you dug out blind'. After spending months at CTCRM this was the first time that I had been praised by anyone. I was chuffed to bits!

A few days later at CTCRM I was called up to the staff room in one of the Nods accommodation blocks. I thought I was in for another severe reprimand from the training team, so I tentatively knocked on the door. 'Come' was the call, so I marched in, halted and said out loud 'Junior Marine Barnes reporting Corporal'. Cpl Watts was the only one in the staff room. He told me to sit down and take off my beret, which was unusual. Instead of me getting a rebuke, we spent the next twenty minutes or so having a heart-to-heart talk. His final advice was, 'If you want something in this life you must give 100% to it and nothing else'. I left that staff room a changed person. The positive comments from Cpl Watts helped motivate me to complete training and earn my green lid. I was, and still am, very appreciative of the guidance Cpl Watts gave to me as a 17-year-old boy. It was upsetting news to hear later of his passing at Mount Harriet; a deeply passionate and professional Royal Marines Commando.

On the 6th May the Canberra headed further south and so did the weather. The glorious clear blue skies and still waters of the doldrums had disappeared. Things on board became more 'military'. People paid attention during briefings and they took advice more seriously. Although Simon Poole and Ged Herd were still up to their pranks. For days, just before getting my head down (going to sleep), I had found in my pit, several round shaped capsules of about 2cm in length and width, with a golden coloured liquid inside. I had no idea what they were and where they had come from. I asked the other three in my cabin if they had found any in their beds and they blandly said 'No'. This went on for several nights. Mnes Simon Poole and Ged Herd after inspecting one 'capsule,' suggested that these were probably insect larvae or eggs and I should change my bed sheets and shower properly each day, to stop them spreading. So, I did. They kept this story up for days. Later, taking a more serious path, they implied that I might infect the whole ship with some tropical disease and therefore should go to sick bay. The prank finished by chance luckily for me just before I took their advice and went to see a medic. One day I had entered our empty cabin on my own to find a brown glass bottle laying on Ged's bed, with about thirty of these larva or eggs inside, the labelling on the outside read 'Cod liver oil tablets!'

I could feel the ship rocking and occasionally shuddering as I sat in the William Fawcett Room. Because the windows had been blackened out I decided to take a walk on the promenade to look out to sea to look at its condition. As I opened the door to the outside, I was hit by pouring rain and strong winds. The Canberra had reached the roaring forties. There were several British military ships, their grey colour camouflaging them against the dark grey sky and water of the same colour. Interspersed with the British military ships was the odd USSR fishing trawler. These relatively small fishing boats were used to gather information on the Task Force sailing south, although this was always denied by the Soviets. The masts, supporting huge aerials on these fishing boats, were three times the length of the ship in height. Far too large for those required for normal 'civilian' communications. I did have admiration for the mainly Russian crew on these trawlers as they endured these horrendous sea conditions. I watched the bow of one boat almost going vertical before it disappeared below the waves, only to rise up again for more of the same; how on earth did they stay afloat? As I was standing on the Canberra with her stabilisers out, we could only feel moderate rocking, I did feel like a fake, a landlubber.

Some lectures were given in the splendour of the Canberra's Cinema. Marines were crammed into every space available. People were sitting in gangways, stair wells, doorways and all the way up to and even on the stage. The auditorium had luxury chairs with ample space to stretch your legs out, that's if you were lucky enough to get a seat. I remember attending a particularly long talk on the flora and fauna of the Falklands. 'Alan bloody Titchmarsh' rattled on about the flora and bored me to tears. The Officer had previously sailed around the Islands and knew the coastline like the back of his hand, which is exactly what I got from a SNCO for nodding off at one point!

Throughout our travels we were allowed to write letters home, however there was, understandably, some censorship. The envelopes were provided for free, as was the postage. These were called 'Blueys' because of their colour. Our BFPO address was, wait for it, 666. Also we were told to write wills. I had no plain writing paper, so I composed mine on a Bluey. This was one of the most difficult things I had had to do. As a 19-year-old, psychologically, this was quite challenging. I remember feeling very emotional but trying not to show it in front of the other lads. The only worthwhile tangible possession I had was my Honda 250cc Super Dream motor bike and it seemed logical to leave it to my older brother Gavin, who had owned motorbikes before and was also a serving Royal Marine. All my other personal effects, including money, were to be given to my parents. I contemplated and agonised for some time over what I could give to my two sisters, Ruth and Rachel. Sadly, I couldn't think of anything they would want so I just simply wrote to my Mum and Dad to look after them. Then I asked Mne Craig Brooks to sign it as a witness. With the April fool's day recall, the 666 BFPO post code and having to write our wills, I really did think that there was something more satanic at work, other than the hierarchy having a lark.

On ship, the reality that we were actually going to land started to hit home when we were told to pack up all of our kit. All non-essential belongings were jammed into our individual green kit bags and taken from our cabins for storage in a hold on the Canberra. I recall thinking I just hope that I have packed the right kit in my bergen and hadn't forgotten something essential. Alas, I had. I had accidently put my waterproof top in my green kit bag. When I realised what I had done, I panicked and ran down to the hold and for the life of me could not find my kit bag. I was returning back to my cabin distraught when I bumped into L/Cpl Chris Pretty. I explained to him what had happened, and he said, 'Don't worry Tel, I've got a spare'. Chris, what would I have done without you down there? Thanks mum!

We were issued with a phial of morphine along with some paperwork to read and fill in. The morphine phial I attached to my dog tags using Pussers masking tape. I thought it was a good idea at the time. However, I did wonder what would happen should I have to take cover, thus landing face down in the prone position, on top of my dog tags and accidently inject the morphine straight into my heart; that would have been fun! The paperwork that we had to carry on our person during the Falklands War consisted of medical details, the Geneva Convention and any injuries sustained. How the hell I managed to keep these dry throughout my time on land I'll never know!

Below, the forms (including the Geneva Convention for prisoners) and medical paperwork we were issued before landing onto the Falklands at San Carlos.

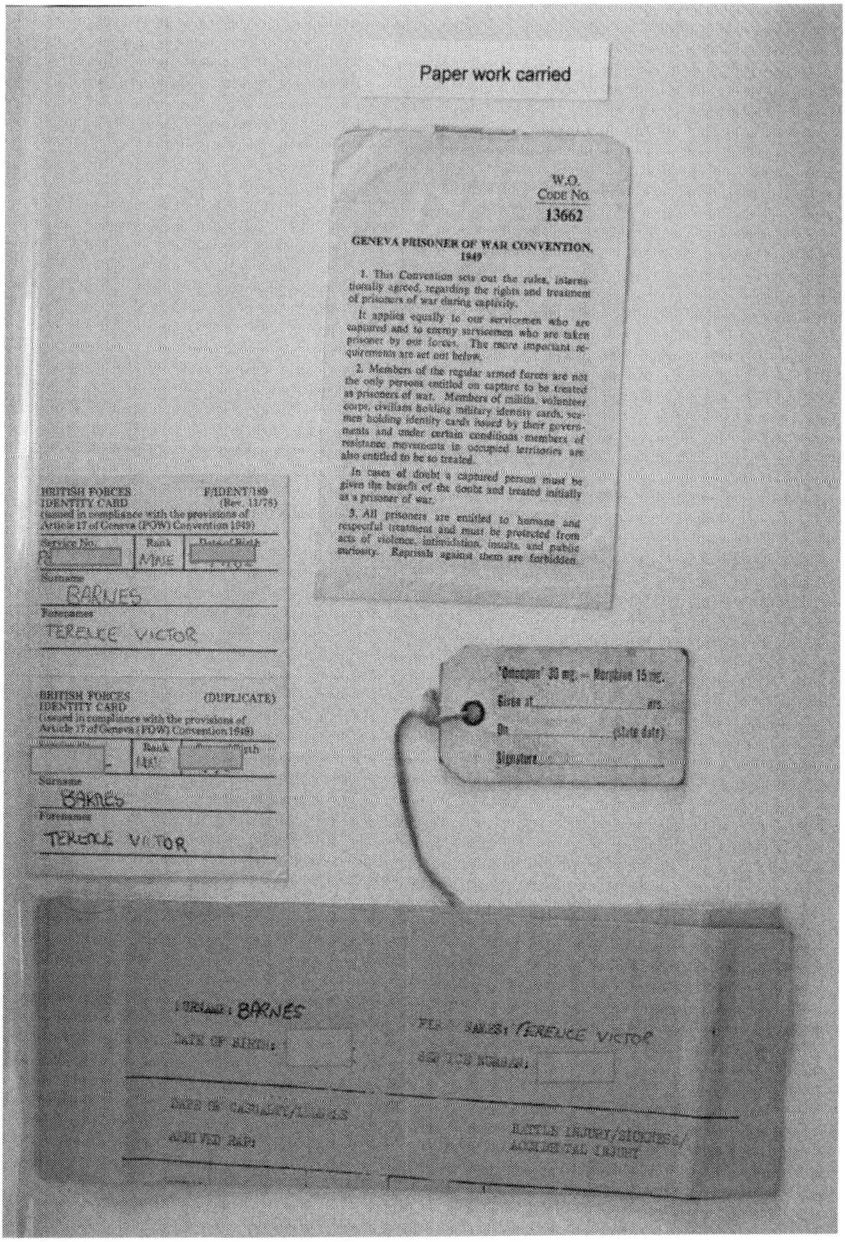

Cross Decking And The First Landings.

After six weeks onboard the Canberra, it was time to leave. On 19th May 1982, 40 Commando RM cross decked off the Canberra to HMS Fearless. 42 Commando RM stayed on ship as reserve. 3 Para went to HMS Intrepid. 45 Commando RM were on RFA Stromness and 2 Para on MV Norland.

For what seemed like ages, we waited on the Canberra, stuck in her maze of corridors, burdened with all our equipment and weapons. Moving at a snail's pace, eventually we passed the Atlantic Restaurant and on through decks D and E. Finally, I was able to see daylight through a door on the port side near the water line of the ship. We had already practiced the cross decking at Ascension Island so were quite confident of an unruffled crossing. One by one we had to jump from the Canberra's galley door, across to a waiting landing craft (LC) that would take us on to HMS Fearless. Unfortunately, the sea swell had increased, making the jump slightly more hazardous than we had experience in our practice back near the Ascension Island. One Royal Marine, from another company in 40 Commando, missed his footing and fell in to the water below, between the two boats. I watched as I thought he was going to get crushed to death, my toes curling up and a chill running through my veins, causing my stomach to knot. This unlucky Marine had no control of his direction or fate, he was at the mercy of the sea. I could make out panic seizing his face. The waves rose and fell as did he. Luckily for him he was pushed out of the gap between the vessels by a large wave, into the open water and rescued by a LC. He was very fortunate that he escaped with only wet clothes and embarrassment. The Marines' soaked clothes gave him the appearance of a wet rat crawling out of a sewer and his facial expression looked like he had just been told by a close friend that his wife was cheating on him. I felt extremely sorry for him as he passed others who made sarcastic comments, having showed very little or no empathy at all for the poor soul.

It was still daylight when we reached HMS Fearless. Onboard, the resident Naval personnel, ships detachment of Royal Marines and 40 Commando RM were crammed like sardines in a tin. 9 Troop were extremely lucky to have been given a mess floor and the odd bunk to sleep on. It wasn't until I went to get some scran and left our accommodation, that I saw how cramp conditions really were. I noticed bodies just lying down where they could, trying to get some shut eye as passers-by stepped over them like they were part of the ship's structure. In the mess we were given our briefing on the landings by 9 Troops' Sgt Nick Holloway and Lt Carl Bushby. Together our two leaders reminded me of Laurel and Hardy. Nick, tall and thin (possibly more like John Cleese) resembled Laurel and Carl, Hardy. To be fair Carl was less plump and cack handed than Hardy but had similar facial expressions! They told us exactly what our order of march was and what buildings we were allocated to clear after we had secured the beach area. The information we were given was very detailed implying that our intelligence was excellent. San Carlos Settlement, Blue Beach 1 was to be our drop off point. We were to be part of the first British troops ashore on the Falklands since the invasion on the 2nd April 1982 by the Argentine Forces. SBS members would signal from the shoreline if the landing was going to be opposed. Some matelots on HMS Fearless who would normally occupy the mess that 9

Troop were in, looked on and listened to our briefing with interest and, I think, a slight sense of jealousy. I however, did recoil at the thought of a landing against an Argentine enemy firing at us and the casualties that might occur. I had watched 'The World at War' TV programmes about World War Two, showing in old, distorted, black and white film, similar actions to what we might have to face. Visions of the D day landings came vividly to mind. Yes, I was slightly scared, but almost excited too. Naive, yes, but well trained, yes. It was almost a privilege to know that 40 Commando RM were to be the first to land on the Falklands Islands.

I cannot remember the exact time and the amount of ammunition each member of 9 Troop received. I had approximately five magazines of 20, 7.62rounds in each, for my SLR, L2 grenades, a (Light Anti-Tank Weapon) LAW 66 mm, some spare link for the GPMG and mortar rounds. On the night of 20th May, on HMS Fearless as we moved forward, through her corridors and down steep stairs, it was very difficult to see. All of the Marines landing had applied camouflage cream and it made identifying other individuals problematic. Because the ship was in total blackout the only light was the occasional bulb giving off a red, dull glow, so as not to affect our night vision. In an unfamiliar environment, using the colleague in front almost as a Zimmer frame, was the only other guidance I had as we headed towards the landing platform dock of the ship. Just as I was boarding the landing craft utility (LCU), I heard a matelot whisper, 'Good luck' and then put his hand on my shoulder.

In the landing platform dock the smell of Marine diesel fuel was strong and the noise of engines seemed exceptionally loud as the

Royal Marine Coxswain reversed the LCU I was in, out into the open sea and thankfully, fresh, cold, air. Luckily the sea was unusually calm. HMS Fearless dwarfed us as we passed by. There was little or no wind, just a breeze caused by the forward movement of the LCU. The sky was cloudless and clear. Because of literally zero manmade light pollution I could see filling the heavens above, many unfamiliar and familiar constellations, and numerous shooting stars streaking by.

9 Troop, along with the rest of Charlie Company, had been crammed into a LCU like stuffing in a Christmas turkey and after a while it started to get a little uncomfortable. Each man was loaded with equipment and ammunition. At one stage I had had enough of someone's flash eliminator (the end of the barrel) from his GPMG sticking into my hip, so I just casually picked it up, put it under my lower leg and laid back to rest on top of my L2 grenades and 66mm LAW. All weapons had been made ready, with the safety catch applied. A gentle knock in the wrong direction could result in a round going off and in that close proximity, god knows how many bodies a 7.62 round would pass through. I could have been a nervous wreck thinking about the number of explosives we were literally lying on and the potential for them to go off accidently. Later, a negligent discharge occurred, luckily with no injuries.

Very few conversations were taking place on the LCU and any that did, were at a whisper, except for the voice of one individual. A Corporal Royal Marine from the PTI branch in 7 Troop, could be heard by all. Quite possibly he was trying to be quiet, but unknowingly his speech seemed to boom out. I had no idea what he was talking about, but there was the occasional giggle from others. Whether this was his way of dealing with nerves, trying to reassure his section, or just portraying a macho image, I do not know. He clearly had an extrovert persona. I just ignored him and besides I had other things to worry about i.e. a potential opposed landing. With all of the equipment we were carrying, along with the additional mortar rounds, if the landing was opposed, it could have been a blood bath as it would have been almost impossible to fire back.

I shouldn't have worried. Although there had been in the days before sightings, luckily at the time there were no reports of Argentine forces close by. As the landing ramp went down, Charlie Company disembarked from the LCU into cold sea water, reaching just below the knee. When we got onto dry land and thankfully dropping off our mortar rounds into a pile, we continued forward. After being so long on board ship it was a good feeling to have the earth beneath my feet, to get the blood circulating around my legs and feel the warmth being generated through my body.

After a brief yomp we stopped and the whole of Charlie Company lined up in our designated sections and troops and approached the buildings in San Carlos Settlement. A reporter for the Daily Telegraph, was attached to us. I remember him making a tremendous amount of noise as he sat with his back against a fence made of corrugated metal and someone telling him to 'Shut the fuck up'.

Suddenly, there was a single shot from about 100m away from my position, some muttering and then quiet. My heart raced as I thought we were in contact with the enemy. Nothing happened. Word came up from a situation report (Sitrep) that someone in 7 troop had a negligent discharge (ND) from his SLR. The best quote I heard was from Chris Pretty saying, 'His heart is in the right place, it's a shame his trigger finger wasn't'!

After the buildings were cleared with thankfully no incidents, 9 Troop yomped up above San Carlos Settlement onto the slopes of the Verde Mountains. We were positioned at the extreme southern end of the beach head troops. In the dark we took off our bergens and started to dig our trenches. Sunrise came on the 21st May and we were still digging. The peat soil was easy to remove, it was the rocks, boulders and the brown, smelly, clouded coloured water that caused the problems and slowed our progress considerably. Most of us gave up excavating and decided to build upwards, above ground level with mounds of peat and granite for defence and tussock grass on top as camouflage. We used small sticks to indicate our arcs of fire, mostly at 10 o'clock to 2, therefore making sure that we didn't shoot our colleagues in the trenches on either side of us. That night and during the day I didn't get any sleep. I had tried to catch five minutes but found it impossible, probably due to the adrenaline still flowing through my body and the immediate necessity of completing our trench. Lying curled up in a ball, inside a saturated sleeping bag, at one end of a half-completed trench that was gradually filling up with water, while your fellow Marine continues to dig, was not the best environment in which to have a kip. Not only was my sleeping bag drenched but so were my feet inside my sodden DMS boots; a result of the previous night's wet beach landing.

My first impression of the Falklands was not good. I thought 'My God it's just like Dartmoor with its famous persistent drizzle, cold, wet and boggy underfoot with a constantly blowing wind'! The unpredictability of the weather reminded me of an English summer except here the elements were more extreme in their intensities. Willows, oaks, beeches and sycamore, common in the UK were totally absent, as in fact were all trees in the Falklands, thus giving us no natural cover or peace from the bloody wind.

During the first day near the jetty at San Carlos Settlement, I saw two or three guys dressed in waxed waterproof, Barbour type Jackets, with long hair down to their shoulders, carrying what looked like American M16's. Guys from my Company went to speak to them when they recognised each other from serving together in other Royal Marines Commando Units. These SBS guys had been here on the Falklands for weeks before any official landings were announced.

A working party was called for and like all good Royal Marines, I ducked for cover, hoping I wouldn't be seen. Assuming that it was to be detailed off for loading or carrying stores, I was pleased that I didn't get 'pinged'. It was not until Mne Sponner (Hall) returned back to 9 Troops positions that we found out he had only gone back down into San Carlos Settlement to raise the Union Flag and pose for some photographs wanted by the accompanying British press. Little did I know that this picture with Mne Sponner in it, was to be published all over the world in the next few days, with the heading 'We're back,' on the front page of many UK tabloid papers.

Below; sketch map 1982 of the landing sites and objectives for Charlie Company 40 Commando Royal Marines. Note A and B companies' location and direction of advance.

Below; Blue Beach on the first day – we built up more than dug down. You can see the wet sleeping bags out above the trenches in an attempt to dry them.

Above; the first wave of bombings by Argentine Aircraft. This view is from my trench looking towards San Carlos Settlement. To the near right Cpl 'Jono' Johnson RM is standing above his trench looking at an explosion in the centre foreground.

In Charlie Company we had two or three Marines join us on the Canberra as we sailed south from Southampton. These Royal Marines had been part of the original NP 8901 group that had put up an excellent defence, against an overwhelming Argentinian Force, during the invasion back in April. One of these Marines joined our section, I can recall another going into 7 or 8 Troop.

The guy in our section I was initially designated to dig in with, we just didn't get on. Was it a clash of personalities? Possibly. We certainly did not have the same sense of humour. I found it hard to find any sense of fun in him at all. He appeared to be very sober, bland and he rarely laughed or smiled and would have been better employed as an undertaker. Conversation was not his best forte. Initially it was like being in a relationship that you were committed to. You put all your efforts in at the start to make it work but, as time passes and the connection fades, in the back of your mind you know this isn't going to happen. We simply didn't 'click'. In the famous words of Private Frazer from Dads Army, we were 'Doomed, doomed I say, doomed!' I had no idea what he thought of me, probably the same, we just did not talk. It's not as if we didn't share the same values or hadn't been through the same arduous training to be a Royal Marines Commando. At one stage while I was digging our trench, I had the notion to put my pickaxe handle down onto his head. I could not live like this. The thought of spending, god knows how long, sharing trenches, scran and wets with this individual was too much to bear. I quietly expressed my concerns to my section commander, and for the better, we were both paired up with different guys. I thought 'Thank the

Lord', there was to be no more psychological suffering for me because of this person, the relationship had finished, and to be honest I cannot recall one single subsequent incident during my whole time on the Falklands involving this 'ex-partner'.

Apart from the basics of digging in, standing to, cooking scran and making wets, 9 Troop also had to man a sentry post. This position was about 20-30 metres further south of our trenches. Laying there in a shell scrape, I felt fairly isolated being on my own, especially at night. While on sentry duty the slightly worrying thought came to me that if a horde of Argentines came over the top of the Verde mountains, down onto our position, it would be up to me to initiate contact and/or warn the rest of 9 Troop. However, having the knowledge of possessing the firepower of a GPMG next to me gave me some comfort. Yet again I went into fantasy mode and I imagined that I was in a foreign country, on the outpost of the British Empire, the last soldier on the flank, protecting my country and fellow Royal Marines.

On one occasion, alone on sentry, just as the last sunlight was fading, I heard a rustle behind me, turned and saw Cpl Dee Irving, my section commander, approaching. He asked me if I had anything to post. Writing letters was the last thought on my mind, but I was keen to let my family back home know that I was safe. So I said yes. Luckily, I had a very soiled 'Bluey' in my pocket and an old pencil. I managed to scribble the address back home on the front and in the dark, dash off two sentences although I couldn't see what I was putting down on the paper. Dee was getting impatient and telling me to hurry up because he only had two minutes left before the post had to go. I handed him my bluey and just hoped that my scrawl of words was legible for my parents.

When the Argentine air raids started coming in, from our trenches we fired at anything and everything we deemed as a threat that flew past. With little chance of hitting the planes, it just felt good to let off some frustration and rounds from my SLR and at least I could say I fired in anger! Green and red tracer rounds landed close to our trenches, fired from the ships in San Carlos Water. Unwisely, I jumped out at one stage and tried to kick them away, burning the toe cap on my right DMS boot!

I watched as Mirage and Skyhawk fighter planes flew over the mountain tops into San Carlos Water, dropping 500lb and 1000lb bombs and I saw plumes of sea water being sent up into the air as, thankfully, they missed their targets. The planes followed the contour of the land as best they could, whilst trying to dodge a barrage of fire from land and sea. Often they flew close by and the roar of the fixed wing jet engines overhead, quite frankly, scared the shit out of me!

I had in a trench nearby, an attached specialist Royal Marine armed with a Blowpipe, a portable surface to air missile. It just didn't work. I think he managed to fire off one or two missiles but the projectile just dropped to the ground about 300m in front of us. The blowpipe was probably one of the worst bits of weaponry I saw taken 'Down South', it just didn't fulfil its purpose. It was about as much use as buying a black and white television to watch the World Snooker Championship Final!

During daylight on the 23rd May we observed more low-level enemy sorties coming in, and several jets get hit by Sea Cat, Rapier or other ground to air missiles, bursting into flames before hitting the water or ground. These were not the first or last we would witness. In San Carlos, stuck in our trenches, warnings of 'Air Raid Red' became the norm and to be quite frank, after three or four days, we became quite blasé about the shouts.

Looking down from my position into San Carlos Water I could see it was a whirlwind of activity, with LC's and helicopters offloading stores from the ships on to Ajax Bay. The helicopters looked like little Bee's going back to their hive, laden with nectar and pollen, slung below their bellies.

On the same day and still at 9 Troop's first location, from where I stood in my trench looking back towards San Carlos Settlement and further on, beyond a peninsula with a small grass air strip on it, I saw the frigate HMS Antelope, stationary in the sea, with white smoke rising from her. She had managed to crawl into the relative safety of San Carlos Water. We were told that the ship had two unexploded bombs (UXB's) onboard. I didn't think anything of it, I was just concerned with life's necessities like cooking, fresh from a tin, my next chicken curry! During the night there was a succession of large explosions and the sky lit up. Initially I had no idea what it was. Though whatever it was, I thought 'Bloody hell I wouldn't have liked to be close to that bastard'. As I looked towards the noise and light I could see the grey outline of HMS Antelope, with a permanent orange glow, growing in size from a fire on board. It was illuminating the whole of the night sky. HMS Antelope was still smouldering and afloat when daylight arrived. On a rare windless morning, huge blooms of white smoke could be seen floating upwards into a nearly clear blue sky.

<u>The Failed And Fatal Attack Of An Upland Goose (kamikaze goose or new mascot?) 27th May – 8th June.</u>

During the Falklands War, San Carlos Water became known as 'Bomb Alley' due to the frequent bombings on the British Forces by the land based, low flying, Argentine jet aircraft. Wreck Point is situated on the north west entrance to San Carlos Water. From Wreck Point, West Falklands is clearly visible across the Falklands Sound. Wreck Point was the site of a Rapier (Surface to air missile) detachment. Strategically placed there because A4 Sky Hawkes and Mirage IIIEA's frequently flew over the position before and after their sorties into San Carlos Water. Just after the initial landings by British Forces there was a genuine fear of a counterattack from Argentina, by their land forces on the British beachhead. For this very reason it was decided that 40 Commando RM was to be Force Reserve and tasked as rear guard for the beachhead. One of the duties was to protect these Rapier sites.

Sadly, during this period 9 Troop heard that there had been a surprise air attack on 40 Commando HQ back at San Carlos Settlement. Mne McAndrews and Sapper Ghandi were killed and several others injured.

Apart from defending the Rapier site at Wreck Point, my section, 33.C, 9 Troop, carried out reconnaissance patrols to gain knowledge of our local environment from our base, called 'The Sangar'. The Sangar had been started by our predecessors from 45 Commando RM. As I have already cited, it was made of granite boulders, soil and turf, roughly circular in shape, with an approximate diameter of six feet. In design, remarkably similar to a castle keep, with a single tactical entrance and exit and enough space for two or three people at once. We built it up to a height and depth so that the GPMG could be placed on top and fired while standing up. We also added a few additional home comforts such as shelves to place mess tins on. Close by, I shared my Artic two-man tent with Mne Ged Herd. Ged was a great person to be around, physically large, matched by his enormous humour. Ged must have suffered being with me because day after day, without a murmur of complaint or surprisingly, diarrhoea, he consumed the gopping looking and tasting scran I had cooked in a mess tin over a Hexi cooker.

At Wreck Point we had the opportunity to zero our weapons using any target we pleased (alive or inanimate). No native mammals or reptiles exist on the Falklands, however there is an abundance of fish, birds and sheep. Much to our disappointment we were told that 40 Commando RM would be staying at San Carlos as a reserve while the rest of 3 Commando Brigade would be going forward. So Chris and I went down to a nearby cove to let off some steam by firing our SLR's at anything, under the guise of zeroing our weapons.

After shooting at sheep up in the hills above the cove, seals out in the sea, and missing them all because we had no SUIT sights (Sight Unit Infantry, Trilux) attached to our rifles, well that's my excuse, Chris and I returned back to our tents slightly less hacked off. The next day I went back down to where we had been shooting and to my horror I saw a dead seal that had been washed up on the beach. I felt so terribly sad. I checked it over but could find no entry or exit wounds. Was it a natural or 7.62 death? This has plagued my conscience for years.

Several decades later while back in the Falklands for a reunion, I spoke to a local farmer and he talked about his loss of a number of his sheep and because of this, a drop in income during and immediately after the war in 1982. The Falklander blamed the Argentine soldiers for killing any wildlife, including his Sheep for food. An accusation I whole heartedly agreed with by nodding my head up and down, while showing not the slightest hint of remorse!

During this period of ours at Wreck Point, the other sections of 9 Troop were distributed nearby, however without any sitrep's we had no idea what they were up to.

I can remember being on duty on my own in the Sangar for several hours at a time. In the dark my focus would waver, and in my mind, not for the first time, I would drift off into a world of fantasy. I had perceptions, again, of being the last man on guard. This time at the Khyber Pass during the first Anglo-Afghan War, with the might of the British Forces behind me and the threat of the Argentines in front. As a typical young heterosexual man, with uncontrollable high levels of hormones, I also had thoughts of the other sex. I would dream that I was going for a date with the Scottish singer/song writer Sheena Easton. She was three years older than me and had experience in life which, for me, added to her attraction. To try and impress her on our first date I would have to recite a verse from her song titled 'Modern Girl'. So I would go over the lyrics again and again. Astonishingly, after nearly forty years, I can still recall some parts of the second verse; (sing along and continue if you can and have the will to!) 'It looks like rain again, She's on the train again to London Town.....etc'. Sadly, back on duty, reality would soon creep in when it started to rain, sleet and snow all within an hour, the discomfort augmented by the constant wind.

The aim of our patrolling, as already stated, was to get to know our local environment, put up defensive measures like barbed wire and to locate likely routes of attack by Argentine troops. It was during a patrol that we discovered, hidden from view, a re-entrant, about one hundred and fifty metres long, that led down from our position on Wreck Point to a bay. The bay was secluded, with steep banks at each end and a sandy beach, ideal for an unopposed landing by the enemy using LCU's. L/Cpl Chris Pretty, Ged Herd and I decided it would be a good place to put a trip wire, fixed to a L2 -A2 grenade, across the re-entrant leading to the beach. My toes still curl up when I recall how, with a steady hand, lying in a horizontal position on the ground, Chris slowly removed the pin from the grenade and then threaded a thin wire through a small hole, to hold the handle in place, one slip could have been fatal. Anyway, the trap was set!

One morning on Wreck Point, just after 'Stand to' (a state of readiness) the whole section went to our given positions for approximately 30 minutes until daylight arrived. Halfway through this stand to, we all heard the thump of an explosion from the direction of the re-entrant. It was obvious to us that the trip wire had done its job and detonated the grenade. First of all, I was shocked, secondly, I thought how dare they (the Argentines) try and land here, bloody cheek! In fear of an attack and slightly excited, we went on the offensive, grabbed our weapons and tactically made our way down to the bay. On arrival half of 33.C were perplexed. There was nothing where the grenade had been except torn, blackened flora, and a collection of feathers scattered on the ground and upon the branches of nearby heather. Eventually the culprit was located, a mature, plump, male Upland goose.

As we picked the goose up, I was surprised at how its body had remained intact after the fatal explosion. We took the corpse back to our position and had a short discussion on what to do with it. One can only make so many varied edible concoctions, some just digestible, from ration packs, even if they have the culinary skills of Rick Stein. Because of the lack of availability of fresh food, some members of 33. C were in favour of eating our new quarry. One physically large member of our section, with an exceptional appetite, who was partial to KFC, could be heard muttering 'Chicken' under his breath. Left for a day, rigor mortis had set in and with a stiff frost, the body of the Upland goose had become rigid and no one had the inclination to prepare it to be cooked. So, it was decided to put the cadaver to use. Without any support, the deceased bird stood upright, at about three foot high. It was placed just outside the Sangar on sentry duty, as a decoy to confuse the Argentines should they dare to do a reconnaissance patrol or launch an attack on 9 Troop 33.C.

To bolster our defences, we put some barbed wire around our location on Wreck Point. I hated the stuff. I remember it taking hours to unravel. I constantly received sharp pricks on my hands and the more sensitive fingertips, resulting in bleeding, even though we were wearing gloves. Also, because it was laid mostly at knee height, it had a tendency to attack you at the shins, just like a snake constantly puncturing your skin with its fangs; the bloody stuff was alive!

As revealed earlier, while at Wreck Point I suffered from trench foot, due to having wet feet from our initial landing at Blue Beach, in San Carlos Water and subsequently the continuous damp conditions on land. I was in agony. I could not walk without tremendous pain. The only comfortable way for me to move around was on my hands and knees. I felt a complete fool, a liability, because I had let everyone down in my section. I took my boots off and examined my feet, they were both swollen, wrinkled and a brilliant white colour. They looked as if they had been submerged in bath water for several days. To say my feet were tender to touch was an understatement. On the 4th June, luckily for me, we had a resupply by helicopter and a medic was on board with his bag of potions and cans of Guinness to aid my recovery.

Mail and old newspapers were also delivered in one resupply and on departure the helicopter took Dee, our section commander, back to Charlie Company's HQ for an Orders Group (O-Group). The significance of having mail cannot be overstated. To hear from your family and friends back home was so important, for me it acted as a morale booster. I remember reading a letter and feeling like I was a bi-polar patient, going up and down with emotions. Yes, I was a little down at not being able to speak to my family, but so happy that I was in their thoughts. The support from home was positive and therefore motivational. We knew our purpose here was being supported back home, well at least by the majority and by my family and friends which personally, were the ones that really mattered to me. Sometime later Dee returned and we waited in excitement for a brief. Unfortunately he had no new news or any information on the possibility of us moving location.

As for the newspapers, well the tabloids were good for two reasons, page three and toilet paper. The broad sheets were past their sell by date, so news of what was currently going on in the outside world was wanting. In one letter from my parents, they told me that my cousin in 42 Commando RM had hit the front-page headlines of the local Ipswich Evening Star, reporting that he had been involved in Operation Paraquet, (the recapture of South Georgia from Argentine military) and I had also been mentioned!

On Wreck Point, the Rapier site was run by some Pongos, this changed later on when they were replaced by the RAF Regiment. Their location was fifty or so metres behind, south west of our position. I can remember one of the operators letting us have a look through their tracking sites, however I couldn't make out much through the grey hue of the lenses. The Rapier missiles, four mounted on the top and sides of what looked like a very large dustbin, reminded me of the robot from the American Lost in Space TV series.

One day in the late morning my section was just going about its business, when yet another 'Air Raid Warning Red' came over the radio. Suddenly there was a hive of activity from the guys at the Rapier. The next thing I remember is hearing a swoosh noise and a Rapier missile flew just above 33.C location and our heads, travelling towards an aircraft. The aircraft was flying at a low altitude as it followed the contours of the land, then as it passed only a few hundred metres west of our position, it dropped down even further, skimming over the sea. The Rapier missile fired from our position hit its target and the plane went diving into the Falkland Sound, sending up jets of water. I can remember grabbing our rifles and going to the nearest landfall site from the downed plane, hoping to catch the Argentine pilot. However, a Wessex helicopter had been dispatched and rescued him from the sea. On another day, we were to witness two Argentine Mirages planes fly past and again our Rapier site hit one, this time on contact there was a large explosion, we didn't think there would be any point looking for survivors.

Personal hygiene was difficult to maintain during the whole time on land. I can recall at Wreck Point, the delights of stripping down to my waist for the first time, washing and shaving in a stream, uphill from the sheep droppings and not too close to a very steep cliff edge. From there, looking west across the Falklands Sound, towards the West Island, I could see a small, isolated, unnamed island and Chancho Point to the north. As the sun set, it was a spectacular view.

Once my whole section was standing around in or near the Sangar, counting our blessings because the weather was being kind to us. There was a clear blue sky and, for a change, instead of a cold wind we felt the warmth of the sun. Then, suddenly we all heard a noise like a rocket taking off and saw a Sea Dart missile rise up from San Carlos Water, heading towards what I thought was a Freddie Laker Airways plane taking holiday makers to their resort. Laker Airways was a British commercial airline famous at the time, until it collapsed in late 1982. I couldn't make out the shape of the plane, only its vapour trails. The Sea dart slowly but surely crept up on its target. It was so far away that we didn't hear any explosion as the missile hit, but just saw the remnants of the plane spiral down towards the earth. I watched on in awe, finding it difficult to believe a missile could shoot down a plane at that distance and altitude. I later found out that this was an Argentine reconnaissance Lear Jet.

Below top; the Upland Goose, friend, or foe (or food) held by me, sporting a Disruptive Pattern Material (DPM) waterproof smock. Bottom; Wreck Point. Building up the 'Sangar' with 33.C Section Commander, Cpl Dee Irving.

Taken by me from 33.C position on Wreck Point. The clear sky over the Falkland Sound showing in the centre, a white circular puff of smoke and trail below. The aftermath of an Argentinian Lear Jet Spiralling down to earth after being hit by a Sea Dart fired from a ship anchored in San Carlos Waters. The Sea Dart has a range of 46 miles, a flight ceiling of 60,000 ft, delivering a war head of 11kg up to the speed of Mach 3.

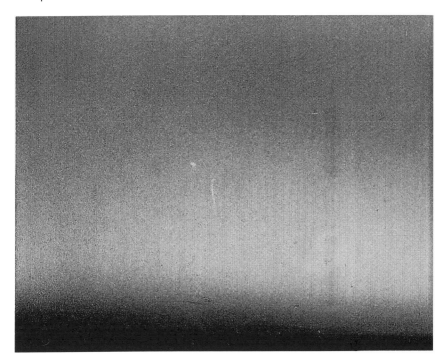

Back To Reality And War.

On the 8th of June we left our cosy two-man tents at Wreck Point and were flown back by helicopter to Ajax Bay. When we arrived there was nowhere for us to go. 9 Troop were told to spend the night under a lean-to, pitched up against the disused refrigeration plant, now being used as a makeshift hospital called the Red and Green Life Machine, after the Red and Green berets worn by the

Paras and Royal Marines Commandos. We were told that there was a 1000lb UXB stuck in the roof, left by an unkind Argentine pilot, flying past in his Skyhawk. During our stay I didn't talk about the bomb, but it was always in the back of my mind. The lean-to was more like a pergola, there was little cover from the rain, but it was better than being up on the hills and exposed to the elements. I was just so pleased to put my feet on solid, dry, and flat terra firma. I was still in pain from my trench foot and the man-made concrete surface seemed to ease the condition. However, the surrounding ground at the Red and Green Life Machine was a quagmire of mud. Paths had mostly disappeared, turning into marshland and where vehicles had driven, leaving ruts, some had become small, elongated ponds. At all costs I avoided getting my feet wet in fear of inflaming my trench foot, so I tried to do as little walking as possible.

Slightly away from the hospital building, out in the open and behind barbed wire (my nemesis), were housed some Argentinian prisoners. It was my first proper sight of an enemy soldier and being so close to them, made me feel on edge. Their prison was oblong shaped, approximately 30 metres in length and 20 metres wide. To pass the day and night the prisoners just walked up and down, defecating where they stood out in the open. It looked like a scene from the Belson concentration camp, except these captives were well fed and their conditions self-inflicted.

Sadly too, at Ajax Bay, it was my first time seeing and later to carry, body bags. They were being carried past us on stretchers to a temporary graveyard only twenty to thirty metres away from 9 Troop's position. As I have already stated, we had heard that a lad, Mne Stephen Mc Andrews, from 40 Commando RM had been killed by a bomb, being dropped by Skyhawks, near his trench at San Carlos Settlement and I did wonder if he had been brought by.

I have no idea what I was doing, nor what the time was, only that it was daylight, however, myself and some other members of 9 Troop were abruptly told to get ourselves to the helicopter landing site and assist in taking the injured off as they arrived. Some of us were lucky in that we managed to find stretchers to carry the injured off the aircraft. Unfortunate others had to drag the casualties off and carry or simply help walk them to the nearby hospital. Some of the Casevac's, (all British), were in a terrible state with burns and limbs missing. When we returned with a gurney, I remember trying to wipe some blood off it before picking up the next casualty. It was extremely hard to hear over the noise made by the helicopter, as it kept its engines and rotor blades working, so instructions were mainly given by hand signals between us, the injured, helicopter crew and medical staff..

As I was carrying a stretcher through the two large doors of the main entrance into the Red and Green Life Machine, I saw bodies on gurneys, and surgeons and medical staff huddled around operating tables. We had to bypass all of this to take the injured to an area on the far side of the building. As I passed by, I could see open wounds as bodies were being worked on, with blood covered surgical instruments and intravenous bags hanging by the side of beds. At first, I just stared at all this blood and gore, I was entranced. I had to divert my eyes, focus on where I was going and the poor soul I was carrying in case we dropped him.

Immediately after the helicopters left, Mne Ged Herd and I got pinged, with others, by a very stroppy Army medic, (what rank he was I cannot remember, only that he was above us in the pecking order) to go back into the building and pick up a stretcher. This time on entering, I just stared straight across to a far wall, not letting my curiosity get the better of me. Ged and I picked up the stretcher we were designated to carry, it had a body bag on it containing a corpse. I remember thinking to myself that it was surprisingly light. knowing that it was possibly a dead Royal Marine beneath the rubber veneer, slightly upset me. We carried the deceased past where we had slept the night before and on to the temporary graveyard. I can't remember Ged or myself saying a word as we walked by the Argentine prisoners and up a slight incline above the Red and Green Life Machine buildings and put the stretcher down. We took the empty stretcher back and put it just inside the hospital doors. I felt that I just had to get out of the building. I didn't talk about it to the others in 9 Troop, I just bottled it up and pretended it didn't happen.

The next day, 9 Troop joined the rest of Charlie Company and moved location up onto the slopes above the buildings at Ajax Bay. 9 Troop were lucky, our position was fairly low down from the peak of the ridge line. One time, working parties from every troop in Charlie Company were detailed off to pick up stores from down in the bay. I remember seeing some lads from 7 Troop passing us while struggling to carry jerry cans of water back to their trenches, all the way to the top; their language was colourful. There was another bonus for us. We were called down to the Field kitchen after 'stand to' in the mornings and last thing at night and because 9

Troop were lower down the slope and therefore nearer, we were always in the queue first and the food was still hot. While standing, eating, I contemplated that the food might get even hotter if a bomb was dropped and hit the ammunition dumps situated right near us. There were tonnes of crates stacked up containing mortar and artillery shells, missiles, grenades, 7.62 rounds and other armaments. I was amazed that they were so close to the Red and Green Life Machine and kitchen. If there was a direct hit, I suppose in a morbid way, at least it would have been less distance to carry the casualties for treatment and no demand for helicopters! Besides the danger, it was an extravagance for us to have hot rations. A grateful day away from the monotonous, menu A ration packs, which unvaried, consisted of a main meal of curried chicken or bacon grill for breakfast mixed in with 'ard bastards' (biscuits AB). Though I did take one part of my ration pack down to the field kitchen to have with a hot wet; my precious, sweet tasting, oatmeal block. After we had eaten scran at the field kitchen it was a case of walking in the pitch black, uphill, to try and find your trench somewhere on the slope above. After eventually finding your trench, if you were lucky enough not to go on sentry duty, you could curl up in your damp sleeping bag and lay in your wet trench or beside it, out in the open air and try to sleep. I can remember once standing in a trench facing towards Ajax Bay, with my legs bend forward pressed against the front wall, my backside resting on the slightly lower back wall, wearing my steel helmet, head tilted forward resting on the front parapet and using it as a pillow. As the hours went by, I got terrible neck cramp but at least I nodded off for a bit.

Below; Argentine Prisoners at Ajax Bay.

'Corned Beef Hash Sandwich? No Thanks Mate!'

I have a dislike of corned beef. Please do not make an assumption that this is because it is a well-known product of Argentina. It is it's bland taste, foul, mushy constituency, and dog excrement like appearance that disturbs me. The globules of white fat reminds me of lard, mixed in to bind it together with some part of an animal. It looks like some concoction made up in a cauldron by Shakespeare's three witches. What is the point? Instead, why not just eat good old plain meat! Corned beef is like celery; tastes of nothing, has no nutritional value, except huge amounts of calories, and I have disliked it since a child. As you consume the corned beef and it gets absorbed by your gut, an explosion of animal saturated fat hits your arteries, soaking your blood stream with high density lipoproteins, your body is yelling 'please stop!' So, I did.

At one point, somewhere near Ajax Bay, I can remember being ravished with hunger. I had only two bags of white sugar left to eat from a 24-hour ration pack. I am not sure who I was with but am certain it was a fellow Royal Marine from 9 Troop, who was just as hungry as I was. We searched through many empty, waterlogged trenches and shell scrapes for food but found nothing. We were just about to give up when we spotted two exceptionally large tins of – yes, you've guessed it, corned beef. My stomach acids rose with anticipation. For what seemed a lifetime after our discovery, we managed to prise the lids off the tins, with our tiny ration pack can openers and then we were in! I can distinctly recall with no dinner manners, plunging my filthy, unwashed hands deep into the tin, grabbing a fist full of its contents and launching it straight into my mouth, again and again. I had visions of my old art teacher at St Albans RC High School looking down with disdain at my encrusted fingernails. Before each art lesson he would line us up in single file, in the corridor outside his classroom and inspect our fingernails for dirt and god help you if he found any. As a punishment he would grab us by the sideburn, then proceed to pull the hair upwards, thus raising us up onto tip toes and making our eyes water with the intense pain.

The corned beef had no immediate adverse effect on me except the contentment of a full stomach after days of emptiness. It wasn't until two days later that I succumbed to the full results of my indiscretion. Diarrhoea for the second time, hit me with a vengeance.

Several months later, on my return to the U.K. I woke up with a hangover as a result from yet another run ashore with the lads from 9 Troop. I found myself on a settee, in a flat I didn't recognise. There were several 'civilians' milling around. One came up to me with the immortal words 'Corned beef hash sandwich?' My instantaneous response was 'No thanks mate!'

The Two-Pronged Attack.

During the land campaign on the Falklands, Major-General Jeremy Moore RM, commander of the British Land Forces, decided that there would be a two-pronged attack from the north and south on the East Island. The northern attack route was to be carried out by 3 Commando Brigade consisting of 42, 45 Commandos Royal Marines, 2/3 Para and attached units. Due to insufficient helicopters available for troop lifts, since the sinking of British Merchant Navy ship the Atlantic Conveyor, 45 Commando Royal Marines, via Teal Inlet, and 2 Para had to 'Yomp' (a Royal Marines term for your own marching pace) or Tab (Tactical advance to battle, an Army term). 42 Commando Royal Marines were lucky enough to be provided with helicopters to air lift them forward, in a slightly more southerly and direct route eastwards than 45. The main bulk of 40 Commando, with The Commando Logistics Regiment, was to remain as rear guard at San Carlos. However, after the loss of forty one troops from the 1st Welsh Guards at Bluff Cove on Sir Galahad, Alpha and Charlie Companies from 40 Commando RM were attached to the 5th Army Brigade. This is where 9 Troop, including me, were to remain for the rest of the war.

The 5th Army Brigade had departed from Southampton on the 12th May, travelling down South on the QE2, and landed at San Carlos on 31st May. The Brigade was headed by Brigadier MJA Wilson, and consisted of 2nd Battalion Scots Guards, 1st Battalion Welsh Guards,1st Battalion 7th Duke of Edinburgh's Own Gurkha Rifles and attached support units, amounting to approximately 3,000 men. It was decided that the 5th Army Brigade would take a southerly route via Darwin, Fitzroy and Bluff Cove. Major- General Moore RM then reorganised the units in the two Brigades. 2 Para joined 5 Brigade, leaving 3 commando Brigade with 42 and 45 Commandos and 3 Para. However, the Gurkhas soon replaced 2 Para who eventually re-joined 3 Commando Brigade.

The Final 48 Hours Plus, For 9 Troop Charlie Company, 40 Commando Royal Marines.

On Friday 11th June Charlie Company were flown to Bluff Cove and joined Alpha Company 40 Commando RM and the 1st Welsh Guards, under the command of Lt Col JF Rickett, as part of the 5th Infantry Brigade's southern advance. As already touched on, we were there to replace those Welsh Guardsmen lost during that dreadful airstrike on Sir Galahad.

Yomp Up To Mount Harriet Attack Start Line 11-12/06/82.

The lack of helicopters available made it difficult for the hierarchy to achieve a balance between the need to unload stores from Ships at San Carlos, thus keeping the vital supply line open, and the demand from the front line to transport troops forward and keep the momentum of attack going. The absence of tarmacked roads, along with the boggy and rocky terrain made it almost impossible for nearly all vehicles to press on. Therefore, for many on the ground of the East Falkland's, the only way forward was by foot. This meant that each Royal Marine or soldier had to carry their own personal equipment, food and ammunition, weighing between 40 – 60 kg, plus any specialised kit. Crop growing in the Falklands is difficult due to the poor soil conditions, and combined with high winds, as already stated, means there are no indigenous trees. Because of this there are large open spaces, making it difficult to conceal your movement on foot from the enemy during the day. Therefore it was tactically savvy to leave any yomping until it was dark.

This period of two to three days in June was the start of what I describe as the 'Yomping stage'. I would not at any point compare it to the arduous northern route carried out by 45 Commando Royal Marines, but it was certainly physically and psychologically demanding, challenging each Royal Marine from Charlie and Alpha companies. 9 Troop's first task, with the rest of Charlie Company, was to yomp and eventually form a start line for 42 Commando Royal Marines to pass through on their attack to take Mount Harriet. Carrying fighting orders, weapons and, stuffed into shared rucksacks, as much ammo as possible, we set off in the dark from a position some miles east of Bluff Cove. It was a typical case of slow down, speed up, and then slow down again as we waited for the tail enders to catch up. This concertinaing of the lines by yomping Royal Marines (the snake), was annoying, which unfortunately, we had all experienced before, whether it be on the training grounds of Dartmoor, Norway or many other locations throughout the world.

During this Yomp, we had our first encounter of negotiating rock runs. The rock runs were like streams of stones and boulders, starting at the top of mountains, flowing into gullies and valleys below, widening as they did, similar to water. These were particularly hard going. I found the best way of clearing these large obstacles was by leaping from one to another using them like stepping stones. However, this technique had its faults and I swore several times after losing my footing and smashing my shins against upright points and sharp edges. Unable to see ahead properly because it was night and also being weighed down with our weapons and kit added to our woes. Some rocks were covered in ice and others seemed to be as big as the famous standing stones at Stonehenge. Some lay horizontally, almost perfectly level and white in colour. They looked like concrete blocks and for some peculiar reason reminded me of a forecourt at a petrol station.

In the dark hours, near the base of Mount Harriet, on one hazardous rock run, 9 Troop came across what was supposed to be the lead group of Welsh Guards. Some of them were sitting down on the rocks. I knew it was the Welsh Guards because, not for the first time, I could hear as they walked, the noise of their waterproof leggings rubbing together, making a swishing sound and worse, a target. This constant and annoying noise was heard by us during the whole war, even after the Guards were advised to remove them. This blatant lack of professionalism riled us, had they never heard of the word covert!

We assisted these Guards who were sitting on the rocks, by carrying their kit over this difficult terrain. I remember picking up an ammunition box and L/Cpl Chris Pretty carrying a spare barrel for a Browning 0.5, which he had found lying on the ground near the feet of an exhausted Welsh Guardsman. As well as a bergen full of our ammunition on his back, Chris, continued helping others, regardless.

Several hours into the yomp we stopped south west of Mount Harriet. At about 50 metres to our right I saw a line of men. For a moment I thought that 'this is it, there's the enemy'. Then to my relief I heard English being spoken by them. To this day I am not sure who it was, but they were definitely friendly forces. Thank the lord it didn't end in a blue on blue incident. Also, Argentine artillery was landing nearby and this was the first time they had been so close to us. I could even feel the vacuum as the air got sucked back into where the shell had landed. Luckily, this time, we had no casualties.

Two other incidents happened on this yomp. Out of total darkness, an aircraft on a sortie, its jet engines screaming as it passed directly over our heads, caused me to freeze like a rabbit at night caught in the headlights of a car. The pit of my stomach vibrated, and I had a temporary loss of hearing. It scared the hell out of me, I had no idea what had just happened until someone told me seconds afterwards that it was one of our Harriers. I could not imagine what psychological effect these planes had on the enemy, even without dropping their bombs.

The second event was when I was looking south and saw a missile travelling along the coastline, fired from the direction of Port Stanley. Later we were informed that this had been an Argentine land based Exocet which hit its target, the unfortunate HMS Glamorgan, tragically killing fourteen of her company.

Just as we arrived at the start line for the attack at Mount Harriet, late due to the issues encountered on the rock runs, we watched the night sky light up with the Navy bombardment from HMS Yarmouth and HMS Arrow landing onto the mountain top as the assault by 42 Commando RM began. Following this onslaught, star shells were sent up to make it easier to locate Argentine targets on the mountain side. Immediately, I could see and hear small arms tracer rounds and Milan missiles being fired. Projectiles were going back and forth as if the gates of hell had opened up and Lucifer himself was spitting red hot lead everywhere. Weirdly, this sight took me back to my childhood, attending an organised firework display at Christchurch Park in Ipswich. Thousands of people would be in awe at the spectacle and there would be shouts of 'wow and cor' by adults and children alike, all enjoying the show. Back to the here and now in the Falklands and my only thoughts were directed towards our fellow Marines who were on the receiving end of some lethal returning fire. I had no feelings of joy at this deadly spectacle. Once I saw tracer rounds from several of our GPMG's focusing on one Argentine target, then a Milan slam into it making an enormous flash and bang. I thought that no one could have survived that. However, within a minute, rounds were coming back down from that enemy position. This scenario went on several times, almost like a cat and mouse chase until eventually there was no response from the Argentines.

At the base of Mount Harriet I can remember digging for my life's worth, a shell scrape as deep as possible, for fear of a counterattack and, with enemy artillery rounds coming in close, no other motivation was needed. Light from the moon made it almost like daytime and because it was a cloudless, windless, cold night, a surface of ice had formed on the ground, making the digging hard going. After an hour or so of being static Charlie Company were ordered to withdraw.

I don't recall much of the yomp back from the start line at Mount Harriet, except feeling knackered and that it was extremely cold. Our new home, south of the mountain, was a little gully that gave us some cover from the constant wind, so at least we could get a wet on. It was day light by now and Chris Pretty took off his bergen that he had carried throughout the night, which was almost completely full of spare 7.62 link rounds for the General-Purpose Machine Gun. He then removed his windproof jacket to reveal where the straps on his shoulders had rubbed due to the weight, causing chaffing and abrasions that had bled on to his clothing.

Ged, Chris, Brian and myself spent the day above the gully looking towards Port Stanley, ducking as the artillery shells flew overhead from both sides and making silly songs up about skipping through the Diddle Dee (a kind of heather), sung to a Scottish folk melody, Scottish accent included. We also saw a sortie of two Harriers fly passed, south of Mount Harriet. The lead plane dropping its 500lb laser guided bomb, while his wing man peeled off. We heard a distant thud as the bomb hit its target. I was so pleased, and my confidence grew, because these guys up in the air were on our side. I knew that we were so close to our final objective, Port Stanley and thought it will only be a short time before we were going to win this!

Guarding Prisoners From Mount Harriet 12 - 13/06/82.

During the next morning we had more artillery land close, but without incident. Later on the same day the whole of 9 Troop were called forward and taken by helicopter to the base of Mount Harriet, to deal with the prisoners. As we landed, I spoke to a couple of Marines from 42 Commando and asked if they had seen or heard of my cousin, also in 42. The reply was 'Yes, he has just left on that Sea King,' pointing at the same time as a helicopter flew off in the distance. I could not believe my luck, but at least I knew he was okay.

As we arrived most of the Argentine soldiers were sitting by a track. I went up close and gazed into their dark Hispanic eyes and it was like looking at two black holes in space, there was nothing there. We had to load them on to Sea King and Wessex helicopters, who then flew them back to Ajax Bay. At the time I regarded myself as young, but some of the prisoners looked like fledglings. Their clothing, although it looked thick and warm, had little or no waterproofing. It was like standing on Fox Tor, Dartmoor, in the middle of a rainstorm during winter with a continental quilt for protection. Yes, it would keep you warm for a while, until the rainwater leaked through to your skin and the windchill hit you. I didn't speak to any of the prisoners, I just didn't want to get personally involved, although I did see others from 9 Troop interact and, surprisingly, heard that some of the Argentines could speak good English.

Suddenly, we got the message that there were no more helicopters available. Unfortunately for the remaining prisoners (approximately one hundred or more), it meant a night out in the open. We had to herd them together and then under armed guard, march them back off the mountain side, over moderately wet, but fairly even ground, to a position about a mile away. It was difficult to see as we walked because as night fell, the landscape had been consumed by a blanket of darkness due to thick cloud cover. Keeping the Argentinian prisoners together while marching was a challenging task. On reaching the final location, just some bleak, open, wild and barren piece of moorland, 9 Troop then had to watch guard over them. As the night progressed and the clouds cleared, the temperature plummeted. I slowly felt the cold getting a hold of my extremities, my hands and feet were going numb. I was bloody freezing and there was no place to shelter from these bitter conditions to try and warm up, even for a few minutes. To keep my core temperature up, I continuously walked in circles around the outside of the gathered prisoners and pulled my neck warmer up over my nose. We did not allow the prisoners to lay down. Some tried going down into a squat to relieve their legs but were abruptly told to stand up. Talking by the prisoners was, as I recall, also stopped. Most of the Argentine soldiers huddled together to keep warm using each other's body heat. Their Commissioned Officers, the two or three that I saw, stood separately from their men.

Before sunrise a frost had appeared, not only on the ground, but also on some of the clothing worn by the prisoners. My warm breath was steaming in the freezing South Atlantic air. The morale of the Argentine soldiers was low. A lack of food, not being used to the cold climate and conflict between the men and officers all might have contributed to this. It appeared that their logistical chain out of Port Stanley was almost non-existent for the front-line troops. In some cases, being without resupply for weeks, the Argentine units on the hills and mountains had to resort to finding their own food and shelter.

In the Falklands, religious thoughts had rarely crossed my mind until I came face to face with the enemy. I am not afraid to admit that my faith in Catholicism had wavered. Long gone were the days of praying, such as repeating the 'Our Father' every morning and night. In Ipswich I had been an altar boy up to the age of fourteen at my local church, where I had been baptised and my family attended most Sundays. At fourteen I thought it was time I left this 'calling', after having the giggles at nearly every mass and getting up to mischief, like setting light to more incense than was needed, in an attempt to smoke out the priest and congregation and also eating several of the holy communion hosts when I had missed breakfast. While at the base of Mount Harriet and taking charge of Argentine prisoners, due to my up bringing as a Roman Catholic, I had what can be described as a slight internal moral conflict. A few of the prisoners had in their possession, pictures of 'Our Lady' (Mary, Mother of Jesus) and I could see several Argentinians holding on to Rosaries hanging from their necks. I didn't have an overwhelming feeling of togetherness in my religious believes with my captives, but I did have some understanding of what I was seeing. Was it pity too? I'm not sure. The comedian Billy Connelly remarked in a book that, as a result of being brought up as a catholic, he had an A level in guilt, was I experiencing this? These emotions did not manifest themselves by me running over and hugging a prisoner, but I did think of home. In my mind I was taken back to my local church, praying, and to some degree, this is what I wanted to do now. There was not an almighty, heaven sent, colossal, blinding flash, but what came to mind was an image of the statue of Mary Magdalene located just outside my Church.

For me, my faith is personal, from deep within my consciousness, not something outwardly ostentatious. Yes, I can see why symbols and pictures might help to focus the mind, but sometimes I find it irritating when people thrust these objects in your face, for everyone to see, as if they are trying to say 'hey look at me, I'm so pious'. I knew that if I had said a prayer out loud it might be seen as a weakness by the prisoners and there would be unrelenting ribbing from my colleagues. The only option, and the one I chose, was to keep quiet. To the outsider, looking at me, nothing would have appeared untoward, possibly apart from my eyes glazing over. As a professional soldier my training kicked in and before I knew it, I was distracted from my thoughts by someone giving me orders to get the captives ready to load onto helicopters, again to take them to Ajax Bay. Also, thoughts of what the Argentinians had done to initiate the war, and that they had killed and wounded my contemporaries, counteracted any thoughts of empathy for the plight of the prisoners.

I believe rumours were rife throughout the lower ranks of the Argentinian soldiers that no good would come to them if they were caught by the British. One story I heard was the Gurkha Regiment, wielding their Kukri knives, would be set free with their captives to do whatever they wished. Was this a ploy by the Argentinian officers on the ground to make sure the lower ranks fought until they died because they had nothing to lose? Or did it have the opposite effect, scaring the average soldier into a state of mental unbalance and fear? This psychological state, combined with poor training, ambient conditions, and a lack of food, might have resulted in some soldiers abandoning their positions at the first sign of hostilities. I could see only fear in the faces of the Argentines standing in front of me, especially the younger ones.

'A Most Unpleasant Night,' Stuck In A Minefield. 13-14/06/82.

On the morning of 13th June, after being relieved from guarding the Argentine prisoners, 9 Troop returned to the gully from where we had originally set off, for the yomp to the start line before the attack on Mount Harriet, two nights previously. After scran and rest, at some point during the day light hours, we were told to prepare for an advance forward by foot, east towards Mount William. We set off at approximately 18.30 in the dark and soon the start/ stop concertinaing yomping began. This time, 9 Troop were at the front of the long file of men and so not as affected by this process. As we advanced, we were under constant Argentinian artillery fire, thank goodness it was inaccurate. As well as the 'crump' from the artillery, I could hear the roar of a Scorpion Tank's engine to our north and was thinking what a large and easy target that would have made and wondering how the hell the Argies couldn't hear them too?

9 Troop's progress was, again, slow due to the rock runs. We had just passed over a small rock run and were quietly walking along in single file when I heard a loud, dull thud behind me and some-one shout 'take cover'. Assuming it was either mortar or artillery shells coming in directly down on our location, I dived straight on to the floor. For a few seconds, immediately after the thud, there was an eerie silence. The next recollection I have is of hearing, what I perceived to be, a very high-pitched, haunting scream com-ing from behind me further down the line. I had never heard a sound from a person, if it was a person, like it before. The noise was akin to some sort of unimaginable, wild beast, caught up in a foothold trap and writhing in pain as it attempted to pull free. Only eventually doing so by leaving a limb behind. It was a mixture of a screech, scream and a cry, all at the same time and of a very high pitch on a loop, amplified by the still air, sending a cold chill down the back of my neck. This still haunts me today. I thought 'who the hell has given permission for, and what on earth is, a female or child doing here? Perhaps it was a Falklander?' Was the answer to myself. Without night vision aids, we had no 'eyes on' what was happening.

In the background I heard a Marine shouting, possibly out of fear of the screams giving our position away to the enemy, 'For fuck sake shut him up'. Just after I got on my feet and back in line, there was another deep, hollow thud of a small explosion, again from behind. This time, I can only recall someone making a muf-fled, abstruse, moaning noise, but obviously in a lot of pain. A chilling message was passed up the line to 9 Troop at the head of the column of men, 'mines!'

It then started to snow. As a child I would have found this downfall exciting, but now I was preoccupied. I stood perfectly still not even moving my top half for what I perceived to be, (and rightly so) as hours. As time passed by I found myself in a predicament. My feet had gone beyond the cold stage. They were absolutely freezing, from my ankles down they felt like blocks of glacial ice and had gone completely numb. I was scared that if I moved either foot just an inch to help get the circulation going, I would set off an antipersonnel mine. So I improvised as I had done many a time while standing to attention on parades; by curling my toes up and down inside my boots, albeit very slowly, after a while some warmth returned.

To my amazement, a Scout helicopter arrived close to our position. I could only hear, not see it due to the pitch darkness and poor weather conditions. It had been called in to pick up the wounded. I couldn't believe it. I thought, such bravery and incredible skill from the pilots, but at the same time they're off their bloody rockers to attempt this landing! Also, I had two conflicting opinions; one was that at least the injured would get medical treatment quicker and the other notion was quite selfish; 'bugger off you're giving our position away'.

After the helicopter took off with the injured on board, I heard Charlie Company Commander Captain Andy Pillar's voice getting louder as he headed forward along the line of Marines towards us at the front. Someone behind him made a comment about it being unsafe and he replied, 'Well I've just walked up and down there and It seems to be okay,' in reference to anti-personnel mines.

Sometime later and still standing in the same position, a message came up the line to us that some Sappers from 1 Troop, 59 Independent Commando Royal Engineers and our own Royal Marines Assault Engineers were clearing a path behind us so we could safely withdraw back the way we had come. After what seemed an age, 9 Troop were given the order to load up and about turn in readiness to move off. I was feeling very nervous about taking my first step and thinking that I must try to follow in the exact footpath of the person in front. I need not have worried because that decision was taken out of my hands. In the dark the Marine standing in front of me swung his heavily laden bergen around to load on to his back. He hit me with it, full pelt and sent me flying. As my heart dropped to my feet in fear and I fell on the ground, I closed my eyes and waited for the sound of the bang from an anti-personnel mine as I landed on it, and then the resulting excruciating pain. Nothing happened. I lay there for a few seconds, as frozen as the ground. Gradually I cautiously got back on to my two feet and back into line. I just thanked God that my footing had landed on untouched ground and there was no explosion. The other Marine with the 'flying' bergen was so apologetic I didn't have the heart to shout out what I really thought. He meant no malice in this act, it was a pure accident.

After yomping some distance, we passed a group of Pongos sitting down, they were the Commando Sappers and we thanked them for their work. Little did we know that they had only sat down for a rest and as yet had not completely cleared the path of mines!

9 Troop had been very lucky, we had walked right over the anti-personnel mines and not set them off. Two Marines from 7 Troop had, the poor souls. I believe that Leading Medical Assistants (LMA's) Black and Kenney did a fantastic job of treating the two casualties until they were evacuated by the Scout helicopter.

The yomp out and being stuck in the minefield took over seven hours. It needed only approximately an hour and a half to travel back to our starting place, the gully near Mount Harriet.

Back in relative safety we heard that apparently, the Welsh Guards Recce Troop had sent us off in the wrong direction. They had neglected to pass on to Charlie Company that we should have yomped north not south of a lake near Mount William, where it was known mines had been laid. Why they did not pass this information on to us that night I do not know, but I do know there were a lot of unhappy Marines. After the war it was discovered that the Argentine Military had failed to keep accurate maps of where they had located their mine fields. The local Argentinian Commanders seemed to have haphazardly buried mines ad hoc and this might have been another factor that led to Charlie Company's bad experience.

Sappers Hill Morning Of 14/06/82.

After what was called by one officer as the 'worst night of his life' (and so far mine too!) and back at our gully, I put on a wet with Chris Pretty, and Ged Herd. Because I was so drained from the previous night, the effort of putting a match to a Hexi block was too much and I lost concentration thus setting light to my artic fingerless gloves, turning them an even darker brown and black; the original white had disappeared weeks ago through the dirt stains. I just couldn't give a toss. I was so tired. So we could get our heads down as quickly as possible without much fuss, together with Chris and Ged we just pulled two ponchos over ourselves for cover against any rain, sleet or snow and also for a little bit of warmth. Unbelievably we weren't even bothered about the artillery barrages flying over our position, from both directions, with the possibility of one landing nearby and wiping us out. I slept 'spooning' with my SLR and 66mm LAW. I had no time to reflect on the sobering experience of last night. Little did I know that this was to be the calm before the storm.

In what seemed like a blink of an eye, Charlie Company were stood to and told to prepare for an attack on Sappers Hill. Sappers Hill was the last high ground before Port Stanley and one of the few positions still held by the Argentine Forces. I thought it was a bite, another hurry up and wait. What I would have given for a few more minutes of Z'S (Sleep). An impromptu and very brief O-Group was given just before setting off.

My Section, 33.C, loaded onto the first Sea King helicopter for the advance and, to be honest with you, I was just so pleased to be out of the cold weather conditions. The aircraft flew at high speed, banking left and right as the pilot followed the contour of the land. At one point when it dropped low and at such a steep angle, I looked out of the door and thought I could almost touch the heather on the ground. Suddenly the Sea King's engines screamed, the airframe vibrating as the nose of the craft almost pointed vertical, then levelled horizontally with the ground and came down to land with a bump, port side facing up hill, and taking up the width of a gravel track.

Just before the helicopter landed, I could hear cracking noises and 'crumps' but thought nothing of it. I was later to learn that these noises were small arms fire, from the Argentines, coming through the fuselage and the 'crumps' were mortar rounds, fortuitously missing and landing on the ground nearby.

As we landed the navigator on board, seemed to be in a bad mood. He grabbed me by the arm, pointed up the hill and then almost kicked me out – I thought, 'what's his bloody problem!'

I was the third or fourth Marine out of the leading Sea King. As the bullets came down towards us I had little time to assess what was happening, the only thought I had was 'where's the nearest cover'. As quickly as I could, with my SLR in hand, I took up a firing position looking up the hill.

Pushing hard on his collective lever, the pilot was in no way hanging around to be shot at further. The roar of the Rolls Royce engines was deafening as the Sea King rapidly took off. The down draft, smell of spent aviation fuel fumes and heat from the exhaust outlets from our helicopter, slowly faded as it left. I watched the second helicopter off load the rest of 9 Troop and also, like the first, do a quick disappearing act. My section had been dropped off almost on top of the enemy's position, not, as briefed, where we should have been, some 5 km back for an advance to contact!

We found ourselves on the edge of a gravel track, facing uphill. Most of us had taken up firing, lying in the prone position. It was difficult to see up hill to where the enemy positions were because of the height of the gorse and tussock grass. I could hear high pitched zipping and deep thud noises all around me. As more fire came our way it was just like being down in the butts, on the live firing ranges, but this time there was no ten foot earth and sand-bag embankment to protect us and unfortunately we were the targets!

Someone was shouting for us to cross back over the track, in a downwards direction, so I did. On this side of the track, we had very little cover from the incoming rounds, only the convex shape of the dirt track which gave us about 8-10 inches protection. I felt very exposed to the rounds coming in, but at least now I could see our adversaries from here, unlike before. We had been informed that on each side of the track antipersonnel mines had been laid by the Argentinians. We were conscious of this especially after Charlie Company's previous night's horrendous experience of being stuck in a minefield. Therefore we were very apprehensive about venturing too far off the hardcore.

Each round that came close carried with it the sound of a high pitched crack as it travelled at the speed of sound and the thought of death too. Although I was not injured, I had a feeling of dread as if someone had hammered a six inch nail into my stomach and twisted it so my lower intestines spilled out. I believed, and rightly so, that If one of those rounds hit me, at such a velocity, I would die instantly. To add to our worries, because of a problem with the whip ariel on the Clansman 320 radio, our troop signaller and officer were unable to send a sitrep. We had no contact with air support, artillery or Company Headquarters, making me feel like we were abandoned. This was augmented by knowing immediate backup by other Royal Marines on the ground might be delayed due to the lack of availability of helicopters.

Bracing myself for an onslaught, I was scared. I lay in a foetal position, experiencing such strong sensations that I had never had before in my 19 years of life. Butterflies in my stomach had the wingspan of an albatross and spread through my whole body. I imagined it was like a child being locked in a cupboard under the stairs as a punishment, with only total darkness for company and no chance of escape. There was no point in calling for help. I just wanted to be somewhere else, right now, anywhere but here, a different place, a different time. I froze for a few seconds. I was overwhelmed by a sudden avalanche of emotions. I had a strong sense of panic. I was struggling to adjust to this extreme fear and as a result I couldn't breathe. It felt like someone had placed a boulder on top of my chest, crushing the air out of my lungs.

I was battling to adjust to this unparalleled burden of fear. The dread of death besieged me. Suddenly an image of my mother and home came to mind. At this point in life I can say that I was not a devout Roman Catholic, but this experience certainly brought me closer to God. I promised to myself that if I survived this, I would go to church every Sunday without fail (if you were brought up a Roman Catholic, I am sure you can relate to this). Having these recollections and thoughts I refocused. I felt the training kick in. Subsequently I gave myself a psychological punch in the face and a metaphorical kick up the arse. I thought that if I was going to die, I wasn't going to do it lying down. Also, I heard an order given by a JNCO on our left to another Royal Marine from the troop to get his head up to which he replied, 'if you think I am putting my head up there you can fuck off!'. This annoyed me, I thought 'Wanker!', especially because this lad believed he was the tough man of the troop. To realise that he was just as scared as me made me even more determined to act.

In what I thought was an uncanny move, CPL Dee Irving (my section commander), who was lying next to me on my left, started fiddling in the top pocked of his wind proof. He pulled out his ear defenders and casually, as if he were out on a Sunday pheasant shoot with family and friends, one at a time put them into his ears.

Mne Mick Thoburn AKA 'Elvis' (RIP) was lying on my right in the same position as me. Dee said, 'You two aren't doing much good there'. So, I raised my head and looked up the hill to see three Argentine soldiers in their grey uniforms. They had their hoods on for protection against the wind, standing up in a trench, with white granite and quartz rock behind them, three quarters of the way up the hill at about 100 – 150m to my 11 o'clock. One of these Argentine soldiers always sticks in my memory because he had a huge Mexican style black moustache and was fat, therefore unfortunately for him made a larger target than the others.

At first my hands shook uncontrollably, and I just fired as many rounds as I could from my SLR in their direction. However, I had a problem, my bloody weapon would not reload. Every time I fired a bullet, I would have to cock it to put another round in the chamber. I knew exactly what the problem was. The gas barrel had come loose previously, while zeroing our weapons back at Wreck Point. I, along with a colleague, had stripped the casing off and fixed it by screwing the gas barrel back as tightly as we could into position. Unfortunately this repair must not have been as successful as I hoped. Trust it to come loose again at such a fucking crucial time!

During this part of the firefight, Dee Irving asked me to pass the 66mm LAW, so I did and thought nothing of it. A few seconds later my whole world went black. It felt like my eye balls had been shot to the back of my head. Every air space in my body vibrated, I thought I was gone, dead, only to regain my consciousness to see that Dee had fired the 66 mm LAW at a target on the hill. I was not so much annoyed with him for forgetting to warn us he was going to fire and did not take into consideration the back blast from the rocket. But what really pissed me off was the fact that I had carried and even slept with that 66 mm LAW from day one on the Falklands and never got to fire it!

I saw another member of 9 Troop, Vince Comb, laying near the centre of the track and slightly higher up than me, with little or no cover. I could hear a deep pounding of an enemy 0.5 gun being fired at us from a position off to our left. Rounds were passing just above our heads and thumping into the ground behind, sounding as if it had been hit by an upper cut from Tyson Fury. Some were falling short, hitting the gravel right in front of our position, ricocheting off and sending debris down on to us. To emphasize how close their fire was, Jock Hepburn was hit in the head with a splinter of a 7.62 round, luckily only requiring six stitches. I heard a crack, looked up and saw Vince had been knocked back and was, with sheer determination and courage, trying to crawl back to his gun. He had been 'zapped', where on the body, at first, I wasn't sure. It was obvious he was in pain. I could see that his eyes were watering and then, some blood seeping through a sleeve on his left arm. Dee told Elvis and me to help. With the strain etched on his face and some considerable effort, Vince had moved near to where we were lying.

Elvis was slightly closer to Vince and therefore started to patch him up. At this point I had to do one off the hardest things I have ever done. Using all the will power in the world to overcome the fear of being shot, I crawled up on to the track and recovered Vince's GPMG. While doing this I could feel my heart banging against my chest as if a hand had reached in through my ribs, grabbed it and squeezed hard. This caused my pulse to raise to astonishing levels. I could feel a loud thumping in my temples and, even though it was freezing cold, sweat pouring down my face. Every movement was sluggish, it felt like I was swimming through treacle. As I slowly edged forward I was fighting an overwhelming urge to withdraw back to safety. But with a mixture of feelings for the protection of my friends, anger at seeing Vince being hit and some self-preservation, I continued forward.

Eventually recovering the GPMG I placed the front tripod on the hill. We just didn't have time to establish proper arcs of fire, it was obvious where my fellow Marines were and also the main location of the enemy.

At 12 o'clock, slightly lower down the hill from the three Argies I had initially seen, there was a sangar type construction, with corrugated tin for a roof and two green coloured ponchos for the sides. I fired several bursts from the GPMG into this. After a while I feared that I was running out of link and shouted for more. Normally a gunner would have a number two to help spot and keep an eye on the amount of belt fed 7.62 ammo left; I didn't.

I looked down to my right and saw Elvis and Dee patching up Vince, their hands a crimson red. The injury on the top of his arm was oozing bright red blood like a sponge being squeezed and soap suds pushing their way out through holes on the surface. Dee was cutting dead cartilage, muscle and clothing away, then with Elvis, placing several first aid bandages tightly on the wound to help apply pressure and prevent any more blood loss. This ad hoc surgery was performed with a Pussers knife! I felt sorry for Vince and proud at the same time because he had grinned and bore the pain; but at this point I had very little time to get sentimental.

My senses were now amplified by the rush of adrenaline going through my veins. Out of the corner of my eye, at about 2 o'clock, I noticed some Argentine Marines jumping through a heavily foliaged area. They were taking cover every so often and firing their FN FAL's (7.62 Light Automatic Rifle), possibly trying a right flanking manoeuvre on us. I switched fire and let loose at them. I could see by my tracer rounds that my fire was slightly too low, so I raised the sights and continued firing at them. To me these were just faceless targets, they were trying to kill me, so sod them. Again, my training had kicked in. Having picked out individuals, with the GPMG I let burst with three to five rounds, stopped, looked up over the sights and, seeing that they had disappeared (at the time whether I had shot them, or they had merely taken cover, I could not say for sure or really want to remember), moved on to the next. I was trying to preserve ammunition rather than just blasting away aimlessly. Dee asked me if I had seen them to the right and I replied, 'Got them'. The Argentine soldier who had led their 'counterattack' was to be later awarded a medal for his actions!

At this stage, I believe (remember the fog of war!) I witnessed a very brave act. L/Cpl Chris Pretty stood up and took his gun team with him, to the furthest right flank of 9 Troop. They were under fire with absolutely no cover, facing away from the main enemy's position. Chris's action was carried out without any direction from a superior and showed excellent tactical awareness and leadership qualities while under fire. This empowerment for the lower ranks, being unique to the Royal Marines, makes military sense and distinguishes the Corps from other services on the front line.

The right flanking attempt seemed to slacken as I saw some Argentines disappear over the horizon and out of sight. So I switched the gun back to the sangar and trenches to my left. After a while, I could not see any more enemy but continued to put bullets into these positions as suppression fire, done to keep any Argentines heads down, stop them from firing back and possibly mounting another counterattack.

Next, there was a call from our left where our troop commander Lt Carl Bushby RM and Troop Sgt Nick Holloway RM were. The order was to cross over the track, moving up hill towards the enemy, in two sections. The section to my left moved forward first while we gave firing cover, then we followed. After this movement by us, the firing from the Argentines eased, then eventually ceased. I can remember seeing a guy from another troops' gun team in C Coy, arriving on the track a few hundred metres away to our left looking completely exhausted, swearing because he had run to catch up, but had missed the chance of letting loose with his GPMG. In the back of my mind I was pleased to see this support arrive. We thought the Argentines had gone to get reinforcements and would be back, but nothing happened. One of the lads to my left, from 9 Troop, pulled out a tiny Union flag and started to sing God Save the Queen, followed by others joining in.

Just after our impromptu singing of the national anthem, a Blues and Royals Scorpion light tank arrived with a couple of high ranking Welsh Guard's Officers onboard. They said something along the lines about taking over from here, possibly using the tanks to their advantage and getting to the top of Sappers Hill first. Lt Carl Bushby and Mne Ged Herd made it apparent to the Welsh Guard Officers, in a very impolite way, exactly what they and the rest of 9 Troop thought, using a few expletives which would make your mother in laws ears drop off. 9 Troop ignored the Welsh Guards, leaving them behind and continued advancing forward along the track, towards Port Stanley. A few metres on I passed a dead Argentine. His body was in the centre of the track, facedown, with some congealed blood visible that had leaked from his head, a visual memory etched into the depths of my mind. Death must have met him swiftly, it looked like the grim reaper had swiped his scythe vertically downwards, removing the whole of the soldiers face.

Sticking to the track and being extremely alert, we tentatively moved on, each Marine being some distance from the other to reduce the target size. As I walked forward carrying the GPMG, I was thinking 'bloody hell, they're going to start shooting at us soon and, being at the front with the gun, I would be a prime target. While out in the open, with little or no cover available, we were extremely vulnerable. If we did come under fire, the nearest potential concealment was the foliage on the side of the track. This meant leaving the relative safety of the roadway, walking/running on to the surrounding ground and taking the risk of stepping on one of those dreadful antipersonnel mines. I had to push such deep, dark, negative thoughts to the back of my mind and focus on the here and now and what was actually in front of me. As we approached the top of Sappers Hill, I found myself deliberating about the peak. With its various nooks and crannies that were great for placing guns, panoramic, unobscured views and almost vertical cliff faces, it was such a good defensive position that the Argentines could have wiped us out if they had put up a good fight. Thankfully they chose not to.

Looking off into the distance, east, to Sea Point, I could make out the coastline and waves crashing onto the rocks. Uncannily, this made me think about going for a swim there when we had finished and were safe. On getting to the top of Sappers Hill, I could see Argentine soldiers looking dejected, some stumbling as they walked on their way, heading east towards Port Stanley, showing no interest in us or anything else that was happening behind them. They seemed like a line of black ants heading towards their nest, carrying whatever they could with them. I wondered what was going through their minds? Perhaps the fear of being prisoners of war and the subsequent treatment they would receive as captives or the welcoming atmosphere when returning home to Argentina, as a defeated army? Maybe sadness at the loss of friends? I felt no pity for them, only anger because they had tried to kill my Oppos and me only hours ago.

Unfortunately, we were told to stop and not to advance on into Port Stanley but stay put on top of Sappers Hill. I'm pretty sure that if we had carried on, 9 Troop would have been the first to reach the capital. When we came to a standstill, I reluctantly returned my newfound friend and life saver, Vince's GPMG, to his number two. I had been so preoccupied up to now that I hadn't even noticed it had been snowing and, worse still, I had given no thoughts to Vince's condition. Afterwards I found out how lucky 9 Troop had been. Several stories came to light as to how close some of the lads were to getting seriously hurt or killed, as we disembarked from the helicopters on to the base of Sappers Hill. Argentine rounds had hit parts of their webbing, helmets and clothing. One marine thought he had been shot in the backside because of the sudden, painful, burning feeling emanating from his rear, only to find out it was a tracer round which had set light to both of his kidney pouches. Another was hit by a round as it went through his ammunition pouch, hitting a fully loaded SLR magazine inside, causing a mini 'explosion' as the spring and casing blew apart.

Later, and still on top of Sappers Hill, we were happy to meet fellow Royal Marines from 45 Commando, who were yomping in from our left (west). The first night spent on the hill, for protection, we got tarpaulin and oil barrels, attached them to an old Argentine position and put together a makeshift sangar . The temperature was freezing, with a blizzard blowing and we had no sleeping bags or refinements, (something we had grown accustomed to by now anyway), only our fighting order. Finding some Argentine long-sleeved t shirts still in their plastic wrappers, I ripped one open and put it on under my windproof top, crept down into a hole and lay close to someone, to keep warm from their body heat. Although it was a very cold, bitter night and I can recollect shivering, I did manage to get a few hours' sleep. When I woke up we found some unopened Argentine ration packs, these were a god send. I can clearly remember opening the brown cardboard, shoe sized boxes, examining the contents and eating some dry cheese flavoured biscuits that were very similar to TUC crackers. I also found cigarettes and a box of matches, which I placed into my mess tins and stored in my kidney pouches in my fighting order, as souvenirs (I still have these today!). A strange choice for a non-smoker. On the outside wrappers of both matches and cigarettes was written in Spanish, 'A product of Argentina' and therefore could not be mistaken as fakes when eventually I returned home. Their rations also had some jam and chocolate, both of which I ate with pleasure however, I shunned the tins of meat because of my recent encounter with corned beef and the resulting episode of diarrhoea!

Another thing I avoided was walking around. I didn't dare stray off far from the summit for fear of stepping on a mine. Still prevalent in my mind were the experiences from the previous night, of being trapped in a mine field close to Mount William and that hideous scream.

A Point Of Reflection.

Why were we, the men of A and C companies 40 Commando RM, sent as spearhead for the Welsh Guards? I believe that the 1st Welsh Guards Commanding Officers had feelings of guilt after their loss of life on Sir Galahad. Also a fear of potentially losing more men from their Battalion must have crossed their minds. I think deep down the officers knew that their men, arriving in the Falklands straight from ceremonial duties, were not, at the time, up for the job. From what I observed it was obvious they lacked tactical awareness and the physical fitness to meet the demands of the environment and tasks placed on them, like yomping long distances. After a night stuck in a minefield, described by Major Rickett in the book by Van Der Biji. N (2007), Victory in The Falklands (PP219) as '...the most unpleasant night I can remember in my life,' I believe that his men were exhausted. By the way, the Welsh Guards were further back, away from us in the lead and where the casualties had been injured. Although we had gone through the same, actually, a lot more before and during that night, (the Welsh Guards had only been on land since the 1st of June), I think, if the Guardsmen had subsequently been put straight onto the helicopters to face the enemy in a firefight, they would have simply just collapsed. The fact was, they were initially intended to act as a reserve for 3 Commando Brigade and stay at the bridgehead at San Carlos.

I can only comment on what I observed and experienced being attached to the 1st Welsh Guards. The men on the ground appeared to be unprepared for the conditions of the Falklands, poorly briefed, weighed down with equipment and lacked the physical fitness of the Royal Marines Commandos and Parachute Regiment. The Welsh Guards, within a short period of landing, looked like their eagerness for a fight had gone - you could tell that most of them lacked motivation and confidence. This was reflected in some of their poor soldiering techniques and lack of 'in-field' discipline. Teamwork looked non-existent and officers, both commissioned and non-commissioned, detached.

I believe Major Rickett quite rightly used the best assets he had at the time and that was the men from 40 Commando RM. As Rickett's comment about A and C companies states, again in the book, Victory in the Falklands, 'Their (Royal Marines) companies were very well trained…'. To be fair, the 1st Welsh Guards had just witnessed some appalling injuries and the loss of comrades on HMS Galahad, and this trauma no doubt had deeply affected some of them.

There has been a mixed response to the issue of whether the Welsh Guards were physically and mentally prepared for the rigours placed on them. When they arrived they had not been 'in the field' as often as they should have, in preparation for such an event. Indeed, Hastings and Jenkins (1983) questioned the decision by the Ministry of Defence to send south any Guards Battalions.

A positive thing to come out of all this for me was that I felt that the amount of stress suffered by us all, certainly in the last 48 hours plus, only served to bond 9 Troop.

These are my conclusions from what I saw at the time, others may disagree!

Below; looking north towards Sappers Hill and the Argentine positions. The enemy had the advantage of looking down on to 9 Troop. This picture shows what little cover we had. To the left is the GPMG used by Vince Comb and me. Just below the GPMG you can see Elvis' and my SLR's, and on the track, Vince Combs' discarded steel helmet. Taken with my Agfa Pocket 1000 Camera, waterproofed by a clear plastic bag from a supermarket! I carried this tiny camera with me throughout the war and later in South Armagh, during my NI tour of 1983 with 40 Commando RM. This photograph was taken just after the firing had ceased.

Above; the dead Argentine soldier we passed on our advance up to the peak of Sappers Hill. I believe that a member of 7 Troop C Coy 40 Commando Royal Marines, behind 9 Troops advance, had rolled the body over, face up. Note the light scattering of snow on the ground which I wasn't even aware of at the time.

The next day, 15th June, with some relief we were flown off Sappers Hill by helicopter to Fitzroy, where we were put into a barn, cramped like factory chickens, but at least out of the appalling weather.

At Fitzroy I recall some Scots Guards were sharing the same accommodation. Jokes about Scots Guards and Royal Marines were slung across from each group, touché! Some comments became out of hand. This vicious banter was eventually stopped when a SNCO had the balls to say enough is enough. In the barn we were out of the wind, making it easy to light a Hexi block and cook. The only problem was space. We had to be very careful not to set light to anyone else's equipment, or them. Also, the toxic fumes from so many cookers burning at the same time was nauseous. I watched blue smoke rising vertically and escaping through tiny holes, made from shrapnel, in the corrugated roof of the barn. The smell of over forty men who hadn't showered for weeks could have been overwhelming if it had not been for the familiar aroma of rations being cooked. The air had a slightly more pleasant scent of chicken curry and bacon burgers rather than the alternative, of stinking humans!

I recall the debriefing given by a Welsh Guards Officer to Charlie Company at Fitzroy after the surrender. He thanked us for our contribution. But what I found astonishing was he apologised because he acknowledged that in some situations his men had not been quite up to the standards of the Royal Marines. I could not believe he had made this statement. To admit this weakness to a different unit, or army regiment would be unthinkable to most, but to a different part of the services! I have always wondered if this was a sense of guilt, due to their inadequacies and, as a consequence, the injuries we then suffered.

On the morning of 16th June, most of 9 Troop jumped into a Sea King and headed north west, back to San Carlos. There was nowhere to sit and strap yourself in, the canvas bucket seats were full of our kit. The helicopter was so overloaded with men and stores that at first the pilot had to travel horizontally, only a few feet from the ground, to make up speed to allow it to take off. We had guys with their arms and legs sticking out of the windows and doors, sitting on top of bergens that were piled up to the roof. To some degree, we and the aircrew didn't care about health and safety; this was war time and everything had to fall by the wayside. Flying by helicopter from Fitzroy over Darwin and Goose Green, looking out of a side window of the helicopter, I saw buildings and planes wrecked by artillery and small arms fire, with pieces of debris scattered about the settlements and a grass airfield. Later on, we also had the pleasure of flying in Bravo November, the only Chinook, heavy lifting helicopter on the Falkland Islands which had survived from the sinking of the ship Atlantic Conveyor, by an Argentinian Exocet missile.

On 18th June the whole of Charlie Company were taken from San Carlos Settlement by landing craft, to HMS Intrepid for some R&R. On board, looking out through the landing platform dock I could see both land and sea. The land flora, with its different shades of green and brown and steep sided crags of hard granite that fell down towards the earth, were in stark contrast to the white and light blue, choppy water of San Carlos Bay. The sea out of the back of the ship was a hive of activity, landing craft and rigid raiders adding to the turbulence in the water. We didn't spend very long on HMS Intrepid. The only other thing I do recall was, for the first time since leaving the UK, chewing on a Rowntree's Nutty bar and bits of toffee getting stuck in my teeth. Later, we were returned back to San Carlos Settlement.

9 Troop spent what was to be our final night on the Falkland Islands in a tent close to San Carlos Settlement. That last night we stood around a brazier made out of an old oil barrel, which some Pongos had lit. I was surprised that tactically they were allowed.

Anyway, it was a complete change from the way we had spent our previous weeks on the island and it was nice to be able to warm ourselves. As we were leaving the Pongos and returning back to our tent, one individual from 9 Troop, slipped an unopened can of bacon burgers into the fire. As the tin heated up and the pressure could not be tolerated, it exploded, sending bits of bacon burgers and charred wood all over the Pongos still standing next to the brazier. It was hilarious. However, there is always a person who takes it too far. One member of the troop wanted to put some 7.62 rounds in to see what would happen!! Thank god we persuaded him not to. For the first time in what seemed an eternity, I drank a can of Pepsi that night and it tasted like nectar. Since then, I have always had a preference for Pepsi over Coke, particularly with a Jack Daniels!

On 24th of June 9 Troop were reembarked on the Canberra.

9 Troop, Charlie Company, 40 Commando Royal Marines, after the surrender.

We were joined by our Company Sergeant Major WO 1 Bill Howie (PTI) Pictured kneeling front, far bottom left. Sgt Nick Holloway squatting front centre and Cpl Dee Irving standing front far right, with his SLR in hand and a map protruding from his left leg pocket,

The enemy at Sappers Hill.

Argentinean Unit Alejandro Koch's 3rd Platoon, M Coy (M/BIM5) on Sappers Hill 5th Naval Infantry Battalion Argentine Marines, (taken May 1982), (Spanish Batallón de Infantería de Marina 5, abbreviated to BIM-5). Three Argentine Marines (Marine Conscripts Roberto Leyes, Eleodoro Monzon and Sergio Robledo) from Koch's platoon were killed (possibly more) and several injured. Marine Midshipman Marcelo Davis's 1st Platoon from M/BIM 5 attempted a counterattack but were beaten back by 9 Troop.

Many **thanks to Marcos Basavilbaso and Fr. Vicentie Torrens for this photograph.**

Two sketch maps of the firefight at Sappers Hill, subsequently drawn up by the Argentinian's. Although the copies are poor quality, you can still see the main lines of attack.

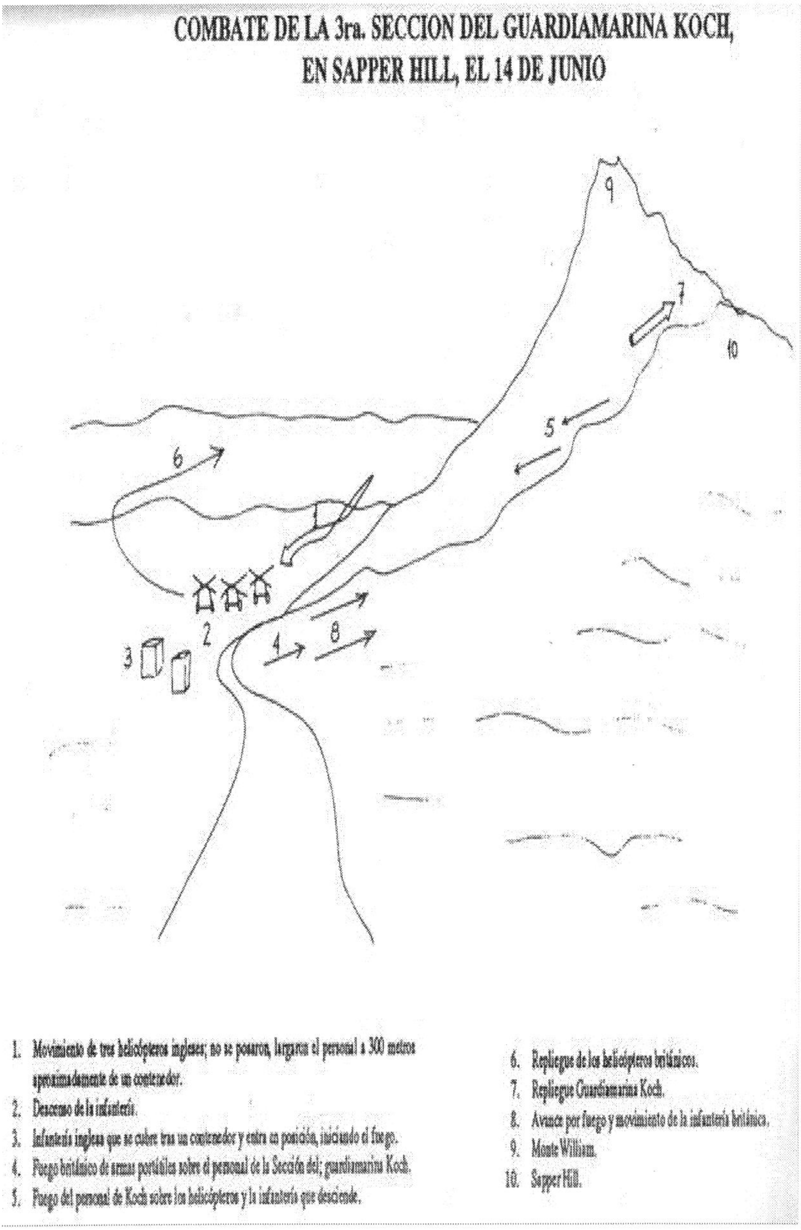
COMBATE DE LA 3ra. SECCION DEL GUARDIAMARINA KOCH,
EN SAPPER HILL, EL 14 DE JUNIO
9
7
10
5
6
2
3
4
8
1. Movimiento de tres helicópteros ingleses; no se posaron, largaron el personal a 300 metros aproximadamente de un contenedor.
2. Descenso de la infantería.
3. Infantería inglesa que se cubre tras un contenedor y entra en posición, iniciando el fuego.
4. Fuego británico de armas portátiles sobre el personal de la Sección del; guardiamarina Koch.
5. Fuego del personal de Koch sobre los helicópteros y la infantería que desciende.
6. Repliegue de los helicópteros británicos.
7. Repliegue Guardiamarina Koch.
8. Avance por fuego y movimiento de la infantería británica.
9. Monte William.
10. Sapper Hill.

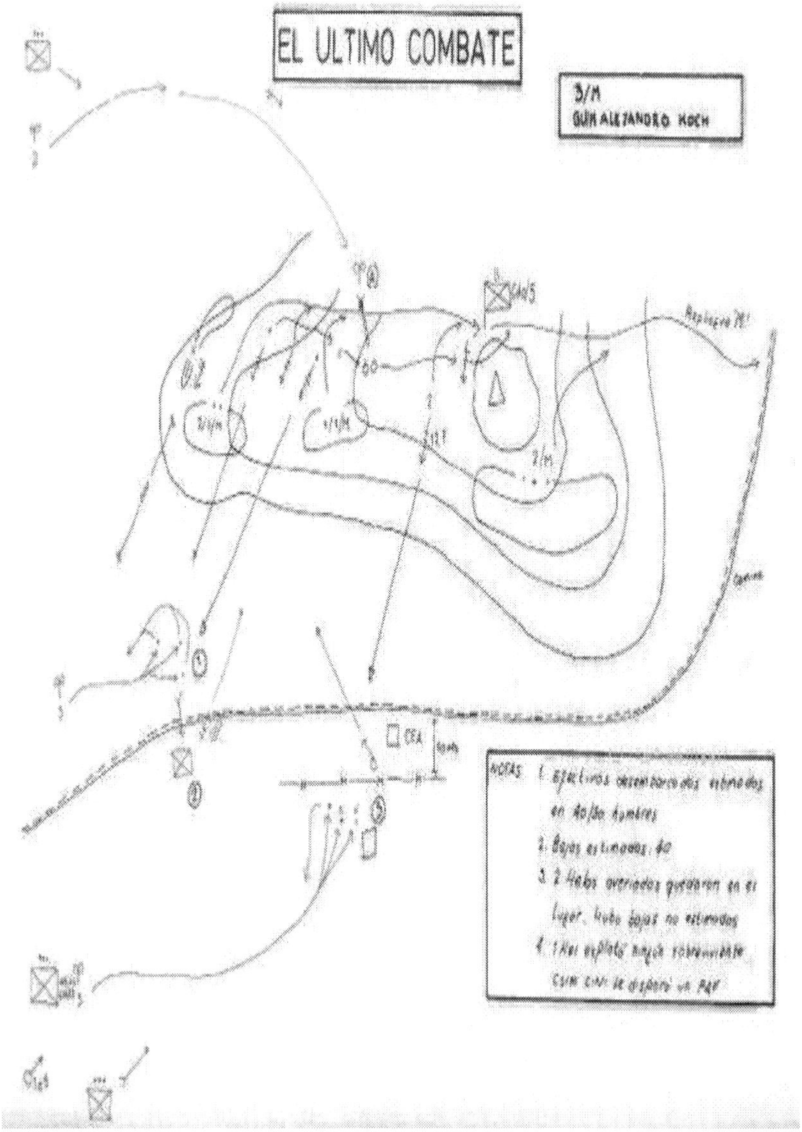
EL ULTIMO COMBATE
3/M

The Home Coming; Sailing Back On The Canberra.

At San Carlos Settlement I jumped onto a helicopter with excitement. 9 Troop, along with the rest of 40 commando RM were told that we were going to sail back home to the UK on the Canberra. As we landed on the flight deck of the ship and then stepped off the chopper, Cpl Mike Peters knelt down, kissed the floor and muttered in his deep Geordie accent, 'You beaut'. It was almost like seeing Pope John Paul II in 1979, visiting Poland for the first time, exiting his aircraft and kissing the ground of his homeland,. Except Mike wasn't as clean or, come to think of it, holy!

As I entered my cabin it felt surreal after being out in the elements for so long. In our new birth and relatively safe environment there was no more wind, rain or snow to compete with, but heating, clean carpets, and a bed made up with crisp, clean white sheets and two soft pillows. It felt irreverent to dirty the place with my filthy clothes, boots and kit. Initially in the cabin there was a smell of fresh linen in the air. However, with the four of us squashed in together there was now a noxious smell. For the six weeks plus on land, none of us had had a proper wash or change of clothing during this time. The product was a room which stunk to high heaven. One Marine, who wishes to remain anonymous, borrowed a pair of scissors to cut his grubby underpants off. The sight of this previous piece of essential under clothing was beyond vile and therefore I will not go into any specifics, suffice to say if they had originally been white and in one piece, they certainly weren't now! He got upset when we wouldn't let him leave them in the cabin's gash bin! In his defence, I must say that the pair of pants I had worn at disembarkation at San Carlos Settlement had disintegrated, no 'exploded,' many weeks earlier and had been discarded on land!

I hurriedly stripped off, wrapped a towel around me, grabbed a bar of soap and dived under what was to be my first shower for what seemed like an eternity. As I looked down at my feet, black water fell on to the shower tray, mixed with dead skin and god knows what else. I could feel my body warm up and see my skin go pink as the blood flow increased to my extremities. Red, burning, dried, skin that had been ravaged for the last couple of months by the harsh wind of the Falklands now started to itch. Wind burn on my face made it look like I had put my head under a sun lamp and overexposed myself to too much UV, or possibly had the appearance of an alcoholic. I strolled back to the cabin listening to piped music, the first I had heard in a long time. The songs included 'Wonderous Stories' by the group Yes, Billy Joel's 'just the way you are', and Supertramp's, 'can we have kippers for breakfast, mummy dear, mummy dear,' a line that still sticks in my head. These songs seemed to be on a continuous loop, interspersed by the BBC World Service news on the hour.

Back inside our small cabin, with four Marines and honking kit, space was always going to be an issue. We were in a hurry to get things stored away. I asked what the hell were we going to do with our pile of dirty dhobi, which was stacked high in the centre of the room. The thought of having to search the ship with literally hundreds of other Marines, just to find an empty sink, some dhobi dust and spend hours scrubbing off the weeks old dirt caked into our garments, was an experience I for one was not looking forward to. Mne Si Poole went to find out what other members of 9 Troop were doing and eventually discovered we could send the dhobi to the ship's laundry for cleaning. What a relief, a huge burden was taken off us. I felt so ashamed sending over six weeks of heavily soiled clothes for some other poor soul to wash. I wouldn't have touched someone else's clothes in that condition, even with rubber gloves and a respirator on! Several hours later after our dhobi had gone off to the laundrette, there was still a lingering smell. so I decided to spray the cabin with antiperspirant and threw some aftershave on the floor. It now smelt more like the inside of a brothel (so I was told).

I was amazed that two days later I found my clothes returned, laid on my bed, immaculately clean and pressed, what a luxury! Putting on my sports kit and being able to relax was an experience of pure pleasure. However, my feet throbbed for days after, (and today still do in the cold) as the circulation started to return. The alien feeling of clean, dry and warm footwear, that I had dreamt of while sitting soaking wet on the Falklands, was now a reality. For over six weeks, all I had seen was military people dressed from head to toe in either DPM or some other shade of green. Their faces and hands blackened by old or newly applied camouflage cream, combined with a layer of dirt. My world had been an endless sea of green e.g. issued sleeping bags, ponchos and even the flora of the Falklands Islands. It was a pleasant change to see civilians on board, dressed in a variety of colours, some seemed so stark, almost luminous when combined with their lily white legs, arms and faces. It wasn't just the sight of different colours, it was aromas too. Shaving foam, aftershave, clean linen; smells that had been absent for so long now returned.

For a keepsake I went to purchase a t-shirt from the shop on one of the upper decks on the Canberra. Sadly, I do not have it anymore, but I recall it being a light shade of blue with two white lines going horizontal across the chest, with the words, 'The Canberra', written above in small font. Anyway, for fear of the t shirts selling out, I rushed up stairs on to the deck where the shop was located. I walked in and was hit by the glorious fragrance of a female steward serving behind the counter, her perfume was like a sweet smell from heaven.

As the Canberra sailed off and out of San Carlos Waters, I was looking back to land spotted my first and only sight of penguins in 1982. I could see them jumping from the land into the sea and back. I laughed to myself recalling my days at secondary school when we used to call the nuns 'penguins'. This was because of the similarity of the black and white colour habit worn by the nuns and the fur of the penguins, also the way they both used to waddle side to side as they walked. However nuns were by far the scariest animal.

As the Falklands disappeared, all I could see was the open ocean and I wondered if I would ever be back. From my green kit bag I retrieved my American detective crime thriller book, took it up on to the open deck and began reading from where I had finished so many weeks ago before landing at Blue Beach, San Carlos. I thought to myself, am I hallucinating? Am I really back here, back to the comforts of 'normal life'? I had the luxury of having my hair cut. It was the first time since training that I had gone for a No 4 crew cut and it felt liberating.

In the following weeks, 9 Troop did a smidgen of PT consisting of running around the promenade deck, but not to the same intensity as on our way sailing down south. Heading north as the weather improved, I spent most of the time sunbathing on the flight deck, lying next to or on top of the chacon containers, with the Canberra's' large yellow funnels behind me. As the grey coloured exhaust left the pipes you could feel the immense power of the engines vibrating through the deck, particularly if she changed course or increased speed. At night, rather than drinking our 'rationed beer' I preferred to go out on deck and watch the sunset off the stern. I enjoyed my own company for a while, and this was where I could find it, although I did have a few beers in the William Fawcett. The bar was often packed, so sometimes I had to go to another one allocated to 42 Commando RM just across the stairwell from the William Fawcett and bring cans of beer back. Some Marines tried to find inventive ways to get around the daily ration quota of alcohol. A few were caught out by the duty SNCO for giving fake names or making out false chits to pass onto the people serving.

A few weeks of sailing and the weather was getting even warmer. Because of the heat in the cabins on the lower decks, someone had left their porthole window open when they went out, to let the cool, fresh air in. Our cabins were on or just above the water line. When this JNCO returned, their room and part of the corridor was swamped with sea water. He was bounding up and down the passageway, swearing at the top of his voice with no one to blame except himself. I found this particularly funny because this JNCO had taken me through training and I had previously thought that all members of training teams were supposed to be perfect!

About this time on board, the whole of 9 Troop had individual briefings with our Troop officer Lt Carl Bushby, Troop Sgt Nick Holloway, Company Commander Captain Andy Pillar and CSM Bill Howie. One at a time each member of the troop entered the briefing room. Sitting behind a large desk were our leaders. I was told about a fund for injured guys and given feedback on my performance. The one thing I do recall is that Lt Bushby said that I had shown grit, determination and guts for taking over the GPMG on Sappers Hill after Mne Comb was hit. This comment was later recorded in my Royal Marines Company Record Book. Because of these positive comments I left the room as pleased as punch. I sensibly kept quiet about these words, but deep down I was happy that I had been recognised for my contribution. I was even dubious about adding this to my written story. Nevertheless, we all played our part, in different situations and ways, some not noted but essential to the success of 9 Troop and Charlie Company.

Concerts on board were performed by the Royal Marines Bands. This included the now disbanded, Royal Marines Commando Forces Band. Sometimes they gave one off, ad hoc gigs in a variety of bars. I recall one musician playing solo's on the saxophone. This was, and still is, one of my favourite instruments, I just love the low, raw sound it creates as it smoothly vibrates through the air. It wasn't just me that enjoyed the saxophone. There were often individual and mob calls from the audience of 'sax, sax, we want more sax'! I particularly liked his part in the rendition of Billy Joel's' song 'Just the way you are'.

Sailing further up the Atlantic Ocean the Canberra eventually crossed the equator, again with no ceremony except for the issue of a certificate to prove what we had achieved.

The certificate of proclamation for crossing the equator on the Canberra in 1982.

All servicemen on board the Canberra were given the order that under no circumstances must we take home any Argentine weapons or ammunition that we had 'proffed 'while on the Falklands. Any such items were to be ditched overboard, from the promenade deck, at a given time when this process could be safely supervised. We were told that there would be a thorough customs check when the Canberra docked, and we disembarked at Southampton. This was to be the one and only amnesty. After the amnesty, if you were found with any unissued, foreign weapons or ammunitions you would be charged immediately. As a result, FN rifles, pistols and bayonets were just a few of the items to get hurled into the Atlantic Ocean off the Canberra. One member of 9 Troop decided that rather than go on the allotted day, he would go in his own time, at night and dispose of his grenades off the stern of the ship. The Marine thought it would be a 'laugh' to pull the pin before he threw each one overboard into the sea below. When I heard that he had done this I couldn't believe how irresponsible he had been. I didn't think it was funny, let alone safe. God knows what would have happened if this individual had brought the grenades into civvy street back home. He would be the type of idiot to throw it under a car for fun and sod the consequences. The only souvenirs I kept, as already stated, were a packet of cigarettes and matches from an Argentine ration pack and a t shirt I found and had worn to keep me warm on Sappers Hill.

One early evening after a concert by 'sax' and some of his fellow musicians, as the Canberra entered the Bay of Biscay, I stood alone on the port side aft of the ship to watch the sunset. Out to sea I observed shoals of porpoises go past the bow of the ship. There were hundreds of them, all heading towards the west where the sun was setting. The cloudless sky changed colour from a clear blue to an orange of different shades, then a deep red hue as it sank below the horizon. The water seemed to shimmer as the almost waveless sea reflected the last light of the sun before it disappeared. I noticed a slight sea mist was appearing. The air temperature was still warm, and I spent the most pleasant time just standing there, reflecting on what had happened and promising myself that, one day in the future I would go on a world cruise and relive this hour.

Mne Ged Herd and L/Cpl Alex (Jock) Hepburn (sitting on the deck chair) sunbathing on the Canberra on our voyage back home.

On the last night before we disembarked off the Canberra, she sailed from west to east off the southern English coastline. When the ship was close to the Devon coast, I witnessed civilian aircraft flying overhead and small boats that had left their moorings and come out to take a look at the Canberra and those on board.

That night all military units and some P&O staff were invited onto the flight deck for an impromptu concert, played, again, by the Royal Marines Band. It was dark when the music stopped and to be honest, I was quite sad at the thought of leaving the Canberra tomorrow. We were expecting to get off the liner with no fanfare, put our kit on four tonners, and jump in the back or if lucky, get onto civilian coaches and head southwest back to Seaton Barracks, Plymouth.

On the morning of 11th July 1982, I had an early breakfast, returned to my cabin, got into shirt sleeved order, grabbed my beret, went onto the promenade deck, only to be disappointed to find it misty. However, within half an hour it had started to dissipate, revealing a clear blue sky above. Helicopters were landing and taking off from the flight deck where, only the previous night I had been watching the Royal Marines Bands give their final performance for the troops. As the morning moved on, more and more boats of varying sizes and types came to shadow the Canberra on her way into Southampton. As we passed the Isle of Wight the number of vessels was up in the hundreds. The Canberra was sounding her foghorn in response to others and also to warn the little boats that she was not able or going to stop for any craft. One buxom young lady sitting on a small boat that was following us on the starboard side, was asked by several Marines on the Canberra to 'show us yer tits,' she obliged. When she pulled her top back down to cover herself up there were boos and calls of 'show us some more'. She then decided, to casually remove her top completely which elicited a rapturous response from us on board;

what a wonderful sight for a home coming!

From where the majority of 9 Troop stood on the promenade deck I could see hundreds of people onshore waving and hoisting up the Union flag and homemade banners, cars and lorries flashing their lights and sounding their horns. On board, someone from Charlie Company ran back inside, down a stairwell into a cabin, grabbed a white bed sheet and scrawled on it (only just legible), 'Charlie Company 40 Commando Royal Marines'. This makeshift banner was hung over the promenade deck safety rails, along with some others with more ingenious and witty slogans, written on any pieces of material that could be found and 'proffed' on the ship. I could hear music being played by a Royal Marines band from the dockside and when 'life on the Ocean Wave' started the whole ship seemed to clap and stamp their feet in unison. Above me, standing on the promenade deck, there were some Marines that had climbed on top of the lifeboats and sat precariously off them with their legs dangling just above our heads. I suddenly had a very obtuse thought. While I had been on board, I had had no money with me. Everything I purchased consisted only of nutty, beer, cans of coke and t shirts. Rather than paying for the goods, I had signed a chit. My thought was how much had I spent and how am I going to pay this money back? I hadn't kept any receipts or records, Was I in debt?

Probably, like all Marines on board, I was excited to get off the ship. When the Canberra eventually docked I went down to my cabin, grabbed my kit and with the rest of 9 Troop struggled to get through her labyrinth of corridors and staircases back to the upper decks. Just before we left there were civilian staff from the ship standing by the doorway at the top of the gangway, wishing us well and looking quite tearful. This had been a trip to the South Atlantic and back home again on the Canberra, never to be forgotten. The most unique voyage in my life, travelling a distance of 8,000 miles one way, almost the length of the earth, in the company and comradeship of 9 Troop. As I went down the gang plank, I remember having to concentrate on my footing and not being able to look at the crowds below on the dockside because the whole walkway was bouncing up and down under the weight of ten plus Royal Marines Commandos and their kit. As I stepped off the gang plank on to the dock, I was given a kiss and a red rose by a young female; I had no idea who she was. I looked up and was astonished to see my mother, father and younger sister, Rachel, in the crowd shouting to me and waving a banner. Despite what we had been told on the Canberra several days before, there was absolutely no customs checks what so ever. There were just a few Military Police in uniform, looking bored, standing next to empty tables, undercover of the dockside sheds,.

I dumped my kit on the floor of a dockside shed and found my family. I had some mixed emotions when I hugged my mother. I didn't feel that tearful, just pleased to see them. I found out that they had shared a minibus with my cousin's family, who was also on board and travelled down from Ipswich that day. Most of the letters which I had written home to my parents were fairly mundane. I had only written once to my older brother, a serving Royal Marine and included some of the more graphic details of my experiences. I just felt that I did not want to expose the others in my close family to some of the distressing details of what I had been through and seen during the Falklands War. As it happened I didn't have much time to speak to my parents because of the need to get back down to Plymouth and hand back stores. I left my parents and boarded the coach with the rest of Charlie Company. There were rumours that we were to get six weeks leave, so I knew I would be home shortly to be reunited with my family and didn't feel guilty about leaving them so soon. The trip from Southampton to Plymouth was remarkable. Every town or village we passed through, the coach was stopped by individuals wanting to jump on and either give us some form of alcohol or a kiss and a hug or both! People had lined the streets and were waving banners and flags. It was as if each place was trying to outdo the other in the magnitude of their celebration. It took so long to get to Plymouth, god knows how many extra hours we sat on the coach, however, I enjoyed every minute of it.

Back at Plymouth I spent a couple of days sorting out, cleaning and returning my kit to the stores and then retrieving my Honda Super Dream 250cc motorbike. I decided to ride home on it. It took me over ten hours to travel from Plymouth to Ipswich, only stopping for fuel. To make things even more time consuming I couldn't use the motorways because I didn't have my full motorbike licence then. I remember it being late afternoon when I eventually crossed the border between Essex and Suffolk on the A12 and yelling at the top of my voice. I was ecstatic that I had actually made it home. If I hadn't had my helmet on, I'm sure the car passing next to me, on the outside lane, would have heard my exclamation of joy.

As I pulled up on the opposite side of the busy road to my parents' house in Ipswich, I had to do a double take. They had covered the whole block of terraced houses with welcome home signs, Union flags and bunting. I could not believe that people had gone to all this trouble for me. I felt really happy. For my safe return home, we also had a party at my parents' house, with friends and relations attending. The next few days of leave were a haze of alcoholic drunkenness. Once, I was carried aloft by friends to the local pub, just across from my parents' house and cannot remember coming home.

At the time, my uncle Reginald Philip Barnes, (Reggie), owned a jeweller's shop. He had lived an interesting life. Joining the Verona Brothers in his early twenties, he travelled to Italy and spent some time in Rome. After several years he decided to return home to England. Reggie was a keen guitar player and formed a group for a few years in the 1970's playing live at a number of venues around town. He also trained and became a skilled jeweller. Designing, making and selling jewellery and glassware in his shop in Ipswich. Reggie was never one for the limelight, so he didn't come to my parents' house to greet me back home from the Falkland's. What he did do though, was leave a pint mug for me on which he had hand engraved the Globe and Laurel (the Royal Marines crest).

Reggie also wrote a poem, printed it and left me a copy:

A SMALL TRIBUTE IN HONOUR OF OUR DEDICATED MEN OF THE TASK FORCE.

For freedoms here in 'Merry England' democracy for granted taken.

These gallant warriors with freedoms sword heroes all, for freedom fought.

The sword was just, not in anger used heroes all, those maimed for life.

Their crimson shed for values grander heroes all, who lost their lives.

By R. P. BARNES (RIP), 1982.

Reggie added two quotes to the piece:

Brave sons of thunder, they restored the light, from darkness brought peace, surrender. ***(Taken from the New Testament).***

They did 'not go gentle' to the tyrannical foe, they rage(d), rage(d) against the dying of (freedoms) light. ***(Dylan Thomas).***

I was told that during the months that my cousin and I were away in the Falklands War, Reggie had made a display in the front window of his shop for the servicemen of the Task Force, with the poem as the central piece.

With six weeks leave I had a lot of spare time and money on my hands. My parents had always rented their TV but unfortunately it had broken down. For a while I was bored just sitting around at home. It was a blessing when a TV repair man arrived at the house to fix it. I got chatting with him and he asked me about my experiences in the Falklands. Just before he left, he said he had wangled it with his company that we would not have to pay for the rental of a video recorder for a few months. He went to his van, brought one back into the house and connected it up to the TV for me; what a good egg!

I also tried to catch up with the news I had missed while in the Falklands by reading newspapers. In one national tabloid newspaper, to my surprise, I came across an article in which Vince Combe of 9 Troop had been interviewed and photographed. The article below described what had happened from his prospective.

The newspaper headline report on 9 Troop, Charlie Company's fire fight on Sappers Hill from Vince's perspective.

Vince, 17, saw bullets coming for him but he kept on firing

CHARLIE COMPANY were still jumping down from the helicopters when the shooting began.

Up on Sapper Hill, the Argentines opened up with machine-gun fire which caught the men of 40 Commando, Royal Marines, completely by surprise as they leaped from the Wessex choppers.

It was a scary situation, dangerous enough to daunt even the most battle-hardened veteran, let alone a fresh-faced teenager not long out of training.

Crouched nervously by the side of the dusty road, Marine Vince Comb, 17, watched the Argentine bullets kick up spurts of dirt as they ripped across the bleak moorside.

Unless the 32 men of Charlie Company's 9 Troop responded promptly with some covering fire, they were in imminent danger of being picked off among the frozen peat bogs.

VINCE: Bursts

Dodging

Lugging his 24lb machine-gun with him, Vince Comb dashed across the road, dodging enemy fire, to a vantage point on the other side.

Hurling himself to the ground, he quickly set up the machine-gun on its bipod and sent bursts of bullets raking across the Argentine bunkers on Sapper Hill, the last high ground between the advancing British forces and Port Stanley.

As the Argentina infantry ducked for cover, the men of Charlie Company scrambled into more advantageous defensive positions.

Young Vince was still firing when two lines of Argentine machine-gun fire stitched their way towards him across the Falkland heather. One bullet hit high up in the left arm. Another sliced through his left wrist.

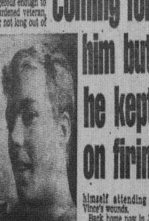

With blood soaking through the sleeve of his camouflaged combat jacket, the young machine-gunner was hurled backwards from his weapon. Clawing his way along the ground, he struggled gamely to get back to his gun. But the effort was too much.

An 18-year-old Marine known universally as "Elvis" scrambled to the aid of his injured mate. Oblivious to the enemy gunfire he turned his back on the Argies and busied himself attending to Vince's wounds.

Back home now in Jardine Way, Dunstable, Beds., Vince Comb insists Elvis was the hero of the day. "It took a lot of guts, patching me up like that while we were still under fire," he insisted.

Vince was one of three 17-year-olds who saw action with Charlie Company. One lost a foot in a minefield explosion near Mount Harriet.

[redacted]

Proud

"People are always running down young Marines," observed Sgt. Nick Holloway, one of Charlie Company's NCOs. "But we can only be proud of the way they performed in the Falklands. Marine Comb's covering fire prevented us taking a lot more casualties."

Still recovering from his wounds, which required more than 60 stitches, fair-haired Vince shrugs off suggestions that what he did was anything special. "There were a lot of young blokes out there," he protested. "Everyone did his share."

The son of a school caretaker, Vince joined the Marines at 16 after an unsatisfying stint fitting tyres and exhaust systems in a car workshop.

He smiles slightly when he recalls how he reacted when he was shot. "I tried to get back behind the gun again, like they always do in the movies," he said.

"In real life things are a bit different."

Being slightly less bored, on the now repaired TV, I watched live, the raising of the Mary Rose in Portsmouth Harbour and at the same time finished off a huge cake my family had made for me to celebrate my return. I truly felt at home.

I remember one morning, in my parents' house, lying in bed when an older cousin came around to see me. The first thing he shouted to me through my bedroom door was 'Did you kill anyone?' I didn't answer him, I just felt like telling him to piss off. After he asked the question several times and had no response from me, I think he got the hint and left. This type of question was posed to me on several occasions during my first few weeks at home. This constant verbal probing by people, whether it was done in good faith or not, became annoying. I found myself becoming distant and physically evasive of others.

Frequently drinking was a way in which I could drift off into my own world, I often left home and went alone into local pubs. I saw several charity boxes left on the bars, asking for donations to support the Falklands injured. I remember almost getting into a fight in a pub with one lad, whom I had never met. He heard me say that I was in the Falklands War and out loud, called me a liar. This made my blood boil. Luckily a mutual friend stepped in and put him to rights.

The six weeks of leave flew passed and before I knew it, I was back on my motor bike, travelling on the A12, heading down to Plymouth. Several weeks later, back at Seaton Barracks I was having a shower. I heard a noise, looked up and saw a fellow Marine I recognised, hopping passed on one leg, a stump where the other foot should have been. I suddenly remembered that night in the minefield.

Below : Canberra arrives home, Southampton Docks, Birth 106.

Above: My Mother wearing sunglasses holding a banner on the dockside.

Southampton Docks Rachel, Mum and me.

Personal Conclusion Of The Falklands War.

The Falklands War was almost forty years ago. A longer period in time than between the end of the Second World War and the start of the military hostilities with Argentina in 1982. Regrettably for myself and other living veterans, the Falklands War has disappeared into the mists of time, and is quite often, rightly or wrongly, overshadowed by the more recent operations such as Iraq and Afghanistan. I do feel some sympathy for those British servicemen that served in Aden, the Suez and Malaya, to name but a few military actions that have happened since the end of World War Two.

These military 'events' seem to have been almost completely forgotten by the media and general public alike.

40 commando RM was portrayed as being the unit that stayed as rear guard in the San Carlos Bay area. I felt compelled to speak out, that this was not the case for all. In conversations I suffered similar to Sisyphus. Metaphorically repeatedly pushing my personal verbal boulder uphill for some form of recognition for 40 Commando's involvement in the Falklands War, only for my efforts to fail and roll back down to have to start all over again for what seemed like an eternity. For the 25th Anniversary of the war, I was lucky enough to be flown back down to the Falklands with other veterans, (I will go into some more detail of this visit later). While there I met several people from other units who were taken back by Charlie Company's exploits during the 1982 war. This lack of acknowledgment was one of the motivational factors for me to write our story.

Below; the new plaque on the stone memorial at Sappers Hill, Falkland Islands, (note the Welsh Guards insignia!)– Is it **time to put things right**? This memorial was placed on Sappers Hill, with much ceremony by the Welsh Guards, (no Marines were asked to attend). There was some resentment from 9 Troop, Charlie Company 40 Commando RM about the original wording. Andy Pillar (at the time our Company Commander) contacted Col Ricketts of the Welsh Guards and alterations were made.

The acute and unpleasant consequences of my experiences such as diarrhoea, trench foot and extreme stress during the land operation, have been covered earlier. The events in the Falklands War in 1982 have had a long-lasting effect on my outlook of life and led to a belief that any war should be avoided, but, I hasten to add, not at all costs. I believe it is the right of the citizens of the Falkland Islands, (indeed, anywhere in the world), to choose how they should live. Time and time again they have chosen to stay as a self-governing overseas British Territory. This choice must be defended. As Mikhal Gorbachev said in his 1987 speech to the UN General Assembly, 'Freedom of choice is a universal principle to which there should be no exceptions'.

1982 was a time when there were no personal mobile phones, social media or immediate access to news through the internet. Information was disseminated over radio transmissions, written or word of mouth and often delayed. As Royal Marines in the Falklands, our only contact with the outside world was through letters from home and the occasional, several weeks old, mostly tabloid newspapers, that had arrived with the intermittent post. Throughout the war, it must have been difficult for the families and friends of those serving. Watching and listening to the news bulletins and daily briefings on TV by the Ministry of Defence, fronted by John Nott MP, as he delivered his prescribed speech, must have caused some worrying moments for people back home in the UK.

I have put pen to paper to hopefully pass on my experiences as a Royal Marines Commando, of lower rank, so that people can empathise with what it was like for us on the ground, on the front line, in the Falklands War. Time seems to have flown passed since

1982, yet in my mind events seem so fresh, as if they only happened yesterday. It appears to me that many Falklands Veterans outwardly in public, show a desensitised shell. It is always difficult to peel back the layers and see exactly what is going on deep inside someone's core. As suggested by the Social Penetration Theory (Altman and Taylor 1973), more intimate feelings are only shown after relationships develop, and I have found this to be true. They say that in stressful situations, the best is brought out in some people. I believe this to be correct too and witnessed this positive behaviour during the relatively short period in time on Operation Corporate. As a result I have made lifelong friends. We occasionally meet at reunions, at a troop or unit level, but these recently seem to have been put on hold as it becomes difficult to keep in touch. Factors such as the Covid epidemic, moving house and of course the inevitable happens, people unfortunately pass on, have contributed to a decline in numbers. It has been at these gatherings where I have had one to one conversation with other members of 9 Troop. Sometimes as the outer layers disappear, hidden thoughts and emotions are revealed. This intimate discourse has been a revelation to me. I really was surprised at how closely my own convictions and fears were matched with my fellow '9 Troopers'. One idiosyncratic habit I have had ever since the Falklands War, is placing my head on the palm of my hand to rest when going to, and during, sleep, wherever I am and on any surface, even if it is a clean, soft, new pillow. I can remember starting this practice when I had no bedding or dry place to kip. By placing my head in my hand, I figured that it raised it off the ground offering some protection from the elements and any insects that might have decided to crawl on me and enter my body via my ears, eyes and/or nose!

I will never forget sailing back on the Canberra and the nostalgic nights when the Royal Marines Commando Band played on the flight deck, and other places on board and listening to one bandsman playing my favourite instruments, the saxophone. Witnessing the flotilla of small boats accompany us into Southampton docks and the welcome we received was remarkable and something truly etched in my memory. Luckily, this event was broadcast live on television and I was fortunate enough to be given a video of it. I have played the coverage several times over, and I can see lots of people I knew at the time but typically, only the top of my head is visible as the picture pulls back to focus elsewhere. There is not one day that passes when I do not think of the poor souls who lost their lives in the Falklands, especially the ones I knew. As in the words of a song by the English song writer and singer Judie Tzuke '...every step that I take, everything that I do, I haven't forgotten you'.

In cold, hard, unsympathetic numbers, two hundred and fifty-five British Servicemen, three civilian Falkland Islanders and an estimated six hundred and fifty Argentinians died in the war. Twenty six were Royal Marines Commandos.

In 1982, 3 Commando Brigade was 4820 in number, with men from 40, 42 and 45 Commando Royal Marines. Initially attached were 3 and later 2 Para from the Army. Also, there were men from the Mountain and Artic Warfare Cadre Royal Marines. Special Boat Squadron Royal Marines and other attached Royal Marines

Units including Commando Logistics Regiment Royall Marines, 1 Raiding Squadron Royal Marines and others. 29 Commando RA, 148 Commando RA, 59 Independent Commando RE, with the SAS and other Army units made up the rest of the numbers. It must not be forgotten the vital role that the Commando Forces Band and the Royal Navy Air Squadrons 845/846 played too.

Unfortunately and unintentionally, the above has ended up as a list, something I hadn't started off to do. I do not want to upset any members of the units that are missing and served within 3 Commando Brigade in 1982, and I want to say that your role was just as vital than those mentioned.

Those in charge of the British land forces in 1982 were Major General Jeremy Moore Royal Marines, Commander of Land Forces, and Brigadier Julian Thompson Royal Marines, commander of 3 Commando Brigade.

If you compare our military numbers to the Argentine forces on land, approximately 11,000, we were heavily outnumbered. Also, they had air support from land-based planes, that were only seven hundred miles away, with seven C130's ferrying stores into Port Stanley, apparently up to 12th June. With these statistical disparities, without a doubt, we should have lost. As I have already suggested, our professional training and motivation was the key. I cannot even advocate this was the case for all of our clothing and equipment. In fact some of the Argentinian kit was superior e.g. their boots. Although sometimes our logistics were stretched, especially with the arrival of the 5th Army Brigade, we were kept supplied most of the time, unlike our enemy.

Compared to the Argentine conscript soldier, we were blessed. Out on the hills and mountains, for them resupplies were rare, if at all. Several stories of the Argentines nearly starving to death have since come to light. With poor military leadership on the ground and by the Argentine hierarchy in Buenos Aires, I wasn't at all surprised at how quickly their forces collapsed at the end. For the whole of the Task Force and me, this was a boon. For the Argentine soldiers on the ground, information was sparse, they had been told they had come to the Falklands (although some had no idea where they were), to unshackle the locals from their imperial British masters. However, they found the Falklanders to be very anti towards them and they didn't even speak the same language nor have the same customs. This must have contributed to the poor morale of the Argentinians. On Sappers Hill, if 9 Troop had come up against a well led and motivated enemy, I feel the death count would have been much higher, on both sides.

Overall Command and Control (C2) was the responsibility of Admiral Sir John Fieldhouse and Commodore Mike Clapp, RN, the amphibious group commander. Initially Commander Julian Thompson, RM was in charge of the land forces. C2 on land soon changed with the arrival of Major General Jeremy Moore, RM, and the 5th Infantry Brigade. Any C2 should have clearly defined structure. Unlike in the emergency services, where they have defined bronze, silver and gold categories, in 1982 during the Falklands campaign these lines of responsibility were sometimes blurred which led to some confusion, as highlighted by Cedric Delves (2018), in his book 'Across an Angry Sea'. On the ground there was a mix of different Royal Marines units and their attachments,

Army Regiments, and later the RAF. Throw in the Royal Navy personnel and it was a bewildering array of units for me to try and comprehend who exactly was in charge and where we fitted in. If you fling together unfamiliar groups with different structures and regimental rivalries, C2 can be difficult to sustain, as happened on Sappers Hill with the arrival of the Welsh Guards' Officers. Luckily, being a lower rank, any problems with the C2 structure were well above my pay grade! Anyway, in relation to C2 I am sure lesson were learnt and changes subsequently made.

As for the politics of the war, well I did not intend to go into this arena. I never thought much about political affairs as a young man back in 1982. I only knew the fact that a right wing, military dictatorship had invaded a British overseas territory. At the time in the UK, some people of a certain political persuasion might say that there was a case of dictatorship in both countries. However, our country was and is a democratic society; this leads me to the old saying, 'you get what you vote for!' The Junta, led by Leopoldo Galtieri in 1982, was responsible for the disappearance of thousands of citizens that did not agree with its military dictatorship policies. Initially, after Argentina invaded the Falkland's with an overpowering military force, taking NP8091 as prisoners, and also just after their 'victory' in South Georgia, huge crowds flocked in Buenos Aires to show their patriotic support for what had happened and the Junta. This victory was short lived.

In retrospect the war did remove the Junta, reaffirm the UK/USA 'special relationship' and more importantly, return freedom and democracy to the Falklanders. For Margaret Thatcher and the whole country, financially there was a bill of approximately £3 Billion. Politically Thatcher was re-elected as Prime Minister in 1983, in a decisive election victory against the Labour Party. She stayed in her role until 1990.

Two mementos from an Argentine ration pack I brought home and still have, (paradoxically I'm a non-smoker!).

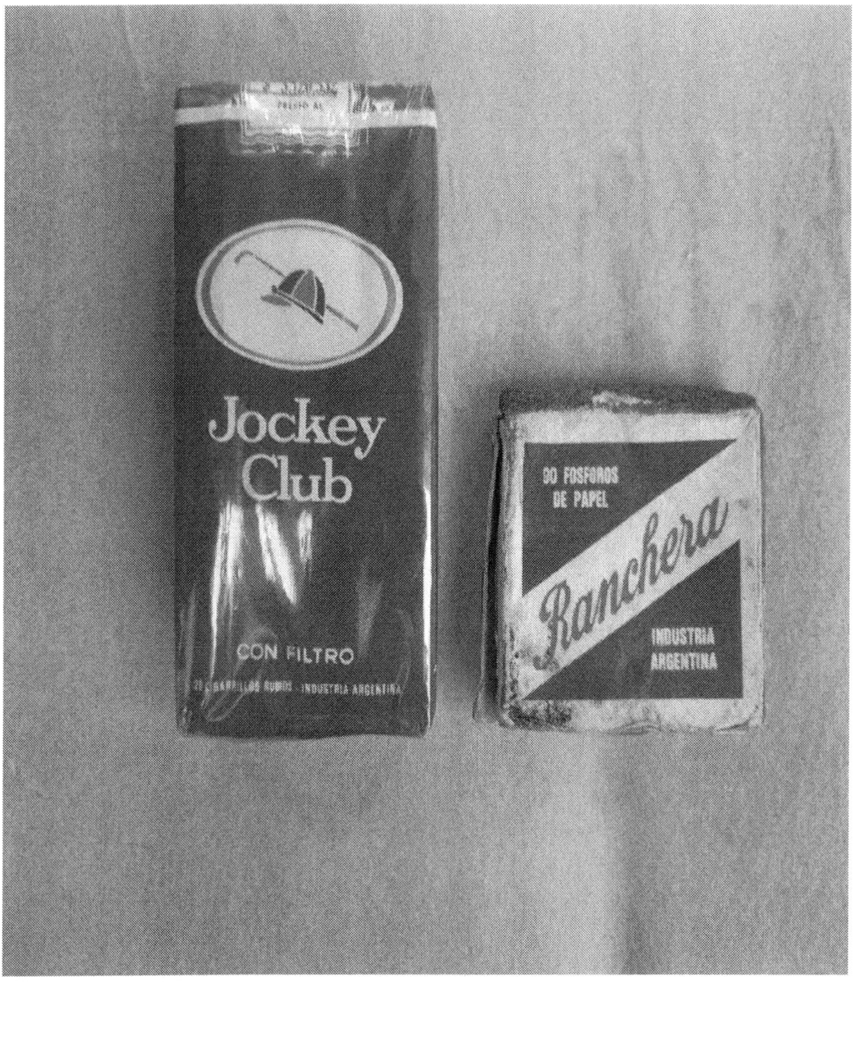

6. South Armagh (Bandit Country) January – June 1983.

After six weeks post Falklands leave, I returned to Seaton Barracks, Plymouth on my trusted Honda Super Dream motorbike. During this period back on camp 9 Troop kept the same officer but had gained a new SNCO, Sergeant Nigel Devenish. Very early on in 1983 the Troop entered two teams into the Rover Trophy, 40 Commando's annual inter-section competition. This involved approximately twenty sections taking part, from all of the companies in the unit, each one being assessed in three areas; vehicle checks, practical navigation and written theory tests. Overall, Lt Bushby's half of 9 Troop came first, and Sergeant Nigel Devenish's came equal second. A cup was awarded on the day to the Troop by the C.O. of 40 Commando; I never saw it again!

Later on in the year, we were told that we were to start pre-NI training in earnest at Lydd and Hythe ranges in Kent, and then on to Thetford in Norfolk. Somehow this deployment to NI had been leaked to the press and comments were made along the lines that 'these boys deserve a rest from active duty, it being so soon since the end of the Falklands'. To be honest we were up for it, back into some real soldiering rather than the endless training.

During 9 Troop's pre NI training we were engulfed with endless lectures and participated in urban warfare stances. One exercise, a role play, was carried out in an old Napoleonic Martello tower at Lydd and Hythe. The scenario was that we had set up an observation post (OP), high up in the rafters of a building looking down on to the entrance of a bar on the opposite side of the road. Nightfall came, a hostage incident took place and we were given permission to fire at any positively identified terrorist. At this point I have to say that the protagonists on the ground in front of us, were all electronically controlled dummies. After hours of boredom staring at the front door of the pub, several people (dummies) appeared, one holding a gun. Well, that was the trigger for the whole troop to let loose with everything we had. Consequently destroying the terrorist, bystanders, and parts of buildings. At the debrief the officer in charge of the range gave us an almighty bollocking for not keeping to our arcs of fire and destroying (the) his dummies.

In mid-October 1982 a small detachment of WREN's joined the Unit. With us they attended the briefings and lecturers about our coming tour in South Armagh. Sometime, in the distant future, one of these ladies was to marry a member of 9 Troop. How he managed to woo her and for her to choose him, I fail to understand, especially when more 'essence' (attractive) Royal Marines like me were around!

After several weeks of NI training, we were given pre deployment Christmas leave. Once again, we had to pack all of our kit, put it into storage on camp at Seaton Barracks or take it home. Because of the amount of gear I had, rather than riding my motorbike to Ipswich, I decided to take the train. I arrived at Liverpool Street Station at rush hour on a Friday, early evening. I was carrying a bergen on my back, a suitcase in one hand and a very large beige coloured issued kit bag in the other. I was desperate to get home so I could get as many pints of beer inside me as physically possible before the pubs shut at 23.00 hours. I ran to the platform from where the next train was about to leave for Ipswich. Most of the train doors had been shut, the whistle had been blown by the guard as a warning of its departure. The train was packed and with all of the seats occupied, people were standing everywhere. Luckily, I found one door still open. The entrance to the carriage was jam packed with commuters. I looked up, thought right this is it. I made an effort to push past some people waiting on the platform who were disappointed they couldn't fit on the departing train and would have to wait for the next. I heard a comment from behind me by a 'Pongo', no doubt trying to get to Colchester Barracks, saying 'you'll never get on mate'. I turned and said, 'You watch'. I raised my large kit bag up in front of my face and used it like a scrum practice pad for rugby training. As I entered the doorway, from behind my kit bag, I could hear grunts and moans from people on the train as they were pushed to the side by my efforts. One poor soul ended up being thrust into the toilet. I was shielded from facial expressions and comments from other passengers by my kit bag; besides nothing was going to stop me and I just didn't care. I turned to make sure my suitcase had travelled on board with me, saw the guard slam the door and an upset Pongo staring at me. I smiled at him and mouthed 'He who dares, he who dares'!

On 21st January 1983, 9 Troop were flown into Aldergrove Airport, just outside Belfast and then covertly transported to Drumadd Barracks, Armagh City, which was to be our base during the tour, although we were hardly there. Most of the time we were out on the border patrolling in what was called 'Bandit Country'. This area derived its nick name because the local population were mainly nationalists opposed to British forces being in NI, a stronghold for the IRA and allegedly a no go for the security services. We spent hours out on foot, led by our trustee ML sergeant who's understanding was the less we stood still, the less likely we would be shot!

One thing happened that undoubtedly pleased others and me. The Marine I have previously mentioned, who refused to get his head up above the parapet during our firefight at Sappers Hill, was arrested with one of his 'hanger on's' by the Military Police just before we left for South Armagh. I am pretty sure that the loss of these two individuals, who were both strangers to the truth, reduced the friction within the cohort and helped the Troop to bond more. I later found out that these two were charged and found guilty of stabbing some poor civilian on or near Union street in Plymouth and I believe one of them was sentenced to eight years in prison.

As a throwback from the Falklands War, I decided that I wanted to be the gunner for my section. This involved carrying the GPMG. The downside was that I was carrying over double the weight of an SLR. The GPMG weighs 24lbs compared to 11lbs of a loaded SLR. Also, after firing the GPMG, cleaning the gas parts was very time consuming. In the Falklands when I took over the GPMG after Vince had been shot, I realised something. Yes, I might be a better target to take out and therefore draw enemy fire, but boy could I put down a deadly rate of rounds on to them and at a further distance than with a normal infantry rifle. This firepower I summarised and hoped, would protect me, my number two and the rest of my section. So it seemed logical for me to volunteer to carry the 'Gun' in South Armagh. The GPMG during our tour was replaced by the older Light Machine Gun (LMG), which was slightly less heavy and had a 30-round magazine rather than being belt fed. I believe it was thought that the GPMG was too heavy to be constantly carried on border patrols. Also, having link rounds dangling from the gun meant they could easily get caught on obstacles as we climbed over them. These might get detached unnoticed, be lost, then possibly be picked up and used by terrorists against us.

Under 2 Ulster Defence force (2 UDR), 40 Commando's Tactical Area of Responsibility (TAOR) covered a large area of South Armagh, which was mainly countryside with a scattering of small towns and villages. Charlie Company were initially allocated Middletown and the Caledon Estate. Roads in our TAOR were narrow and renowned for improvised explosive devices (IED's) hidden by roadsides, in drainage ditches, culverts or tunnels beneath the highway.

Caledon Estate was built in the late 18th century and home of the Earls of Caledon. We were deployed there to protect the current owner and his assets from terrorist attacks. The house could really be described as a sizable mansion. Surrounding the mansion, the estate owned a large area of farmland, with the river Blackwater flowing through its grounds. The mansion was ringed by a ten foot plus high fence, topped off with barbed wire. Entering inside this tangible parameter was out of bounds for us; we were the defence ring on the outside. There were several exterior flood lights which, at night, illuminated everything inside and outside the enclosure, making weird and sometimes spooky shadowed patterns off the fence on to the grass below.

Arriving at the Caledon Estate in covert vehicles for the first time 9 Troop found our new accommodation a little bit neglected and totally lacking basic facilities, compared to the luxury of that inhabited by the owner. He had given us the privilege of using his old, disused stables. Well at least they were dry, and we had our sleeping bags to keep us warm. As we arrived, there were some guys from the army in the stables and I noticed a private was sitting down on the floor, polishing several pairs of boots. I asked him if he was being punished and his reply was 'No this is normal. We always have to clean the boots of the JNCO's'. I was not shocked at all. Even out on active operations the army continued with their strict regimental rank structure. Little or no autonomy is given to the lower ranks in some regiments. To not let a Marine think and act on his own would fly against the whole ethos of the Corps. Also, this state of affairs throws up a mental barrier of ' them and us' and could have disastrous affects where teamwork is essential, especially when lives are at risk.

'Our brick' (a team of four Marines) in South Armagh was Sgt 'Ginge' Devenish, Ricky Miller, 'Mitch' Mitchell and me. 'Ginge' as a nick name could have applied to nearly the whole brick; three of us were red headed, the other wasn't!

Out On Patrol.

In South Armagh the Rules of Engagement (ROE) were different compared to Operation Corporate. While out on patrol and on sangar duty, adhering to these ROE guidelines was always in the back of my mind. In NI you had to be one hundred percent sure before shooting. Identifying and opening fire on a legitimate target required a certain amount of confirmed criteria. You could not just blast away randomly. Recognising the enemy in the Falklands was relatively easy, unfortunately, not so in NI.

My first patrol was carried out almost completely on the land owned by the estate of Caledon. We only ventured out of the boundaries once, on to a country road for a few minutes. Yes, I did feel slightly nervous and was probably being over vigilant. The thoughts of past atrocities crossed my mind. I once shared a taxi from Ipswich railway station with my brother and a guy from 2 Para. Some months later the Para was murdered with seventeen others by the IRA at Warrenpoint. Also, to raise my blood pressure even higher, the message came through that an off-duty police officer had just been shot, point blank in the face with an Armalite rifle while he was leaving a fish and chip shop, nearby, in the small town of Keady. The murderer vanished as quickly as he had appeared.

9 Troop spent our earliest days familiarising ourselves, not only with the local topography but also buildings within the Caledon Estate. There were various disused out buildings, a tennis court with a pavilion and of course the old stables, our home. Being such good Marines and carrying out our job to the word, on one night patrol we were checking places where we suspected explosive devices might have been left. To the rear of the mansion, and outside the perimeter fence, we found a drain cover. With my companion we managed to prise the lid off and then carefully and quietly, place it to one side. We looked inside and saw that the drain headed towards the mansion. It looked fairly clean, dry and there was just enough space for a person to crawl along. With a torch in my hand I slid myself in with some ease and scrambled along commando fashion for several metres. At the end of the drain, it opened up into what I thought was just a small, dark, and damp room. As I pulled myself out of the drain and entered the room, I found a light switch, flicked it on and there, below the single light bulb, directly in front of me were racks of unopened bottles of wine. It was winter and we needed to keep the chill out while on patrol, so I proffed a couple of bottles for the lads! A few weeks later our troops TAOR changed. We gained the town of Keady and lost the Caledon Estate. I am glad we never met the owner because he might have had a sad on when he discovered his best bottles of wine were missing!

Travelling by road in military vehicles, such as Land Rovers, was deemed to be too great a risk for moving us around the border area, so we mainly used helicopters for transport. Sometimes, when they were available, we would fly several thousand feet above roads, spot a vehicle(s) that looked suspicious and we wanted to check out. From the heavens above the helicopter would spiral down like a cork screw, level out and pass at great speed directly over the top of the cars, no doubt scaring the living day lights out of the occupants. We then would be dropped off further up the road, so we could form an impromptu vehicle check point (VCP). On one occasion, just before embarking back onto a Wessex hellcopter after one such VCP, I saw the infamous 'Jock' Hepburn bend down and pick up something from the wet, grassy ground and put it into his pocket. It was a bit strange but I thought nothing of it.

The helicopter climbed to an appropriate height and hovered. A new target was spotted, so the pilot carried out the same manoeuvre and started spiralling down. It was then I noticed Jock gesturing to the navigator, who was standing by the open doorway. Jock was holding his stomach and puffing his cheeks out as if he was going to be sick. The navigator looked confused and approached Jock. When they were face to face Jock pointed to his mouth, opened it as if to vomit, but instead of sick. a frog jumped out! I held my breath in disbelief then roared with laughter until my face turned bright red. The frog sprang out of Jock's mouth and landed on the floor of the helicopter. The navigator swiftly booted it out at an altitude of a few hundred feet, into the fresh air of South Armagh, shaking his head and muttering 'Fucking Marines'.

As we yomped through endless small holdings and their fields, we had to navigate our way over a variety of different types and heights of boundaries. Mostly the fences were made up of barbed wire or at least topped off with it. After a few weeks we were thoroughly fed up with having to negotiate these fences every time we crossed a field. It was so time consuming having to pass kit and weapons over to each other. To add to our frustration, if you were caught by the barbed wire, accidently attaching itself to a particular part of your anatomy, it was often quite painful for a male. Hence, every time we went on patrol we took a pair of cutters with us and simply cut through the barbed wire. This made the going faster and so much easier, particularly for me carrying the gun. I no longer had to unstrap the bloody thing from my shoulder every time I climbed over an obstacle. However, after several complaints from local farmers to the police (who were based in the same police station as us), we had to stop this practice. As a sobering thought, the only fatality from 40 Commando RM during our tour was an accident caused by a Marine carrying his gun, as he attempted to climb over a fence.

With us on one patrol was Cpl Peters,' AKA DOTL and his brick. It was night time and DOTL was in the process of straddling one of the many fences we had come across. Using his weapon to hold it down, he suddenly let out a yelp as sparks, arcs of light and subsequently laughter rose up into the South Armagh sky. 'What's up?' someone sarcastically asked from upfront. 'You bunch of twats, you could have told me it was an electric fence!' was the reply from DOTL.

I found myself going headfirst into my new role as a gunner during our tour in South Armagh. This was my niche and I wanted to be the best. I practised stripping the gun down and putting it together, loading, unloading and blockage procedures. To make carrying the extra weight of the gun easier, I improved my muscular endurance by using a set of dumbbells to do endless bicep curls, shoulder press and other upper body exercises, sometimes along with Ricky Miller and Mitch for motivation and guidance. I had an affinity with my gun, in fact I was obsessed, almost in love! It was during this time in Charlie Company, when 9 Troop's nick name started to be used, the 'fighting 9'. It came from our exploits in the firefight at Sappers Hill, during the Falklands War.

We spent some time in the first few months of our NI tour trying to hunt down the famous racehorse, Shergar. Shergar was taken by an armed gang on 8 February 1983. Thoughts were it had been taken by the IRA to sell and so raise funds for their campaign. Every horse, donkey or mule (sometimes cow) we saw grazing in the fields or in barns raised our hopes of finding Shergar, but to no avail. Someone high up in the military even suggested we stopped and checked all vehicles carrying cans of dog food in case it had been butchered!

While out on a particularly long patrol somewhere near the border Ginge the ML 'yomper' decided to take a break. We removed our bergens and put a wet on while Ginge went off to do a recce. Ricky and I thought about how we could stop, or at least slow down the pace and distance Ginge was doing. He had the adage from his ML training, 'get height and then distance'. Thus every hill he saw we had to yomp to the top. I decided that the only course of action was to slow him down. Stopping him completely would have to be done by something drastic and he wasn't going to fall for anything that wasn't real e.g. a member of the brick feigning an injury. I found some large rocks nearby, and with Ricky's assistance, emptied Ginge's bergen, laid the rocks in the bottom of it and stacked his clothes back on top. I then replaced his bergen exactly where he had left it. A few minutes later Ginge returned from his recce, we loaded up and began yomping, again. I kept a close eye on Ginge in case he noticed a difference in the weight of his bergen; to my relief, nothing for now.

An hour or so later we stopped by a minor road, formed a harbour position and started to get a wet on. Ginge stood in the middle of our location and started to unpack his bergen to get a jumper out. He reached all the way to the bottom. I looked up to see him pull out one rock after another, saying 'What the fuck'. Ricky, Mitch and I burst out laughing. Ginge bellowed out 'Barnes!' and ran towards me. Like any good Marine, never leaving his weapon, I grabbed my LMG and ran for my life out on to the nearby road. He continued to pursue me as I ran trying my best to escape. As I was going hell for leather, I passed some civilians who were looking out from their gardens and wondering what was going on. I continued running as hard as I could. I heard a clunk and thought nothing of it, my immediate worry was that Ginge would catch me. He shouted 'Stop you twat'. At first I thought he was saying this so he could try and slow me down. A few steps later, my right arm, which was carrying the LMG, suddenly felt lighter. I looked down to find only the barrel in my hand. The main body was lying in the middle of the road some yards back! It had detached, just as I had passed the civilians watching. They were 'gob smacked,' to see one of Britain's finest, abandoning his weapon as he was being chased down by a red headed devil!

Caledon House, South Armagh, 1983.

Inside The Wire!

Sometimes 9 Troop would be based in police stations close to or virtually on the border with Eire. If we did stay in these locations, we had to man the sangars, main gate, and traffic crossings coming out off and going to Ireland. We could regulate the traffic coming through the boarder by using a set of traffic lights, sighted where the road narrowed from two lanes into one as it passed our location. If we wanted to stop a vehicle, we could simply change the lights from green to red. If this failed, then we had the use of two sets of caltrops (spikes) that could be raised by a lever in the lookout post and were guaranteed to puncture any vehicles with pneumatic tires. One day a colleague of mine was on duty at the main gate, watching the road through TV monitors. Brian was a large Marine over six-foot- tall and had been brought up in the North East of England. He had a very dry sense of humour, which I clicked on to and enjoyed. Brian took no messing around. A wedding procession was ready to cross the border from the South to the North, about ten cars in total. The front chauffeur driven car was carrying the bride, her father and bridesmaids. This lead car 'jumped the gun' and went through the lights when they were on amber, Brian wasn't happy. He pulled the lever for the caltrops. The car went through the first, then the second set but failed to get any further. With the tyres deflated and a queue of cars behind, the wedding procession was halted. Helpers got out of their vehicles and pushed the lead car off to the side of the road so others could pass. Unlike the rest of the UK, the police stations in South Armagh, and throughout the rest of NI, were heavily fortified against terrorist attacks. High fences topped with razor wire, manned OP's, CCTV and large secured gates were typical. There was a knock on the front gate of the police station. Brian went to investigate. He opened the peek hole. Standing there was a man from the wedding party, distraught because of the delay. He asked, 'Have you got anything to fix punctures with?' Brian with no empathy and with the wit of Bob Monkhouse replied, in his deep Geordie accent , 'We don't fix punctures we only make them, now fuck off!' and slammed the peek hole shut. I don't think there is any need for Brian to apply to the UN for a role as an ambassador for peace keeping!

Some of our time was spent manning the sangars protecting the outer edge of the police stations. These were frequently shot at by the IRA, from across the border in county Monaghan. I spent hours on duty just staring out of sangars through protected glass viewpoints, occasionally drifting off deep into my own fantasies, searching for inspiration to help me stay awake. One sangar had the benefit of looking out onto one of the main roads leading into the centre of Keady. Sometimes you could see people walking into town. I often kept a careful eye out for young, attractive, women. If I was lucky to spot one, I would zoom in with my binoculars. It was a welcome distraction and helped to pass the time.

It was a relief to break the monotony of guard duty and go out on patrol. On short, semi urban patrols, my brick would go with minimal kit, carrying only Armalites, and spare magazines in our jacket pockets. While patrolling I cannot recall how many back gardens we climbed over, but it took me back to growing up in Ipswich and my 'garden hopping' adventures. However, this time we seemed to take down more washing lines, sometimes on purpose. On our return to the police station from short patrols, we would always go into the galley, turn on the ovens, cook and then devour egg banjo's (sandwich), sometimes, swimming in tomato ketchup; what an indulgence and a gourmet's delight!

Inside one police station there was a tarmacked, rectangular shaped landing pad measuring about five by ten metres, built for small helicopters, like Gazelles or Scouts to land and take off. This rectangle had a large perimeter of grass, then a high fence with a sangar facing the boarder therefore offering the helicopters some protection. If we had any spare time, which was rare, I would put on my sports kit, go onto the helipad and literally do hundreds of grid sprints and various exercises. I eventually devised my own fitness circuit. I soon found the grid sprints monotonous. So, with guidance from Ricky Miller I started to learn how to skip. Ricky's skipping rope was made of leather and often it was soaked in water to stop it from knotting or twisting out of shape. Every time I failed to do the correct technique, I would be rewarded with a very painful whack on either the back of my head, neck or legs. It left red marks on my body and it looked like I had been to a S&M party. The training helped me to relax, sleep easier, improve my cardiovascular fitness while learning the new skill of skipping (albeit painfully). Even in the total darkness of night, I would go out and train. Being very close to the border with County Monaghan, any lights would, well, light up the area and make us an easy target for snipers to shoot at.

In Keady Police station the accommodation for 9 Troop was basic. I shared a cabin with Mitch and Ricky. Ginge being a SNCO had his own room. Our heating consisted of a single, mobile, Calor gas heater. If we forgot to turn it on before we went out on patrol or sangar duty, we would return to a freezing room. Conversely, if we did leave the heater on for long periods it left an aroma of gas in the room that penetrated your clothes. If I went for a dhobi and left my wet towel on the back of a chair and the fire wasn't left on it would take days to dry. If the fire was on, my towel would dry quickly but have the fragrance of sulphur. The cabin had no windows therefore the only natural light came from the doorway. Even during the day, it was difficult to see what you were doing under the single electric light bulb suspended in the middle of the room. It was like a dungeon. At least we were dry, relatively warm, could have a shower and got hot food cooked for us, sometimes by a chef. Our cabin benefited by being slightly out of the way from the rest of the troop and we didn't get disturbed when there was a change of guard, or a section was going out on patrol. Also, when stepping out of our grot, the helipad was right in front of us, so I didn't have to go far to do my fitness training.

In Keady during my breaks from manning the sangars or front gate I would sometimes go to the television room, located in the basement, right in the centre of the police station. The room was accessed by steep stairs and could only accommodate approximately five people at once. I never met any police officers there, which was great because we had the monopoly on what we wanted to watch. One Marine almost made the television room his home. He used it for his personal grooming, even going as far as making it his own pedicure room. He would always sit in the front row of chairs, turn another chair towards himself and use it to rest his feet on, often obscuring the television screen. It was almost disturbing to watch as he would go through his revolting routine on his feet, distracting the rest of us from concentrating on the programme we were trying to focus on. As if that was not enough, he would leave his toenail clippings and pieces of dead skin on the floor and chairs. After a few days we had had enough. He was physically lifted up and promptly thrown out, only to be allowed back into the television room when he was chaperoned, and he had promised not to carry out this nasty habit in public, ever again.

There was a VHS video player in the television room, however there were very few videos and nowhere to get any new ones from. The most popular film watched by most of 9 Troop, including myself, was National Lampoons Animal House starring John Belushi. We repeatedly watched the film simply because we could relate to some of the exploits carried out by the fraternity. Some of the scenes in the film, of wild, drunken parties where people did outrageous acts, reminded me of runs ashore in Plymouth's infamous Union street. It was as if we had an affinity to the cohort of undergraduate students portrayed in the film. We stole some of their ideas and later, back from our tour in South Armagh, we would relive them e.g. toga run's ashore. It might be worth mentioning that there was another film that touched our psyche and was also very popular at the time, again starring John Belushi; The Blues Brothers!

Wally The Goffer Wallah.

At one station in South Armagh, there was a 'tuck shop' run by a civilian called Wally. He was from Afghanistan and told us that he had been an Afghan 'freedom fighter' against the USSR, after they invaded his country in late 1979. He would often come out with stories of his heroic deeds. He even produced a photograph of himself with his cousins in Afghan, all holding very old looking rifles. Some of his exploits bordered on the ridiculous, from firing RPG's (Rocket Propelled Grenades) at T52's (Russian Tanks), missing and then taking them out with rifles, or rolling underneath the tanks to attach mines.

To test out Wally's military prowess with a weapon we asked him if he would like to fire a rifle in the small indoor range on site. He said he would love to. If my memory serves me, the range was about 15 metres in length and It was made out of a pair of concrete pipes that reminded me of the smarty tubes on the Endurance Course. They were about five feet in diameter and buried beneath several metres of topsoil. The firing point was a small, sealed room, just enough for two or three others excluding the person shooting. Any noise in the room was amplified by its square design, the metal panelled walls and roof. There was Phil, a JNCO and Chalky, a SNCO and me in the room. As Wally lay down in the prone position at the firing point, we made the American Armalite ready for him to fire. Standing behind I watched unknown to Wally. Just as he released the safety catch, Phil was about to stop him and pass him a pair of ear defenders. Chalky, standing close to me, caught the eye of Phil and shook his head side to side. We all tried not to laugh. Five shots of 5.56mm were fired by Wally. Even with ear defenders in I could hear the ringing in my ears and felt, deep in the pit of my stomach, the sound waves as they bounced off the walls and echoed around the room with each shot going off. Wally finished firing and Phil took the weapon from him and made it safe. As we went outside Wally said in his heavily Asian accent 'Very good, very good, but sergeant, **my ears, they are killing me, killing me!'** This became another infamous quote used time and time again by 9 Troop.

Thoroughly annoyed with Wally's claims some lads tied him up in a white mattress cover and threw him outside the main gate. He lay on the pavement motionless. There were shouts to Walley from the lads, 'Watch out Wally they're going to shoot at you." Although it was a bit over the top, it was funny to watch as he tried to kick and punch his way out of the mattress cover. After he was released and let back into the police station he approached our leader to complain about his treatment, ***'They're going to kill me,'*** referring to the Marines not the terrorists!

Once, we were out on a foot patrol close to the boarder with Eire. 9 Troop set up an ad hoc VCP at a road T junction. Ricky, 'Mitch' Mitchel and I were doing the vehicle checks. I stopped a car and sitting in the front passenger's seat was a prominent and angry Sein Fein member. He asked, with some venom in his voice, 'How much time is this going to take?' One of our lads replied, 'I'm sure you know that this is a terrorist hot spot, we need to make sure your vehicle and the road ahead is clear and safe for you to continue on your journey'. So, to the frustration of the car's occupants, we did a thorough check which took a very, very long time.

On another foot patrol we went to Tynan Abbey just on the outside of the small town by the same name. In January 1981, the owner of the Abbey, an eighty-six-year-old past Speaker of the UK Houses of Parliament, and his son, were murdered by the IRA. After the attack the house was set alight in an attempt by the terrorists to hide their crime and possibly wipe the family name out of Irish history. Their bodies were later found in what was left of the structure.

Tynan Abbey was an eerie place, a shell, completely burnt out, you could still clearly see the scorch marks left on what little was still standing of the two hundred year old building. It looked more like a Victorian folly than what it had once been; a functional home. The incident had only took place two years previously but it looked like it had only happened a few days ago. I could still see curled up pieces of wallpaper, charred pieces of wood that had once been furniture and up close, hanging in the air, there was still an odour of smoke. It would have made a fantastic location to film a gothic horror or ghost story. The age of the building, its architecture, with some grotesque stone gargoyles above the main door and the tale of its final demise would have made the setting complete. The strange thing for me was the coincidence of the site and my primary school headmaster's name, Tynan (spooky!)

March Or Die!

During the eight years I served in the Royal Marines, I met a variety of people with different characteristics. Some Marines that I have purposely chosen to try and forget, others that have been permanently embedded in my memory, in a pleasant way and will stay there until my last breath. Certainly, Alex 'Jock' Hepburn is up there with the best. I have already mentioned Jock in previous stories, but it's worth looking at him and his escapades in a little more detail.

There is one picture of Ricky Miller and myself standing by some gorse and it reminded me of a famous quote given by Lance Corporal 'Jock' Hepburn. The story goes like this. We were near the end of our tour in 1983. 9 Troop had been sent out on a four-day foot patrol in the rural border lands of 'Bandit Country'. But before I continue, I must describe the protagonists. Jock Hepburn a newly promoted Lance corporal, who was slightly older than most of us, had a hint of a Scottish accent, a flower of Scotland tattoo on one of his forearms despite being brought up in Clacton, Essex, (hence the nick name Cockney Jock, no offence meant Alex!). He had a very sharp and dry sense of humour. Attached to Jock's brick was the famously named 'Pigsy' who was given the role as troop radio operator. His nickname came about because his face was the spitting image of Pigsy, the character from the Japanese television programme 'Monkey,' shown around these times. Also, he was no stranger to a jam roly-poly with custard and therefore he was slightly overweight for an active Royal Marines Commando.

Back to the story – we had been given a pickup point to be withdrawn from the patrol by helicopter. The landing site was on top of

possibly one of the steepest hills in the area. At the base and continuing all the way to the summit, it was surrounded by various obstacles such as streams, hedges and fences. My brick had reached the bottom of this hill and were resting before we made the climb to the top. While we were resting, we heard that an advance party including Jock Hepburn and Pigsy had gone to the top but had been told that the pickup was cancelled and so they were making their way back down. However, once this brick met up with us at the bottom of the hill, the orders had changed, and the pickup was back on. This meant that they had to climb back up the hill for a second time. I have a vivid picture in my memory of Jock leading Pigsy off back up the hill. Pigsy, feeling tired, (possibly because he had to carry the additional weight of the radio and his own fat!), hungry and wet was dripping (complaining) to Jock about how unfair it was. We stood watching from a distance as they walked ahead. When they reached about a quarter of the way up the hill, we followed on. In disbelief our brick could still hear Pigsy moaning about his plight and expecting some sympathy. By time we caught up, Jock had obviously had enough of the dripping. He turned around and shouted at the top of his voice, an adaptation of the famous quote taken from the French Foreign Legion when a troop had been marching for weeks, out in the depths of the Sahara Desert, with no water to drink or rations to eat. '
Pigsy you know the score, it's march or die, march or die!'
Ricky, me and the others that heard Jock, laughed so much that I'm sure we could have compromised our position – Pigsy's face was a picture. The saying has stuck with 9 Troop and is always brought up at reunions.

Jock was second in command (2i/c) of a brick and was known to be a bit of a disciplinarian, 'Pussers' in other words. He would often go around the police station to check on his subordinates. Sometimes he would go to extraordinary physical feats to check that they were fulfilling their roles correctly. Once he was out checking the sangars just in case someone was nodding off. To get to one sangar the conventional method of access was via steep, wooden stairs, and once at the top, you entered the sangar by lifting a hatch that opened inwardly. This normal way of entry made a lot of noise and easily warned the Marine on duty that someone was approaching. Jock, trying to be cunning and catch someone asleep decided to scale the outside of this particular sangar rather than use the stairs thus, giving no warning to the occupant that he was on his way. On this occasion Brian Edmunds was on duty, and wide awake. Brian was looking out of an observation slit, saw Jock trying to scale up the outside of the sangar and said, ***'What the fuck do you want Sir Hillary Hepburn?*** '(the name after Sir Edmund Hillary, the famous mountaineer). Much to Jocks frustration and annoyance, but to our hilarity, the name stuck and was even posted on notice boards when rotas were drawn up during the rest of the tour.

Our final place of residence for the last month of the tour was back to 9 Troops starting location, Drumadd Barracks in Armagh City. It was almost, but not quite, like being back at Seaton Barracks in Plymouth, except for obvious security reasons we weren't allowed ashore. However, to keep our fitness levels, we could run a loop inside the camp, use a weights room to train in and we even had

the luxury of access to a sauna.
I attended a mass carried out in a small chapel on camp. The only people at the service apart from the priest were myself, another Marine and the Company Commander, with two other officers from Charlie Company. When I returned back to my grot, several other members of the troop asked me where I had been. I unashamedly lied and said, 'Oh just to the sauna'. I knew that if I had told the truth I would have probably been put in the 'God squad' category of weirdo's and be on the receiving end of some stick.

Although 9 Troop weren't allowed out of camp for any reason unless on patrol, we were able to buy alcohol on camp in the NAAFI bar. Because it was drawing close to the end of our tour, we decided to have one too many beers and it did get a little bit out of hand. I cannot remember why, but for some reason I found myself, with the assistance of another Marine, picking up the juke box and then throwing it on the floor. Tables, chairs and beer glasses were flung in the air by other Marines and came crashing down all around. Then suddenly it just stopped. It was a few minutes of utter madness followed by complete silence, like a twister passing in the mid-west of the USA, leaving chaos in its wake, the water-spout being replaced by beer! Someone found cleaning equipment and before I knew it I was mopping the floor; how peculiar! Was this melee a result of pent-up frustration that had been stored up over the last six months and had just been released?, or the joy of thinking we would be home within the next few days?, I have no idea.

One of our last foot patrols was in Armagh City, close to the Cathedral. Accompanying 9 Troop was a search dog and its pongo handler. The dog and handler were with us so they could help confirm or clear anything of interest e.g. an explosive device. Several months later while back home on leave I was drinking in a pub in Ipswich and in walked the dog handler. At first, I thought I was delusional, that I had had too many beers and it had affected my eyesight. I walked up to him and he recognised me straight away. Needless to say, we sank a few more beers and have been friends ever since.

I certainly gained confidence during this tour of South Armagh. I think a lot of this change was due to my physical development. By carrying the added weight of the gun and doing extra PT, I increased my muscle mass. I had been skinny before this extra PT. I can remember some other lad commenting that I was the only Marine he knew that had hips wider than his shoulders! The increase in physical stature changed the way other people looked at me too. I was no longer classed as a sprog and did get some respect from other Marines. I must also thank Ginge and Jono Johnson for my development. In the past I was happy to just blindly follow my leader. They actually took time to explain what we were doing and why. On one patrol they even gave me a map and explained our exact position so I was able to follow our progress on my own. I felt comfortable enough to ask questions, something I was shy of doing in the past.

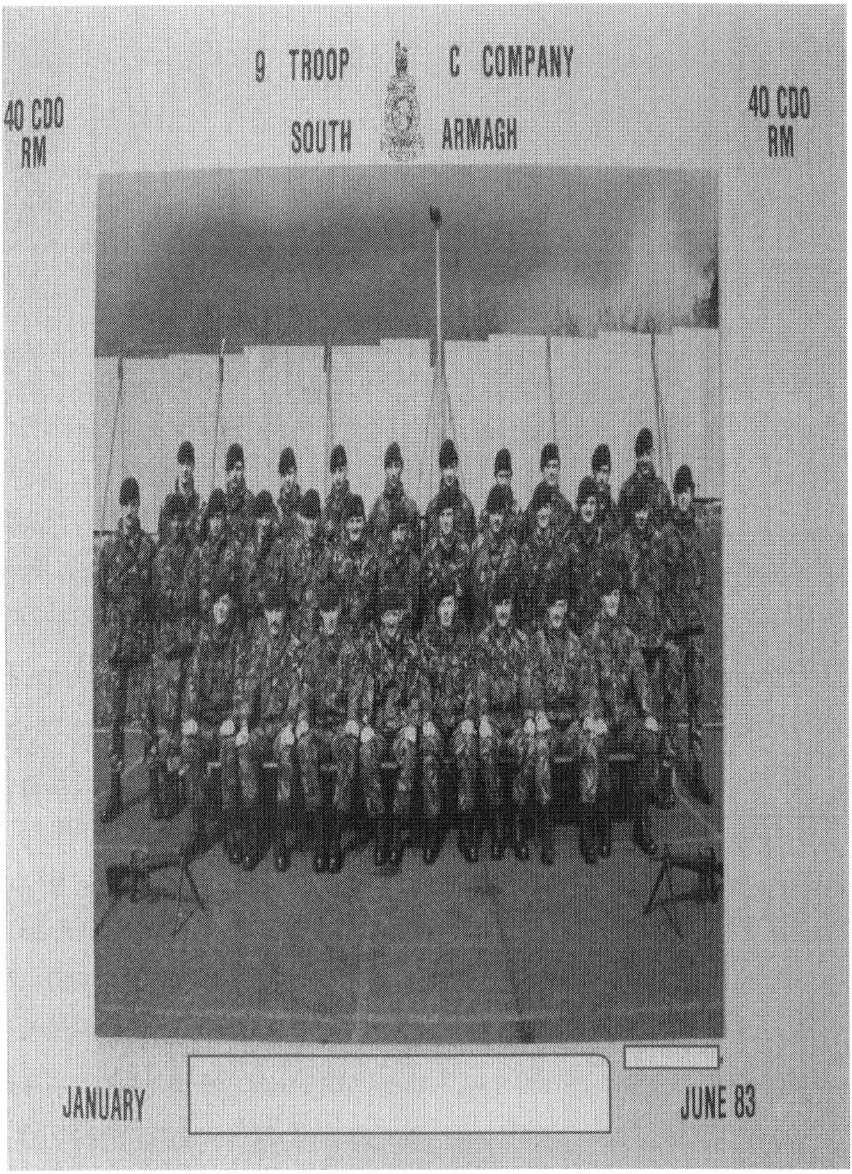

Middletown, South Armagh.

Two 'Bricks' from 9 Troop. Taking a break, out on patrol in 'Bandit Country', 1983.

L-R Ricky Miller, Ginge Devenish, Mitch and me. Our Brick, Keady, South Armagh, 1983.

Binge Drinking.

Our tour of South Armagh finished on 6th June 1983 and just like after the Falklands War we were given extended leave, this time only four weeks compared to the six. My drinking binges on leave became heavier and to be honest that's all I wanted to do, consume alcohol. My Father thought I was an alcoholic and quite frankly I was unable to function normally without it when I was home on leave. I used to wake up with a can of beer by my bed or drink shots of vodka from my father's drinks cabinet, before going out to the pub ready for opening time at 11.00. The drinking sessions on leave started as soon as I got on the train from the South West, heading to Paddington. I would go straight to the buffet and get several cans of beer, drink them quickly and then buy some more. This would continue in the buffet carriage on the train from Liverpool street to Ipswich. Before I had reached home, I was always drunk or at least, very nearly.

When I was back in Ipswich there was always somewhere and someone to drink with. If the pubs were closed, I would often end up in some house or dingy flat, I didn't care where, as long as I could drink. I had no real favourites for my choice of pubs in town, it was the locality that mattered, the closer the better. My drinking always started in pubs on the outskirts of the town centre, close to my parents' house and as the night and the drinking progressed, I would slowly creep towards the centre of Ipswich, eventually discarding pubs and ending up in wine bars, simply because they stayed open later. There was one trendy wine bar that I used to go to called 'The Butts,' fortunately I didn't find it as boring as the butts on the range at Altcar!

At first, my nights out started off by meeting up with friends from school, but as my drinking got worse these friends dropped out and I simply continued with anyone in the pub that would talk to me. Some people just latched on to me because they knew that I was home on leave for a short time and had money to spend. This however was not the case for all. I made friends with some great characters that I feel privileged to have met and trusted. Martin was a window cleaner. His round was exclusively retail shops in the centre of Ipswich. He was only ever known as Yank. He had arrived in Ipswich in the mid 1970's from Bridgewater in Somerset. At first people had difficulty understanding what he was saying because they were unused to his heavy, south west country accent. They wrongly assumed that he was an American serviceman, from one of the United Sates Air Forces bases close to Ipswich, hence the name Yank. He always wore denim, a beard, had a constant red glowing smiling face and was in his mid-thirties when I first met him. Apart from window cleaning during the day he worked as a security guard throughout the night. I remember him once showing me a very large burn on his leg. It happened when on duty. Drunk, he had fallen asleep on a heater and only woke up when he felt the pain soaring through his body and smelt the acrid air of his own burning flesh.

A friend of mine who was also the landlord of a pub called The Golden Lion in the centre of town, allowed Yank to store his ladders and cleaning materials in a shed out the back. Whenever I was home, I could guarantee that Yank would be in the Golden Lion. Together we had some heavy drinking sessions. On my own I would start drinking at 11.00 and knew that at some stage in the morning Yank would walk in. He was one of the funniest people I ever met. Once I was delayed and arrived at the pub slightly later than usual. It was around lunch time and I saw Yank standing at the bar, surrounded by three or four young ladies who were laughing hysterically. On the bar Yank had placed a small purple coloured, velvet pouch with two string ties at the top. One woman had asked him what was in the pouch. Yank told his audience that it was a 'secret, I can't tell you, but give it a gentle squeeze'. The woman picked it up in her hand and squeezed. Yank immediately let out a cry, crossed his legs, had a shocked expression on his face and reached down to his scrotum. He then said out loudly, as if he was in excruciating pain, 'I said gently!' Later, for effect, I found out that Yank had placed two large marbles in the pouch.

This was a time when the pubs, during the day closed at 14.30 and then reopened at 17.00. To carry on drinking between these hours I would go to an off licence and buy some alcohol then take it to the shed used by Yank at the back of the Golden Lion. This became known as the afternoon 'Shed Club' and Yank was given the title of landlord and only invited what he classed as VIP's to drink there. He was such a popular guy that often there would be far too many people to get into the shed so we had to spill out onto the nearby pub carpark. This was an advantageous position as these people could act as lookouts in case the police were nearby who would break up our illegal gathering. Visiting pubs and cleaning their windows was part of Yank's job. Some landlords had such a trust in Yank they gave him keys to their pubs so he could get access out of opening times to clean inside, but, unfortunately, also to free beer on tap at any time of the day. Going into pubs was part of his work and social life, he just enjoyed meeting people. At one point Yank confided in me that his doctor had advised him to stop drinking or else it could lead to serious health problems. Sadly, in the end too much alcohol consumption led to his death, far too early, in his mid-forties. I was genuinely shocked and upset when I heard of his passing. Yank was irreplaceable. Martin left a wife and son and I am ashamed to say it, but I never really knew them. Without Yank, run's ashore back home in Ipswich would never be the same.

I too had several warnings relating to my excessive alcohol consumption, not from a medical practitioner, but my own body. I suffered from delirium tremens (DTs) including all the shaking, shivering, sweating, awesome headaches and several times I felt pains in my chest, exactly where my heart was located. I knew these were not good signs, especially for a young, fit male adult.

My addiction to alcohol became out of hand. Often, I would catch the last possible train back to camp, the midnight sleeper from Paddington Station to the South West. This allowed me to get drunk before I left Ipswich, in an attempt to prevent the immediate effect of suffering from DT's on the journey. Back on camp I would sometimes fall in on a Monday morning hung over and sleep deprived. Why did I drink so much? Well yes you can blame some of it on the Royal Marines culture, but not all. I felt that I had to let off steam, and apart from doing physical exercise, (in Ipswich there was no one to do this with), drinking was an easy option. It nulled my anger. An anger that I still have difficulties with today. There are some parts of my life that I wish I could take a sledgehammer to, smash them to pieces and then to dust, so that they can be washed away by the rain and in time, disappear into the earth and from my memory, forever. I once went teetotal for a while, and consequently even the smell of alcohol made me feel sick. Now I don't trust myself. I feel that it's all or nothing, one drink is a waste of time. If I am going to consume alcohol, I have to do it in a big way, there's no half measures.

1983, Back To Seaton – For The Last Time.

On our return to Seaton Barracks, Charlie Company were put on the top floor of an accommodation block, with Alpha at the bottom, Bravo in the middle, a reverse of how it had been before our tour in NI. Rather than having to run down two flights of stairs in the morning to ditch the gash (put out the rubbish), we threw it out of the window aiming for the large cylindrical bins situated outside, near to the main entrance to our accommodation building. As the gash sailed its way down two floors, we shouted either 'take cover' or 'incoming'. This was to warn the guys from other companies, or our own, what was on its way down, so hopefully they could avoid it. After several weeks we didn't have to shout anything. Every time Marines had to pass below our windows, they automatically looked up. Due to our poor aiming, the gash would frequently miss the bins on the ground, particularly in high winds. This meant that someone had to go down and pick it up, so in the end we stopped this practice because it was counterproductive, oh, and we were spotted by a SNCO who gave us a right bollocking!

One day we had an Inspection of the accommodation and because Chris Pretty was a L/Cpl he had to stay and present our grot. My bed was missing the front left-hand side leg. Taking the initiative, I used two suitcases to prop the bed up, but unfortunately it was far from being horizontal, in fact, it was at such an angle that the front left-hand side touched the floor. Captain Pillar walked into our grot with some other inspecting officers. As they surveyed the room, Captain Pillar stopped and said to the other officers and Chris 'what fucking nutter is sleeping on that excuse for a bed'. Chris replied 'Barnes Sir' and they shook their heads in disbelief but weren't shocked that it was me!

During the summer of '83', if 9 Troop had time off while at Seaton Barracks, we would take our own cars on the Torpoint Ferry across the river Tamar and head down to Looe in Cornwall. It had a lovely white sandy beach and it felt (well almost) like you were abroad, particularly when the sun shone. One time during the working week, we were accompanied by our troop officer, Carl Bushby. He ordered four tonners to take us to a site a few miles out of Looe. The troop had to do a small yomp along the cliffs overlooking the sea, as you approach the town from the east. We carried bergens but instead of anything military inside all they had were towels, swimming costumes and sun block. I believe that Mr Bushby used the yomp as an excuse for him to see Looe for the first time.

Whenever we returned back to Seaton Barracks from Looe, come to think of it any time we were back on camp, it was almost like a continued summer holiday. If the troop didn't go to Looe then we normally carried out fitness training, showered, did some dhobi, went for scran, played music in our grots until sunset and then went ashore. I can always remember Chris Pretty blasting out songs at an annoying level, particularly 'I'm still Standing' from Elton John's newly released album. It was a great time for me to be in 9 Troop. I felt comfortable, not only with my fellow Marines but also with myself. I was confident in my soldiering abilities, fitness levels and I didn't miss home at all.

At one point 9 Troop did an advance party for a week, up to what was going to be our new home, Norton Manor Camp in Taunton, Somerset. Norton Manor was just outside Taunton on the A358 to Minehead. It was surrounded by countryside and, compared to the compact Seaton Barracks in Plymouth, our new camp was spread over a large acreage and buildings were interspersed with greenery. There were tennis courts, a firing range, football pitches, assault course, athletic track, unlike at Seaton Barracks there was also a separate parade square from the MT yard and even a small forest! The buildings were archaic, and little had changed on site since the end of the Second World War. I could see that there had been little or no financial investment for years. Some old, unused Nissen huts had moss growing on their corrugated roofs, guttering hanging off and were far from watertight. To think that this was going to be 40 Commando RM's new base was beyond belief, it was a shit hole!

During our week as advance party at Norton Manor, we stayed in the guardroom and only went ashore once to the nearest pub called the Cross Keys which was about a mile away from camp. It was an environment with outdated décor and furnishings that reflected the few locals that were drinking at the bar. We had one pint, left and strolled back to camp wondering if that was a reflection of the night life in Taunton.

On wandering patrol duty around Norton Manor, I did several 'walks of discovery' to orientate myself and find out what was in some of the derelict buildings. I had great fun kicking in and pushing down doors and windows in the old stables just to look inside. In one Nissen hut we found old American signs left from the time of the Second World War when it had been used as a hospital and more recent belongings from the previous owners, the Junior Leaders Regiment.

The Officers Mess in the main Country Manor was some distance from the rest of the camp, set in the middle of a forest and was soon due to be updated. The Manor is a gothic style, grade II listed building and was in poor condition after years of neglect just like the rest of the camp, but it was still functional and used to accommodate any officers. 9 Troop's Officer refused to sleep in the Manor saying it was filthy and decided to stay in a single cell, in the guardroom, for the week with us instead. We all thought that he had bottled it for two reasons. The first because he was the only person staying in the Officers Mess overnight and therefore had no company. Secondly, he had overheard some stories, innocently and with no malice intended, told by us on the coach on the way up, of mysterious noises and visions of spirits wondering the empty corridors and rooms during the night!

Four lads from 9 Troop who had missed the advance party, under their own ingenuity made their way up from Plymouth to Taunton to do a recce for themselves on Norton Manor Camp and Taunton's night life. They decided to hitch a lift and thought that if they split into two two's they would have a better chance of getting picked up. One pair were successful and while they were travelling along the M5, talking to the driver, they found out that he was on his way to sell the car they were in. They decided, although it was a wreck, it would suit their short-term purpose and decided to buy it. They paid cash, then dropped off the driver, turned around, went back and picked up the other two Marines then drove on to Norton Manor. Showing their identity cards to the main gate guards (pongos,) they easily got on to the camp with their new car and took a look around. At the bottom end of the camp, they found an athletic track. The track was old and the surface made of cinders. Using the car as if it was in a stock car race, they thrashed it around, churning the track to bits and also the surrounding grass where they had spun off. I believe they abandoned the car, or what was left of it, at Norton Manor, then ordered a taxi to take them to Taunton railway station to catch a train back to Plymouth before they were apprehended by the provost on camp.

I recently went on a family holiday down to Cornwall, stopping off in Plymouth for a few days, staying in a hotel on the Barbican, near to the National Aquarium. For purely sentimental reasons and a little bit of curiosity, I took a drive to see Seaton Barracks. I drove on the dual carriageway, out of the city, passed the camp on the other side of the road. I did a 360 degree turn at a roundabout and approached the camp on the same side of the road where the main gate used to be, on my left. There was no main gate just a slip road into an industrial park. Every building that had once stood on the site had been knocked down and replaced by business units. All had gone, even the relatively new swimming pool that had been situated to the rear of the camp and was used by civilians when not required by the Military. The only thing still visible of the original camp was part of the tarmacked MT carpark. This was where I had, on many occasions, stood on parade during inspections for spearhead and just before leaving on Operation Corporate in 1982. I wondered what had happened to the statue that stood on the camp and how was this allowed to be done to such a historic site: weren't the buildings listed? To add to my astonishment there was no brass plate or mounted blue plaques commemorating the site and military units that had been based there, absolutely nothing. It felt like a piece of my history, along with the buildings, had been demolished. This had happened without my, or any other previous Royal Marines that had been based there, consultation or permission. I left the site with a heavy heart, some pleasant memories, and a sentiment that nothing lasts forever. I took a drive down a nearby cul de sac and found that the old officers married quarters were still standing and inhabited, now by civilians.

Drafted.

40 Commando RM were informed by the new C.O. Lt Col Donkin, that they were going to be living up to their nick name of the 'Sunshine Unit 'by going on an exercise in the Mediterranean. The trip involved a ten-week deployment on HMS Hermes, taking part in a NATO exercise and visiting countries from the east to the western side of the sea, calling in at some ports for runs ashore. Unfortunately, just before the Unit left, I was drafted. I was gutted but fortuitously I was to stay in Plymouth. My new home was to be at Stone House Barracks, sometimes called the spiritual home of the Royal Marines. Located near Union street, for the single Marine, it was a great place to be based for runs ashore. My place of work was to be at Hamoaze House, Devonport, HQ for the Major General, Royal Marines about a mile away from Stonehouse. I was accompanied by another Royal Marine from Charlie Company too, Tony Brown, so it made the move a little easier.

As for the work, well it was a pen pusher's dream but not for me. I worked from 09.00 to 17.00, with an hour for lunch, I might as well have been a civvy. Dressed in half Lovats, my task was fetching and replacing confidential files from folders, as requested by officers wishing to read them. Apart from Tony and me there was another Marine working at Hamoaze House. He had been there for nearly two years, was married with two children and had been permanently medically downgraded. It was an ideal situation for him. Every other weekend I had to stay on site acting as security and, like the day work, it was as boring as spending one year in quarantine. During the day I would put files and paperwork back under the wrong titles on purpose to make out that I was useless at the job and hopefully they would move me on. My ploy never worked, they were all too nice. One day, still drunk from the previous night's run ashore, I used a little bit of 'Dutch Courage' to ask for a chat with the Major who was responsible for me. He invited me into his office, and I told him calmly that I hadn't joined the Royal Marines to do administration and frankly that if he didn't send me back to a Commando Unit, I would do something stupid (what exactly this thing was and how stupid it was going to be, I didn't know myself).

Within a week I was drafted back to 40 Commando RM, now based in Taunton.. I couldn't pack my kit quick enough. I sent most of my possessions in a box to be transported within the next few days by MT to Norton Manor camp, but I still had a large bergen to carry on the train. On the day of my draft I cycled in the dark from Stonehouse to Plymouth Railway Station at 05.30. Because of the combined weight of me and my bergen on the bike, the bloody chain snaped about half a mile from the station. Then it started to rain, it just had to. Anyway, to compensate this early morning misery, deep down, I was as happy as one of Snow White's Dwarfs at a mini skirt convention, simply because I was going back to be with my oppo's.

7. BACK (HOME) TO 40 COMMANDO R.M.

I was going back to 40 Commando, to normality, but in reality, well, at first, my happiness was misplaced. Only a few guys I knew from the past were left on the rear guard while the rest of the unit were still on their Mediterranean Exercise. This rear party grew in size as Marines were drafted in, a majority straight out of training from CTCRM. The then rear guard CSM treated us all like Nods. He had us parading at any time of day, doing guard duties, fatigues and inspections of accommodation, nearly every other day.

On one Monday morning during rear party, the CSM had us on parade and wanted to know who had trashed his office sometime over the weekend. Most of the windows and nearly all of his furniture had been destroyed beyond repair. Unsurprisingly no one admitted to doing it but everyone was laughing behind his back and offering to buy the offender a wet on the next run ashore.

This whole episode of being on rear party was not what it should be like in a fighting Company. The lads straight out of training didn't know any different. Like in training, it was normal to them and they carried on like rats following the pied piper, completing every task set them by the CSM. As I had been in the unit before, predictably, but relentlessly, the new lads asked me what it would be like when the unit returns. I would reply 'Nothing like this load of bollocks!'.

After what seemed an eternity, in late November 1983, when the main unit actually return back to their new Camp, Norton Manor, I was told that I was going to be in HQ and not Charlie Company. Luckily at the time I knew someone in the records office and he suggested if I could get somebody to swap Companies, it would be fine. So, I did. I was going to be back in Charlie Company!

I was about to march into the office of Charlie Company's Sergeant Major to find out what troop I was going to be allocated to, when my old sergeant, Ginge Devenish, saw me. Ginge followed me into the office, told the CSM that he wanted me back in his troop. So there you have it. I was back for at least another eighteen months with my beloved 9 Troop, and yes, I did have a charmed life! It was great to be with all of the lads. I moved all my kit into a ten-man grot with my oppos. I was back home!

As I have previously mentioned, the site had the appearance of a typical Second World War camp. Most of the buildings at Norton

Manor were constructed out of wood, with asphalt roofs. The accommodation for the general ranks was located in blocks called 'Spiders'. In the centre of a spider block were the ablutions and off these were three legs or ten-man grots, each side, all six interlinked by interior corridors. Each Spider held almost a whole company of men (approximately 80 plus). These buildings had apparently been identified as unsuitable for human habitation, by who I do not know, but we didn't care. The floors in the grots had been recently carpeted and the showers were hot and close by. 9 Troop were allowed some freedom to re arrange the furniture as we liked. I had two lockers and two bedside cabinets; you were only supposed to have one of each. I made a man cave. It was almost like living in my own personal flat. By now we had the luxury of being able to use continental quilts (bought out of your own money) on our beds instead of the itchy issued blankets. In my grot we made a lounge area, rented a TV and video player from a local shop in Taunton and watched endless films. Our Spider was right next to the Galley and close to the Camps' perimeter fence. Outside the perimeter fence there was a small woodland that we used for honing our hunting and shooting skills. The fence was in a poor condition and it was easy to climb over or break through should we wish too. In the past it was obvious that camp security had not been a priority.

Chris Pretty was the first to purchase an air rifle and soon several others followed suit, including myself. I bought myself a second hand 22 with telescopic sights fitted. Chris soon got into the swing of things and returned every day from the small woodland with a kill. The population of birds must have decreased considerably.

One day I went out on a 'patrol' with Chris. We put on our camouflage jackets, climbed the camp perimeter fence and spent some time wandering through the woods. We covered quite a distance from our grot, the sun was starting to fade when suddenly I spotted a man, dressed in a Barbour jacket and hat, leaning up against a large oak tree. Chris had seen him too. We both moved closer and saw that he had two shot guns. One was propped up on the tree by his side the other resting in his hands and several dead wood pigeons at his feet. Chris and I beat a hasty retreat. How he hadn't seen us I do not know, especially after the noise I made when I got the giggles. What was more worrying was that someone could, (even if he owned the land) with a loaded weapon, get so close to the camp undetected.

Another fun activity we did to pass the time was fish in the open water tanks, located between each spider. The tanks were sunk into the ground, rectangle shaped, measured about ten metres in length by five in width, with a concrete rimmed wall about one metre high around the outside. We could never see the bottom of the tanks because of the colour of the water, a rusty brown. I believe they were used for water storage in case of fires when the camp was originally built. It must have felt like heaven for the fish when we threw in bread. They went on a feeding frenzy rising to the top so we thought we would try and catch them with a line and hook. The fish we caught were generally small roach or sometimes perch, how they got there is a mystery, let alone survive.

We soon became bored with fishing in the conventional way. So we tried throwing in several thunder flashes weighed down with stones, held together with Pussers tape so they would sink. On detonation, the noise felt like artillery landing close by, I could even feel the ground vibrate, rising up from the depths of the water tank. I'm sure if it was measured on the Richter Scale it would have had the magnitude of a small earthquake. Unbelievably no dead fish rose to the top, not even a semi-conscious one swimming in circles, possibly with concussion or at least a headache. I concluded that either these fish were very hardy, had the blessing of Poseidon or the water tank reached to the depths of hell where they hid.

Carl Bushby our Troop officer during the Falklands War and South Armagh tour, left 9 Troop and was replaced by Lieutenant Eddie Musto in November 1983. Several decades later at a reunion, Eddie Musto told me how he had looked at the troop's individual personal reports (Form R. 141 for those of you that are paperwork geeks) before, during and after the Falklands War and thought my god, what the hell am I letting myself in for! Eddie was in his second year of training, still on probation and this was his first command as a troop officer. Also, he was a little apprehensive, if not intimidated, meeting 9 Troop for the first time because we had had the experience of actually going to war and he hadn't.

It was around this time I heard that a new member had joined the Corps at CTCRM, Prince Edward. He didn't last long, unlike Eddie Musto who had a distinguished career in the Royal Marines.

Captain K. L. De Val, Charlie Company's new Commander joined us too on 10th January 1984. Not long after 9 Troop were out on exercise again. Sennybridge Camp is in mid Wales, surrounded by bleak moorland, close to the village of the same name, with little other signs of human habitation for miles. Geographically it is not that far from South West England. By road simply up the M5 then across the Severn Bridge on the M4. After that the major roads end and that's when your trouble starts. If there is inclement weather, particularly snow, travelling down the winding roads is very difficult, if not impossible, let alone finding the isolated camp.

I can remember once being on Sennybridge Camp, looking out of a window from a Nissen hut and seeing the snow starting to fall and thinking, no praying, please Lord stop, I don't want to be stranded here in this hell hole. It was used as a transit camp for units like 40 Commando RM to stay at for a few nights while carrying out live firing exercises on the extensive ranges. The accommodation blocks were relics from the Second World War period if not before. Beds were bunks and mattresses stained, with gopping pillows to rest your head on and no heating. Going to the heads meant a trip out in the fresh air. I couldn't imagine what it would have been like if Sennybridge Camp were our home base. After only a few days I would be swinging off the trees through boredom. At least Norton Manor was close to Taunton where you could escape military life. There was a NAAFI on site, but it was rundown, musky and only had an old black and white TV that could just about pick-up BBC 1. During my career I was unfortunate enough to have been sent to Sennybridge Camp three times and beforehand I always had that Sunday evening blues before the working week started, a feeling of dread in my stomach.

My last ever 'appearance' at Sennybridge was with 9 Troop on a seven-day live firing exercise, early on in 1984. We did endless section, troop, and finally one Company attack. The Company offensive was launched from low down in a valley, following parallel to a ' babbling brook', then steeply ascending, with our final objective being several miles away up on a bleak hilltop. To soften the enemy, 81mm mortars were fired on to the hill, landing and exploding with great effect. When the mortars ceased, Charlie Company was ordered to advance. In 9 Troop I was the GPMG gunner, I had my number two and Chris Pretty as the gun commander. As we started to move forward, Chris immediately found a perfect position to place our gun, on top of an embankment, with foliage for camouflage and above the main Company's advance. I put live fire down on the targets ahead. There happened to be a flock of sheep right in our arcs of fire; unfortunately for the sheep very few survived. For once it wasn't raining, well at least at the start but by time we had finished it was pouring down.

As Charlie Company advanced, my gun team zig zagged forward through streams, bog and sheep droppings to new firing positions. This process happened for well over a mile, until we reached the final objective on top of a barren, windswept, hill. When the attack eventually finished, we unloaded our weapons. I then looked at myself to find my clothes were covered in mud, animal poo, sweat and I felt absolutely shattered. Although exhausted, I was exhilarated at the same time because I thought to myself that this is what I had joined up for, doing the job I was paid to do, firing shed loads of live ammunition from my trusty GPMG!

On our slow walk back down from the final objective we saw that there were a few unlucky sheep that had caught a round but were still clinging on to life. I watched as they were hastily dispatched with a 7.62 from a SLR by our compassionate, new Company Commander.

Back at the start line we were debriefed about the attack by a SNCO, who had been acting as a range safety officer and followed my gun team throughout the assault. He had nothing but praise for us. I truly did think that this is what I wanted to do for the rest of my life. In the back of my mind 'Letting rip' with the gun did take me back to the Falklands War, particularly on Sappers Hill. I knew how a well targeted GPMG can be an effective method of not only destroying the enemy's confidence and numbers, but at the same time protect my friends. When advancing, the only thoughts I had was focussing on getting to a good fire position and putting rounds down onto the target. I had no feelings, just a cold, black, numbness, I was on auto pilot, in the zone.

For two days on the 15/16th February 1984, 9 Troop had to do security at the Royal Albert Hall for the Mountbatten Festival of Music. At night we stayed in the Union Jack Club, near Waterloo Station and travelled to and fro by coach each day. Before the concert started, working in two's, we had to do security checks looking out for any threats in the Albert Hall. This meant going into every room, including the Royal Box and their rest areas behind it. Once I was bursting to use the loo, so I got my partner to keep a look out while I took a dump in the toilet designated for VIP's and Royalty. I just couldn't resist the temptation. At Christmas parties in discussions with others that's one of my many claims to fame!

Not only did we check rooms, but we also had the tedious job of looking under every chair in the main auditorium. While I was doing this check, Jock Hepburn was down on the main arena. Suddenly he let rip with the loudest fart I have ever heard. It echoed around the hall, vibrating through the airwaves like the sound of a trumpet. He disappeared quickly from the main arena by diving for cover down a stairwell that performers could use if they needed a quick exit or entry from the audiences' view. With the main arena now empty, the fart noise caused anyone in the vicinity that had heard it to look up towards the seating and because I was the only one up in the auditorium, assume that it was me who was the guilty offender. Awkwardly for me, at the time, the place was teeming with civilian contractors! From way below and out of sight, I could hear Jock laughing like a Hyena.

On day two, before that night's performance, all of the musical instruments were left in situ on the main stage by the Royal Marines Band. While on duty again, Jock Hepburn got hold of the two play sticks that had been placed on top of a very large bass drum and decided to give us a personal rendition, of how he thought the beat of a particular song should be played. The sticks were going up and down as if they had a life of their own. Jock looked like the mad drummer, Animal, from the Muppet Show and only stopped this onslaught to our senses because his beret slipped from his head on to the floor.

9 Troop had the final night off. We went ashore and of course headed straight for Soho. The lads couldn't resist going to see a sleazy peak show. As we entered, I saw a well-dressed man in a suit, sitting in a cubicle with the curtain half open, I shouted, 'Isn't

he an MP?'. He left immediately much to our amusement. The inside of the peepshow was poorly lit, the carpet stuck to your feet and it smelt awful. To watch a show one person at a time was supposed to enter a small cubicle with a single seat, pull a curtain behind them and put a coin in a slot for the drapes in front to open. Five of us piled in one cubicle and put a coin in the slot. In front of us, behind a smeared glass screen sat two women who were well past their sell by date. In fact, one was sitting down doing some knitting until she realised she had paying customers and suddenly threw her needles to the floor, jumped up from her chair and started to go through her dance routine dressed in only her bra and knickers. Her colleague noticed that there was a crowd of us in the cubicle and shouted 'Oi, only one at a fucking time'. We left, not because she told us to, but simply because the pair of them offered absolutely no sexual pleasure to the eye, and so we told them so as we walked off laughing.

Back to Norton Manor and it was not long before there were the inevitable arrests of the odd drunken Marine in Taunton by the Avon and Somerset Constabulary. The first, within a few weeks of the Unit arriving in town, was on a Saturday afternoon. The drunk offender was caught, riding (or at least trying to) a stolen motorbike, with no helmet, through the River Tone, close by the Town Bridge in the centre of Taunton.

However, the most memorable arrest was in 1985 and it was even reported in the national broad sheets. This time it was by a Marine friend of mine, who never drunk alcohol because he was a dedicated body builder and monitored his nutritional intake. He wasn't tall but he was very muscular. His arms were the size of my upper legs. He never got over excited but laughed a lot and had a notable Northern Irish accent. The new film Rambo II had just been released and to promote the picture there was a large mock-up of a helicopter mounted on the cinema roof in Taunton. My Irish friend scaled the cinema building, removed the helicopter. With his accomplices, who, unlike him, were drunk, took it for a pretend flight down the main road, mimicking airborne attacks on the local inhabitants, detaching it's fake armaments, throwing them at the shoppers and making bombing noises.

In early 1984 I decided to run the Taunton Marathon thinking that this would distract me from going ashore. I stayed on camp at weekends while others got drunk or went home. Often at night on my own I got bored. To help alleviate this I did some shooting with my air rifle outside and in bad weather, indoors using the full length of our grot. Sometimes I missed the target and hit the walls. This left marks from the pellets and if found by an officer during an inspection I would probably get charged, not only for the repairs. but also for firing a weapon indoors. Luckily I found that pieces of spearmint chewing gum almost matched the colour of the paint and could be moulded to fit nicely into the holes.

I did a lot of additional running training at weekends on my own or sometimes with a team of fifteen Marines from Charlie Company under the guidance of Sgt Marcantonio, a P.T.I. It all became very professional. We were given seven week programmes, had a pasta party the night before the race and even sponsorship from a sports shop in Plymouth, where I believe one lad from Charlie Company 'Blue Young' had connections. Before the Marathon I was allowed lots of freedom to train on my own while the rest of 9

Troop had to fall in and do ‘military stuff’. One morning the troop officer sent a young sprog Marine to my grot to see if I was free and ask if I could possibly attend one of his essential lectures with the rest of the troop. As I lay in my bed, my reply was ‘Tell him I’m far too busy’. The sprog stared at me in disbelieve and stuttered as he said, ‘But I can’t tell him that’. ‘Yes you fucking can’ I said back, rolled over and covered my head with my quilt; life was great!

Once 40 Commando, including me had to go to Altcar Ranges (again), shooting for a week and to pass the Annual Personal Weapons Test (APWT). I was annoyed because it interfered with my running schedule. Addicted to training, just like a junkie hooked on heroine, after one day’s shooting, at night I found myself running down a country road in the pitch black and having near misses with cars. Running was everything. I even listened to the Chariots of Fire film theme music on my Sony Walkman to go to sleep.

Distances increased over time and we finished our training with an eighteen-mile run, leaving Norton Manor Camp and for some part, going over the Quantock Hills before returning back to camp. This was probably the fittest, well at least cardiovascular wise, I had ever been in my life. Also, it was the first time that I had ever bought and used a ‘specialist’ pair of running training shoes, Hi tec Silver Shadows. I believe they were the first mass produced ones available in this country. Before I purchased these, I used to scoff at people who thought that footwear could have any effect on, or even improve your running performance. How wrong I was. Previously I had just used my old issued white plimsoles.

On the day of the marathon, Charlie Company's team finished with an average time of Just over three and a half hours. The money raised for our chosen charity was collected. To the delight of the children, some members of Charlie Company abseiled into a school, to hand over the cheque for £500 to representatives of a local children's charity called the Opportunity Group, (See, I did previously tell you that I enjoyed abseiling).

Charlie Company Marathon Team 1984, Norton Manor Camp. Sgt Marcantonio front row centre with mostache, me, back row furthest right. For this picture we were all forced to wear the sponsored shorts and shirts!

Doing the marathon meant that I had to spend some of my summer leave in Taunton. After running the marathon, I returned home and back to the drink. My cardiovascular fitness suffered greatly and I went from a racing snake to a fat knacker in the space of four weeks.

There used to be another type of 'sporting' competition, within and across troops and companies within 40 Commando RM. The aim on a run ashore was to see who could trap the ugliest 'gronk' (female). To prove that this had been achieved, evidence had to be provided in the form of a photograph of this unfortunate female, no oppo's witness statements, verbal or written, were permitted. This photograph then went on a 'gronk board' and was displayed for everyone to see. After several months the winner was decided on by either a vote by all, or an N.C.O. I heard that in a different Company, one sergeant thought it was hilarious and frequently checked the gronk board until the day he saw a picture of his wife, fully exposed.

Sometime before we left for Cyprus in June 1984, we had been joined by some new or returning Marines, that had been drafted to 40 Commando. Dave Pither returned from his stint on ship with his Ford Capri, used as the Troop's run ashore vehicle, and Joe Goff also off ship. Rod Roden had come from 45 Commando and Mike Gower from CTCRM.

One day Mike Gower had to go on a course for a few weeks and asked Rod to look after his car for him. While Gower was away, Rod used the car for his own purposes, but mainly to take the rest of 9 Troop ashore, particularly at weekends.

On return from his course Gower asked Rod for his car back. Rod replied' I haven't got it', Gower said 'why not?' Rod replied, 'I had to sell it so I could have some money to go ashore with the lads'. Mike looked at him for a second and even without asking for the money back said 'Oh, okay' and walked off. For me this typified the closeness we had in our troop at the time. In 9 Troop we were so tight that we didn't care about tangible things, possessions and money didn't matter, what did count was our 'oppos' comradeship.

Our JNCO's, people like Glen Thompson, Ken Whitefield and George Bates were all part of our team. A far cry from when I was in training and had first arrived at 40 Commando. I can quite honestly say I felt like part of a family and since then I have never been so close to others as these Marines. One time I never went back home to Ipswich for just over a year, I felt I didn't have to. My new life was soundly grounded here in 9 Troop. Some lads had been fortunate, like me, and had served together in the Falklands and NI, and soon another tour, to Cyprus, which would only help to bring us even closer.

As I have already stated there is a saying in the Corps, 'Once a Marine, always a Marine' (OARMAARM). When you take off your uniform and go home you still continue to be a Royal Marine. It's not just a job, it's a way of life. After leaving the Royal Marines you are still classed as part of the family, you still feel this bond, a closeness that I have never experienced in any other organisations or sports teams. Until my death song, I will be very happy and proud to say that I belong to this unique group of people.

My runs ashore at weekends in Taunton were probably some of

the finest and outrageous that I ever had in the UK. Taunton is a relatively small place with a population of only 60,000, but not too far off the beaten track and stuck in time, that they still put on trial and burn witches. Taunton has a very homely feel, I really did like the town centre, the surrounding countryside, and its people. When I now visit, I still get that warm feeling of being in a comfortable and friendly environment, for me it's like returning home.

There were quite a few pubs in Taunton town centre in the 1980's in which we used to go to for a drink, but the one we called our own, was named 'The Light Bob'. The Light Bob was situated on the pedestrian section of the high street. It had two bars, one was on the ground floor, a couple of steps up from the front door. Hardly anyone used it except if there was a massive queue at the bar downstairs and they didn't have the patience to wait. The downstairs bar was where we lived, loved and some could say, survived. I only ever saw Marines in there, the few civilians were all females, wives, girlfriends of Marines, and brave, stupid or a combination of both, groups of young ladies. The landlord was very clever, he employed Marines to serve behind the bar at weekends to help prevent any friction that could arise with civilian staff. Also, the Marines working would be used to our behaviour and could deal with anyone getting out of hand.

9 Troop went through a phase of drinking cans of Foster's lager and stacking the empty cans on the bar or table, some reaching a considerable height before being taken down with a karate chop or kick. Why Fosters and stacking? Well it was Chris Pretty that started both off. I believe it was because he had an inclination to visit Australia one day in the future and drinking their Fosters beer

gave him a 'taste' for the continent. Secondly, he liked to build things up then smash them down.

One run ashore, memorable for its ridiculous consumption of alcohol, started on a Saturday by knocking back shorts with Rod Roden, Bob Harper and Andy Langdale (aka Burger). It was lunch time and we decided to leave the Light Bob and go elsewhere. We ended up it in the Turks Head Pub, on St James' Street, near the River Tone in Taunton. In there we met a couple of lads, (civilians), who wanted to buy us drinks. We ordered vodka's and all together 'sank' them in one, alongside pints of lager. The drinks just kept on coming at no financial expense to ourselves. At 14.30 we staggered out of the pub. I could hardly see, let alone walk straight. We decided to get some scran and set off in a drunken haze. I had never before consumed that amount of alcohol in a lunch time session. Rod, Burger, Bob and I made it to a fish and chip take away near the railway station. Rod ordered first, got his scran and wandered off outside. Burger, Bob and I got our scran and walked outside to see where Rod was. At first, we couldn't find him anywhere. After several minutes and yards of staggering by the three of us we saw Rod, in broad daylight, lying in the gutter of the busy Station Road, unconscious, face down in his takeaway. Rod was truly legless. We never made it back to the Light Bob nor the night time drinking session. I don't even know how the four of us got back to camp. I only remember waking up on Sunday morning with a tremendous headache, oh, and a bag of chips for a pillow!

The Winchester Arms in Taunton was another pub that we frequently used but sometimes due to its clientele appeared a little too posh for our liking. Once again 9 Troop had another toga run ashore. Still drunk from our lunch time drinking session, we arrived outside the Winchester. Because the landlord had not opened its doors promptly at 17.00, Chris Pretty and George Bates, both JNCO's, in their togas, picked up a nearby bench and started to ram the wooden front door of the pub in an attempt to smash it down or before this happened, encourage those inside to open up. It could have looked like a scene from the breaking of the Roman siege on Jerusalem. Only, the pub had what looked like fake medieval turrets, was situated next to Taunton's Norman Castle, lit up with electric lights and of course the lads were wearing brightly coloured underpants and issued boots! In the end the ramming and swearing only achieved a bollocking from the landlord, (who afterwards, surprisingly, still let us in), and wooden splinters in the hands from the battering ram.

In pubs, the one song I can remember 9 Troop constantly playing on the music video juke box screens, (these video juke boxes where a new phenomenon in the early 1980's) was Chaka Khan's single ' I feel for you'. The part of the song where the vocal goes 'Ch-ch-ch-chaka-chaka-chaka Khan', was adapted by Marines and sung very loudly with, Ch-ch-ch-**chukka-chukka-chukka boots!** Chukka boots was a reference to the suede desert boots worn on military ships and more commonly, for runs ashore by Royal Marines. In the 1980's, like most Royal Marines of my age, I had cropped hair, wore Chukka boots and jeans. When at home on leave in Ipswich, much to my annoyance, I was frequently accused of being a skinhead!

Before returning back to camp, after nearly every run ashore I habitually had to go to the Taunton Kentucky Fried Chicken (KFC) to get some scran because the Duchy's at Norton Manor closed down a year or so after our arrival. I loved to eat the KFC spareribs that were covered in a delicious red spicy sauce, served with chips, sweet corn and coleslaw. I would return back to camp in a taxi and devour most of it in my grot while sitting on my pit. However, I frequently woke the next day not just with a hideous hangover, but also with half the contents of my takeaway in my bed. It looked like I had had an erotic night with my spareribs. Half chewed bones were everywhere, even in the far end of my bed, next to my feet. The white sheets were covered in mayonnaise from the coleslaw, grease from the butter spread on the sweet corn and chips, but the nightmare was the red spicey sauce from the spareribs; it was hell to remove in the wash.

8. UNITED NATIONS TOUR OF CYPRUS.

Early in June 1984, Charlie Company left Norton Manor Camp and travelled by coach to Brize Norton. From there we boarded a RAF TriStar plane and approximately four and a half hours later we landed at RAF Akrotiri, in Cyprus.

40 Commando were the first Royal Marines unit to be back on the island as a cohort since 1979. For the first three months of the tour, Charlie Company were on duty on the Green Line, as were Alpha Company who were to the west of us, based in the 'Box Factory'. The Green Line is a United Nations Buffer Zone between Greek and Turkish Forces. In 1974 there was a Turkish invasion of Cyprus, and after some serious heavy fighting, a cease-fire was declared. The result has left Cyprus being split in two. The Turkish Republic of Northern Cyprus in the North and the

Greeks in the South. There has been a stalemate since and tensions on both sides are still high.

As part of the British Contingent (BritCon), for the United Nations Peacekeeping Force in Cyprus (UNFICYP) our job was to patrol, man OP's, record and report any infringements carried out by either of the two sides.

From Akrotiri Airport Charlie Company went straight to sector two, on the Green Line. While there for three months we had to wear light blue berets to show that we were UN troops. It seemed odd seeing the lads in 9 Troop not putting on their famous green commando ones. The funny thing was we were given these new light blue berets straight out of their boxes as soon as we arrived on the Green Line therefore, no time to shape them. We had no choice but to plonk them on our heads and set off looking like Nods, or boy scouts; unstylish and very unprofessional. Charlie Company's CSM was the brunt of sniggers and jokes. His beret, which was far too large for him, looked like a toque (chefs' hat) that had been plonked on his head, it flopped around as he moved and it was dubbed the 'aircraft carrier'.

Next Page; Charlie Company, 40 Commando Royal Marines UN Tour 1984.

Charlie Company's base on the Green Line was named Bravo 18 (B18) and located on the outskirts of Nicosia. B18 had once been a primary school, later it was modified to house troops. Some of the walls still had bullet marks, left from the fighting in 1974. It was located only a few hundred metres between the Turkish and Greek lines. Most of my time was spent in a continuous four-hour cycle; four hours on an OP, four hours on standby, another four on rest, then repeat.

From B18 we were taken by Land Rover, along a single dirt track that divided the two opposing lines, to OP's Bravo 19, 20 and 40. While hurtling along the dirt tracks to your location or heading back to B18, if the air vents on the Land Rover weren't closed and you were sitting in the front you would get covered in an orange coloured, sandy dust. It was even worse if you were driving behind another vehicle. This was a nightmare if you were going out on duty because it meant spending the next four hours picking pieces of sand out of your hair, clothing, weapon and equipment. Those that were returning back to B18 in the Land Rovers and unfortunate enough to get blasted by the sand, could be seen walking back to their grots, coughing and wheezing with only the whites of their eyes visible and snot pouring down from their noses.

One time I was part of a section of Marines that had to escort some Armenians to a cemetery stuck in the middle of the Green Line, so they could visit, tidy up and lay flowers at their relative's graves. It was quite a sombre event seeing these people having to get permission and an escort to see their beloved ones. However, this was not the only cemetery I went to in the Green Zone. There was one maintained by the Commonwealth War Graves Commission and in it were buried several Royal Marines who had died fighting on active service, during the four-year Cyprus Emergency from 1955 to April 1959.

The temperatures in the central plain of Cyprus, where Charlie Company were based, are the hottest on the Island and we were there during the peak of summer. While on duty in the OP's, local Greek farmers, I guess feeling sorry for us, in a kind act would bring us large watermelons to help try and keep us cool. These were very refreshing and made a pleasant change from the plastic tasting and warm, if not hot, water from our issued black bottles worn on our webbing. During our four-hour stint on the OP's, we were not allowed to eat so there was the issue of removing the evidence of the watermelons in case an officer came to inspect the site. Seeds were undigestible therefore they had to be spat out and collected along with the skins. The juices were very sticky and because there was no supply of water to wash our hands with, rather than waste our water bottle reserve, our hands remained covered in a pasty, clear fluid for the rest of the stint.

The difference between the Greek and Turkish armed forces on the ground was quite defined. The Greeks, only a few metres to our south and like us based mainly on roof top buildings, were totally relaxed and carefree to say the least. They had their shirts unbuttoned or off, weapons on the floor, berets used to keep the sun off their faces and they blasted out the latest hits from portable radios.

We, as UN peacekeepers had to keep a slightly more professional approach than the Greeks. To the North of us, the Turks. Their soldiers were out in the open, barren, mainly flat, abandoned fields, catching the full blast of the sun's rays and heat, with some of them having no or very little shade to take cover under. They stood behind man made earth embankments, almost to attention, with their rifles slung across their chests, hands on or near the trigger and never removed any clothing or head gear. The Turkish soldiers occasionally walked up and down their line to stop the boredom and stretch their legs but most of the time they just stood still, staring towards us and the Greeks. The Greeks would always shout to us in English and make jokes. In stark contrast to the Greeks, there was not a murmur from the Turkish side, their discipline was strict.

I had to learn by rote, a briefing that was to be given to any officer visiting our OP's. As part of my verbal brief, I was to ask the officer if he would like to look through a very large set of binoculars, mounted on a tripod stand. This was so he could identify objects, especially up in the distant Kyrenia mountains. I used to get the giggles because I imagined that I had pointed the binoculars directly at the hot Mediterranean midday sun. The officer visiting and listening to my brief would take a look through the eye pieces of the binoculars, and from where I was standing behind him, I would see smoke rising from the top of his head as the magnified rays burnt holes were his eyes used to be!. Sadistic, yes, but it felt like it should have been in a sketch from the sitcom 'It ain't half hot mum'.

For most Marines, a consequence of being on duty in the OP's for long periods of time was boredom. In each position there was a logbook where any military activity, especially by the Turkish or Greek Forces would be written down as an official record. Marine Mike Gower took this order to the extreme during his moments of monotony in B20. During one four-hour stint he included everything he observed and did, from picking his nose, swatting a mosquito then smearing the squashed insect on a page in the logbook as evidence and seeing a Turkish soldier urinate. A week later Charlie Company's Commander ordered to see Gower in his office because he had received a slap on the wrist by the UN hierarchy. Every logbook was sent to the UN HQ and looked at for any useful information. When they came across Gower's accounts they were not very happy, nor was our Captain.

The most ridiculous thing that we had to do while on duty was present arms whenever a vehicle or helicopter passed by our OP. This was because under UN Standard Operational Procedures, (SOP's) it states; 'Pay compliments to all vehicles and aircraft which approach your position…' We had to practice this manoeuvre on Norton Manor Camp's drill square before we left England. 9 Troop was standing in a square facing inwards. One by one each Marine was asked to present arms to the SNCO taking the drill. Jock Hepburn, facing directly opposite me came out with the famous Dads Army quote 'They don't like it up em,' as he raised his rifle in the air as part of his demonstration. I got the giggles and by the time the SNCO came to me I was so weakened by laughter I could hardly lift my SLR up, let alone carry out the drill. To make it worse, over the Sergeants shoulder I could see Jock laughing at me. Tears were rolling down my face, I had no control over my body, and I started to shake as I tried to hold it in but failed miserably. The SNCO, who stood in front of me even let a little snigger out, then gave up, took a sidestep and went on to the next Marine. It was like one of those childish situations when you start to get the giggles and just can't stop whatever someone says or does..

In between time on duty I would go and train in a makeshift gym in the basement of B18 or go for runs along the dirt track on the Green Line. We were only allowed to go out and do these runs if we wore UN vests and went in pairs. Due to the afternoon heat while running, we would sometimes remove the vests in an attempt to keep cool, but we always maintained a careful eye in case any white painted UN vehicles carrying officers was travelling along the track towards us. Once I was out running with Rod and Gower along the Green Line, when our Company Commander Captain approached in a Land Rover, driven by one of our fellow Marines. Rod and I were wearing vests but Gower was topless. The Land Rover caught up to us, stopped and Gower was told by the captain to put his vest back on. Gower received a bollocking and then the captain told his driver to continue. As the Land Rover drove off in the distance, Gower said 'Sod this' and took his vest off again. Unfortunately the officer was looking in the rear-view mirror of the Land Rover and saw Gower. He shouted to the driver, our fellow Marine, 'I'll not have insolence in my Company', ordered the vehicle to be turned around and came back to confront Gower. When he reached us, he went ballistic at Gower, but the funny thing was the Captain couldn't pronounce his R's very well, so every time he said Gower, it came out as 'Gowew' making us double up with laughter. It was a bit like the scene from the Monty Pythons film The Life of Brian when the Roman nobleman, Biggus Dickus, also unable to pronounce his R's addresses a crowd. If you are unfamiliar with this scene, where have you been???? and secondly, I suggest you go and watch it on YouTube!

One other telling off by an officer, that is vivid in my memory, was when Gower was caught phoning his girlfriend back in the UK without permission. Someone had discovered that if you used the phone in the Captains' Office at B18, you could get a direct line to the UK anonymously and for no financial cost to anyone except the UN. When all the officers were off site, Marines would sneak into the Captain's office and make calls back home. One day Gower took advantage of these free calls and was in the office, talking to his girlfriend back in Taunton. Gower had his shirt unbuttoned, trousers belt off, was sitting on a chair and had his feet on the company commanders' desk. No one had warned him that the Officers had returned back to B18. When the Captain opened the door to his office, he saw Gower and said 'Oh, sowwy Gowew for the intrusion'. He went to turn around and leave Gower in peace to carry on with his call, but instead suddenly stopped to think about it for a moment and said, ' Hang on a minute Gowew, I'm not bloody sowwy, what the hell do you think yo'we doing'? I could hear the severe reprimand going on from where I stood on duty above the office.

While on the Green Line and with time off, we were occasionally taken by four tonners about twenty minutes ride away from B18 to a swimming pool. All UN contingents could use this facility. Using the pool were groups of military personnel from different nations e.g. Danish Contingent (DanCon), Finland (FinCon) and Sweden (SwedCon) as well as British (BritCon). The factions from Scandinavia had women serving with them, and often they could be found sunbathing by the pool wearing bikini's, which was an added incentive to go there. The water serving as a method to cool off from the heat of the sun and the sight of such beauties!

Several times while at the pool we happened to see and speak to Brigadier Duchesne, the Commander of BritCon who, for some reason enjoyed our company, possibly because of the antics we got up to. The swimming pool was normally packed with serving people. Some of the British Army and RAF personnel had two year drafts to Cyprus accompanied by their families for their whole deployment and were regular visitors to the pool. The swimming pool measured twenty-five metres in length, approximately four lanes in width and a deep end with a diving board. One Marine had represented GB in trampolining. He was showing off doing various dives (that I could only dream of carrying out), from the diving board into the deep end. After one spectacular demonstration of a dive, which included a forwards somersault, he went to get out of the pool. Not using the steps, he lifted himself up with both arms onto the side and was facing outwards. In this vulnerable position, two Marines behind him pulled his swimming trunks off with some ease, leaving him naked. They wouldn't return his costume, in fact they hung it off the top edge of the diving board like a piece of laundry drying in the wind. To hide his embarrassment from everyone watching, he lowered himself back into the water and swam the breaststroke up and down the pool for half an hour. All you could see was a bare white bottom bobbing up and down the pool, before someone took pity and gave him his trunks back.

B18. Our grot in the old School on the Green Line. Mark 'Rod' Roden and me.

Ayia Napa.

After a month of monotonous OP duties on the Green Line, my section of 9 Troop was given a two day leave period and headed down to Ayia Napa in the south east of the Island. It was like being on an 18-30's holiday. To save money, one Marine booked and paid for a single room in a hotel or bed and breakfast and we all used it as a base, to wash, shower and sleep even if it was on the floor. We spent most of the day on the beach, swimming and sun-bathing and then went into the centre at night to drink. Unlike now, in 1984 there were only a few bars and two or three night clubs in

Ayia Napa. However, the atmosphere then was just as lively as it is now. It was a great place to let my hair down; alcohol, music and girls, heaven! I also had the comfort of knowing that at the end of the night there would be a fellow Marine to make sure I was safe and drag me home to 'crash out'. The next day the only thing my fellow Marines couldn't offer was a cure for the painful suffering of a hangover, that was amplified by the heat and bright sunlight of summertime in Cyprus.

Israel.

At some point, again while on the Green Line, Charlie Company were offered free flights on a Fokker plane to Jerusalem. About eight Marines, including myself, were lucky enough to go. When we arrived at our hotel in Jerusalem, Ged Herd managed to arrange for a taxi driver to take us on a tour of all the famous sites in and around the city. We also went further afield to Bethlehem, took the cable car up to Masada Fortress and had a swim in the Dead Sea which almost ended in a mud fight. Apparently, the mud there is supposed to have detoxification properties and people smear the stuff all over their bodies. We followed this ritual and threw the mud all over our bodies, but it didn't stop there. Anyone or anything close by was deemed a target and hit by mud balls. The similarity was akin to my days at primary school throwing mud around in the main hall.

At the time I believed, correctly, that you could even buy the mud in packages at cosmetic shops such as Boots. When I returned back to the UK I contemplated on a missed entrepreneurial opportunity. I had an idea of under cutting the prices for the product by current suppliers to retailers by coming up with ways of how to smuggle the mud back into the UK. I thought that by using human 'mules', who would hide the mud internally or externally, in secreted packages possibly around their waists, might just work. However, I had visions of these traffickers splitting the wraps and as the mud dried out, falling as dust onto the floor, leaking the goods and my profits. I even thought about diluting the dead sea mud by fifty percent by adding soil from my back garden. But like all good business ideas, with some tiny flaws, nothing happened!

What did surprise me while walking around was the number of young Israeli men and women in military clothing, carrying loaded weapons. They were everywhere, particularly in the Old City of Jerusalem, in such locations as the wailing wall and the Dome of the Rock. The sight of these Israeli military never unnerved me, in fact it made me feel more secure by knowing that if anything life threatening did happen there would be a swift response to the threat.

I was very pleased to visit the Church of the Holy Sepulchre and stand on the Mount of Olives. Places I had only heard of in the bible and talked about at masses and during Religious Education lessons at school. Thank the heavens above that we did these visit on the first day, because, as usual for Bootnecks, the next couple were taken up by drinking.

There were three things that I brought back from Israel: a yarmulke (a Jewish skull cap), a small, marble box and a badge. The badge was the size of a fifty pence coin, had a white background and written in black bold on it was 'Too drunk to fuck'. While we were still in Jerusalem, unknown to me and obviously to outdo me, Gower, went back to the same shop later on and purchased a similar badge. This time it displayed '**Never** too drunk to fuck'. Once back in Taunton and on runs ashore, Gower and I frequently wore the badges, much to the amusement of some women that took the time to read them. I figured that the message sent out by my badge was why Gower always trapped and I didn't!

On our way back to Cyprus, at the Airport just outside Jerusalem, while waiting in the departure lounge we were called up to a counter one at a time to have our bags searched by the Israeli military. The rest of our party sat down with nothing else to do but watch. When it was Gower's turn he went up to the counter and for some reason looked nervous. By the sound of his accent, the person in charge of the customs search had been brought up in the USA. He reached down into Gower's holdall and pulled out a plastic carrier bag. As he was opening the carrier bag the American cum Israeli asked what was in it. Gower timidly said 'Dirty washing' just as the foul smell of four days soiled washing rose up to hit the searcher's nose. As the dirty clothes almost crawled out of the bag, the custom's man turned his head away in disgust and said in a very loud voice so we could all hear, 'Get that nasty thing away from me'! The rest of us fell about laughing as Gower, looking totally embarrassed, sheepishly put his offending dirty clothes back into the carrier bag, then into his holdall and took the humiliating walk past us and other passengers, to sit back down.

Me standing by the Wailing Wall, 1984.

Back in Cyprus and on the Green Line, every two to three days a section of us from 9 Troop went to man OP B41- A. This OP was in the centre of the former International Airport. Old civilian aeroplanes, hangars and the runway could be seen from our new position, just as they had been left in 1974. B41- A was located some distance west on the Green Line from our base at B18. Because of this we stayed and slept over in accommodation nearby. For scran we drove Land Rovers to a nearby RAF mess. On entry to the RAF mess for the first time we thought we had walked into the Savoy. The mess was very spacious. There were tables with neatly pressed and folded cloths on top, cutlery laid out, pictures on the walls, carpet on most of the floor and light classical music playing. As we cautiously approached the counter, I could see a huge variety of hot food was on display. The biggest surprise was when the chef asked if there was anything special we wanted to eat and referred to us as 'Gentlemen'! The environment, food and courtesy shown was alien to what we had been used to for the last few months back at B18. To be honest we would never have expected this level of luxury at Norton Manor's galley. At the time I thought if this mess was for the lower ranks of the RAF I couldn't imagine what standards of opulence were to be seen in the officers' mess.

9 Troop at the end of our stint on the 'Green Line'.

Below ; a sketch of the base and OP's on the Green Line that were maintained by Charlie Company. Bravo 18 was our home for the first three months of the tour.

Cyprus 1984, on the Green Line, Bravo 18. This picture was taken looking north, out to the Turkish Sector, showing the close proximity of their trenches on the opposing hill.

Down 'South'.

In September 1984 Charlie Company were sent south from B18 to Dhekelia, Alexandra Barracks, located in one of the Sovereign Base Areas (SBA). With some pleasure we removed our light blue berets and replaced them with our 'green lids.. Dhekelia had its own schools, church and shops, just like a small town. Alexandra Barracks were just across from the main site. I was quite envious of the Army and RAF ranks which had been posted to Cyprus for a long stint of two years or more. They seemed to work short days, live in relative comfort, had BFBS radio and television and in their time off, which seemed to be often, they had the whole of Cyprus to explore.

In contrast, at Alexandra Barracks I shared a packed room with eight other Marines, had cold showers, no heating, and believe it or not, towards the end of our tour it started to get quite cold, especially at night. During this time my personal report states the following, ' Good conduct strip was given on 23rd March 1984, deprived 29th September 1984, then reinstated on 6th Oct 1986'. Let me explain why. During my birthday run ashore in Ayia Napa there had been a fight between Marines and locals at a night club. Four tonners were dispatched from Alexander Barracks to pick us up along with cars containing several members of the Royal Military Police (RMP). As I stood waiting on the road close to the back of a four tonner, happily ready to be driven back to camp and not paying for a taxi, a MP told me to get on the truck. So I did. However, he pushed me as I climbed up, so I immediately, jumped back down and with the help of one of my clenched fists, I 'gently' pushed the MP out of the way, knocking him to the floor. I thought to myself, no, I'm not allowing you to spoil my evening. As I went to walk off, I heard him say 'Come back here you nutter!' I turned and saw several other RMP's give chase, therefore I ran. Ten minutes later I found myself hiding in a bush by the side of a road. I thought it was all clear, hence I got up and started walking back to the centre of Ayia Napa to continue my run ashore. Suddenly I heard a screech of tyres from behind me and four RMP's jumped out of a car, one saying, 'That's him'. I was arrested and taken to the Military Hospital in Dhekelia for a medical check, before being put in a cell for the night. The next day I was released, picked up and taken by a Land Rover back to Alexander Barracks.

Several weeks later Charlie Company was fallen in for a morning briefing. At the end, the Company Commander stopped halfway through a sentence and said, 'Oh, by the way Bawnes this arrived today' (remember he couldn't pronounce his R's very well), holding a very large file, raising it in the air above his head. He then went 'volcanic' and started to spit lava in my direction, finishing with 'Happy fucking biwthday Bawnes!' The rest of the company let out a laugh.

Still in Cyprus, a month later I found myself in a military court. As I marched into the court room and halted, flanked by RMP's I saw sitting in front of me several officers/judges behind a desk. The RMP I had allegedly hit gave evidence and I could see that he was more nervous than me. The officer residing asked if I had any questions and I turned and said that I was sorry, and could he ask the RMP whether he thought that I was drunk. The question was asked, and he replied 'No'. I said to the bench, 'That's not true, I have half the company that can give evidence that I had been drinking all day'. This put some doubt in the mind of the officers regarding the truth portrayed by the RMP. The only thing I couldn't deny was my behaviour in the car on the way from Ayia Napa to the hospital. In the written report by the MP's it was recorded that 'Marine Barnes, sitting in the back of the car, placed his arms around the neck of the driver whilst pushing his knee, hard into the back of the chair. When asked to remove his knee and arms Barnes replied, 'That's not all you're going to get you bastard!'

Much to the dismay of the Pongo MP's I was only given seven days in cells and that this was to be served in Alexander Camp, not theirs, where they could have beasted me all day. I heard that my Company Commander had put in a good word for me. He later said, 'Bawnes don't expect me to do it again, you've used up all your lives'. The description of my arrest was typed up and put on Unit Weekly Orders, pinned on a notice board and read by other Marines with some amusement.

Believe it or not, on the day I was released from prison, at night I went out for a drink and ended up getting arrested again, by the same MP's. The driver of a taxi I had been in claimed we had hit him and 'done a runner'. For a change it wasn't me that was accused of committing the crime. However, the RMP's gave me a hard time and tried to get me to snitch on my fellow Marines. I just laughed at them and after a couple of hours was released with no charge.

It's funny how songs can remind me of certain places. In the 1970's I was a great fan of Queen, Dire Straits and ELO (and still am to this day). During the Punk phase I listen to the Sex Pistols, the Stranglers and then progressed on to the Specials, The Jam, and any Two-Tone music then finally New Wave. During my time in Cyprus I listened to soul, R&B, some dance and Wham. The one record that stood out for me was Ghost Busters from the film of the same title. There is a line in the song that goes '....I ain't afraid of no ghost'; I replaced it with' I ain't afraid of no MP'.

Crete.

By chance, I was due two weeks leave just after these incidents with the RMP's. So off I went with my oppos from 9 Troop to Crete. This was yet again another one of those drunken voids. I can hardly remember much about Crete except, when the bars closed, crashing out in my sleeping bag on a beach only to wake up in the morning surrounded by sunbathers and swimmers.

The one time in Crete when I managed to stay sober, Rod, Burger and myself rented trials motorbikes and went up towards Mount Ida, in the centre of the Island, then returning back along dirt tracks. It was great to feel the freedom of not wearing helmets and roaming around the island, covering distances that would have been impossible by foot and inaccessible by car or bus.

Two weeks in Crete and we had almost ran out of beer money. Rod sacrificed his Seiko Divers watch and sold it to a waiter in a bar. Sadly, but pleasing to my liver, time had run out too. Scrap-ing together enough money to hire a taxi, we went to Heraklion to catch the ferry back to Cyprus. On our arrival at the port, we were told that the ferry was cancelled and the next one wouldn't be for days due to a storm in the southern part of the Mediterranean. We decided to head north and go to Athens. Some lads immediately went to a travel agent when we arrived and booked a flight that day, directly back to Cyprus. Rod and I thought to hell with it and decided to stay in Athens and visit the Parthenon. On the first night in the city, we slept in a park, hidden under a large bush, where two people started making love until they heard Rod snor-ing. The next day we found a hostel with a spare two-person room for the equivalent of £2.20 each; we didn't want to slum it in the dormitories at 50p cheaper. Regrettably, again for my liver, Rod and I found an Ouzo tasting bar. All different types of Ouzo were on display in inverted bottles behind the bar and dispensed by optics. Why they bothered measuring the amount of Ouzo you drank I didn't understand, because as a customer you paid a flat fee and asked for (or in our case, pointed at because we couldn't speak Greek) the drink you wanted. Once empty, your glass was refilled again and again until you had had enough of that flavoured Ouzo and wanted to try another or just couldn't stand up!

Because we were a day late back from leave, I thought it was a good idea to go to the British Embassy in Athens, contact the military attaché there and inform them that we couldn't get back to Cyprus. Once we had passed all the security inside the building, Rod and I spoke to a civilian worker who said that our military unit would be informed therefore we assumed everything would be ok.

After two days of getting drunk and visiting the Parthenon (at least we achieved something positive) we went to Piraeus (Athens' Port) and got on a ferry to return back to Cyprus. Once on the ship, we settled down on the top deck in our sleeping bags. A few hours later, a large storm hit us, people were being seasick everywhere, on gangways, stairs and in the toilets. The captain had no choice but to divert and dock off Rhodes for one day, making us even later back to Cyprus. In the galley on ship very few took up the offer of free food because of the delay and their sea sickness. Rod and I ate like kings and found it funny as we watched trays of food on tabletops slide from left to right and back in time with the rocking motion of the boat as it was battered by waves.

Me doing my Steve McQueen pose on the island of Crete, 1984.

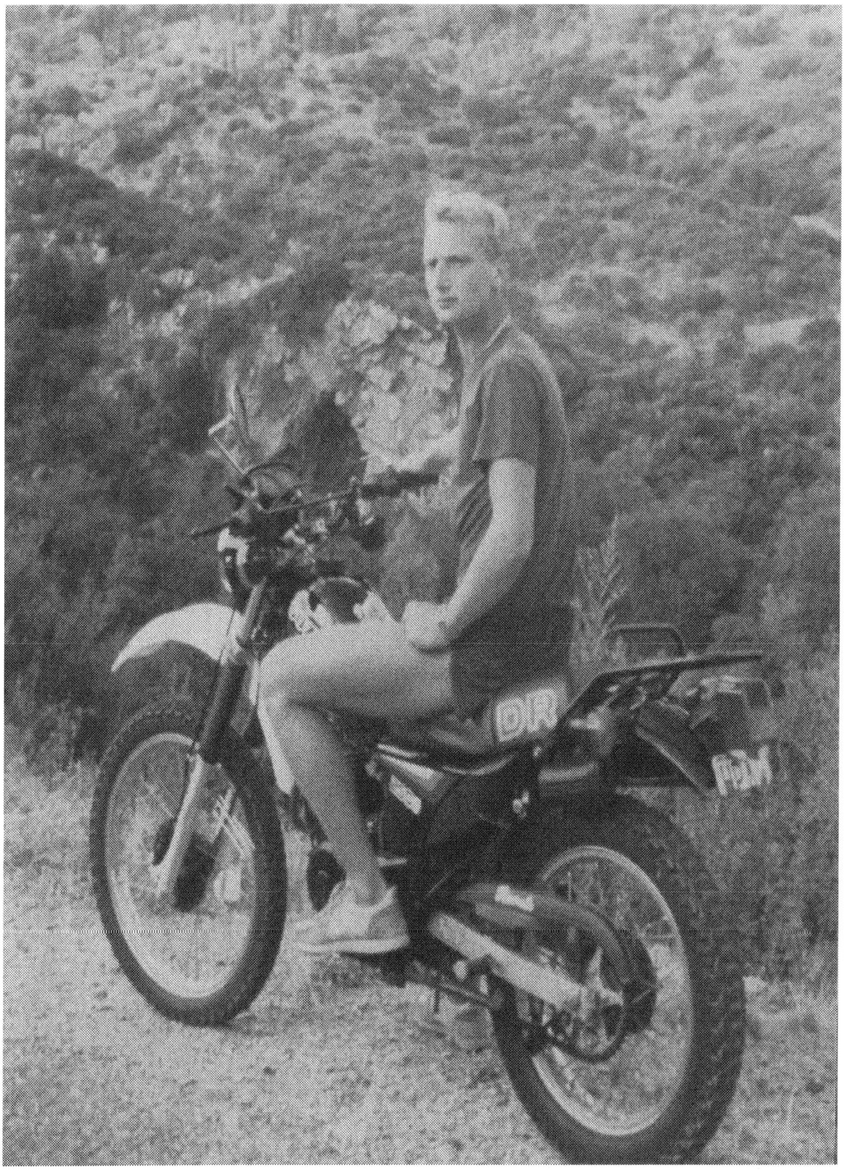

Near the Acropolis of Athens. Me with a hangover.

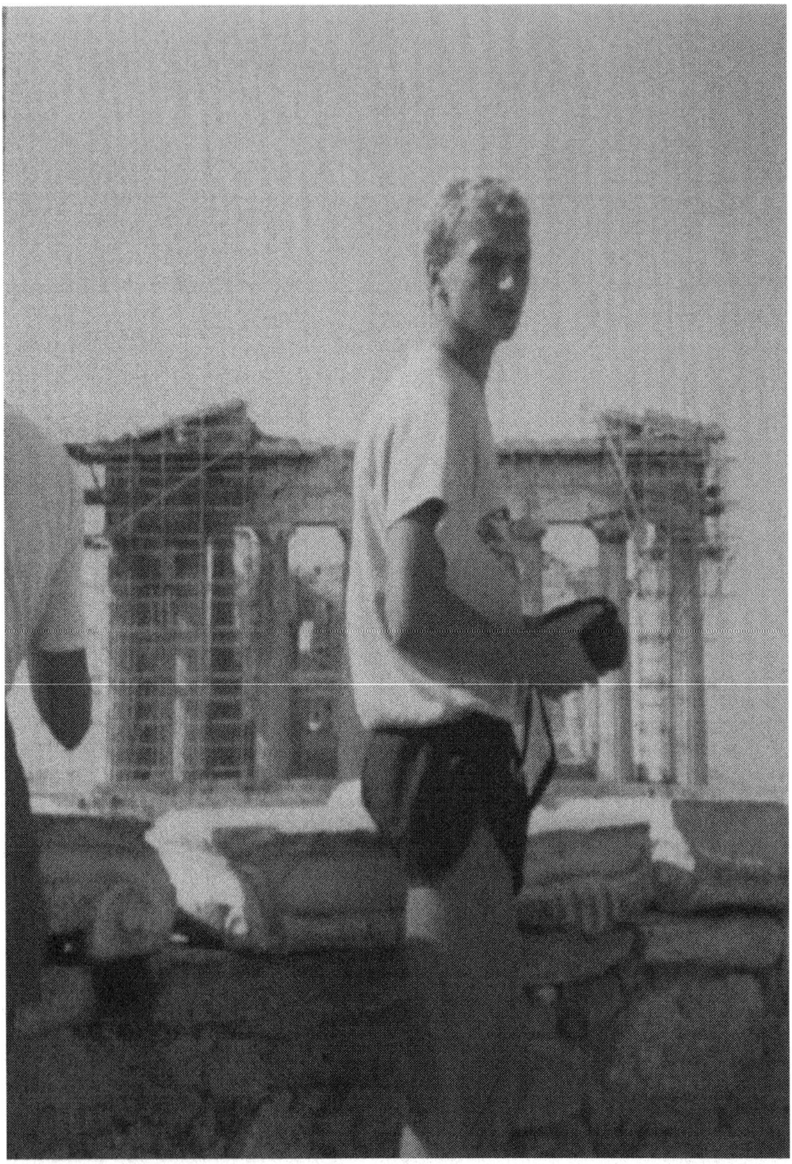

Safely Back In Cyprus.

When we eventually made it back to Alexandria Barracks, I was told that if I hadn't been on that ferry I was going to be charged with being AWOL. I thought great, that would have been another encounter with the RMP's. As I walked into my grot on the first floor of the accommodation block, I saw that the lads had packed their kit ready to go on exercise. After almost three weeks on leave and with an awesome hangover, it was the last thing I wanted to hear. Anyway, there was a reprieve, the next morning the heavens opened up and there were floods making roads impassable. We spent a couple of days just hanging around camp before loading on to coaches to take us down to the south west part of the Island.

When we arrived in the exercise area, we were expected to play the role of enemy against a whole Army Unit. During this one week exercise, 9 Troop were literally given free range on when and who we attacked. My section found a cave on a beach and used it as our base. Launching attacks as we pleased, we high jacked a Land Rover from some unsuspecting Pongos and used it as our own. The funniest assault we did was a hit and run strike in broad daylight on their HQ. We targeted their galley, which was under a large tent, at the optimum time of usage, lunch! The attack began with Andy Gaunt throwing into their galley a smoke grenade, followed by a thunder flash and then the rest of our section letting rip with everything and anything we had available to fire. Those on the receiving end had no idea what had hit them. The result was hilarious to see. Pongo's were jumping out of their skins, running around like headless chickens and spilling the contents of their mess tins over themselves and others as they tried to scramble to safety. The best thing of all was to witness officers not only being on the receiving end of our fire, but giving out conflicting orders making a chaotic situation become worse. We returned back to our cave with not only camouflage cream but also wide grins on our faces.

While staying in our cave we found an unmanned, nearby shack, located on a rocky pinnacle in the same bay. In the shack, Burger and I found a working fridge, opened the door and saw inside cans of beer. I couldn't believe my luck! Not looking a gift horse in the mouth, we proffed a few cans and returned back to the cave and shared them with the rest of the section.

Our last day on exercise was spent fighting off the Army who were on the offensive. They did attack, but with little success. During one skirmish, Andy Gaunt confronted a Scottish Guardsman who was running towards him. Andy threw the best punch I had ever seen, hitting the recipient straight in the face and dropping him to the floor like a rag doll.

There is a saying that Royal Marines Commandos should be kept locked away from civilians and only allowed out in times of war or national crisis. After some of our appalling exploits on runs ashore, this statement should have been enforced during our six months in Cyprus. The funny thing was that on our return to the UK, 40 Commando RM was awarded the Wilkinson Sword of Peace for its work during the Cyprus tour of 1984!

For our last month in Cyprus the weather had changed from hot to cold. On some nights, we looked out from our balcony on the first floor, across the sea to witness spectacular displays of lightning starting on the horizon, gradually getting near but never actually reaching us on land.

9 Troop spent the last few weeks packing our personal and Company's' kit and of course getting drunk in a nearby NAAFI. As a consequence of the early packing, we were left with very little bedding. I just had one single sheet and consequently got cold at night as the sea breeze impregnated the grot through windows which couldn't be closed. Burger was in the bed next to me and halfway through one night while he slept I stole his sheet for extra warmth. When I woke up in the morning, I saw Burger laying on his bed, in the foetal position, bloodshot eyes staring at me, suddenly realising why he had been so cold in the night and in a monotone voice muttered 'Barnes you bastard!'

During the final week, Joe Simms (RIP) would go out every night to the NAAFI and come back to the grot drunk as a skunk. Incapable of making it to the heads from his pit, he would swamp in the nearest thing, often someone's locker, and most of the time it belonged to one of the unfortunate sprogs' in the troop. Cries of 'Oh no not again' could be heard along with the sound of urine splashing into the locker and landing on its contents, then running down onto the floor, accompanied by a wicked giggle from Joe. He also had this fetish of catching insects of all different sizes and, using a needle, threading them through a piece of cotton. Joe made several insect necklaces and hung them from his locker and bed headboard, why? Joe only knew!

Cyprus had been an experience that I would never forget. I certainly captured the times that I had first perceived would happen, back when I was a teenager travelling out to Malta accompanying my brother and lads from 41 Commando RM on runs ashore. Fit, tanned, full of vitality and testosterone, Cyprus 1984 was 'the time of my life'. In 9 Troop I felt safe and part of a family; I sincerely never wanted to leave.

Travelling back to the UK, we were diverted to a civilian airport. Almost the whole company were stood around a carousel waiting for our luggage to arrive. After about half an hour of waiting, out popped one solitary suitcase and everyone was staring at it as it was carried along. No one claimed it. A Marine took the initiative, picked up the lone suitcase by the handle, read the name of the owner and shouted across to the waiting men, 'Barnes. T.V'. Some wit in the crowd immediately shouted out 'Barnes transvestite, Barnes transvestite, where are you?' I tried to make my way surreptitiously through the crowd of Marines to recover my suitcase. I was unsuccessful and much to my embarrassment and hilarity of the on watchers, I was identified.

Our Section's last exercise in Cyprus. 'Playing' enemy against the British Army.

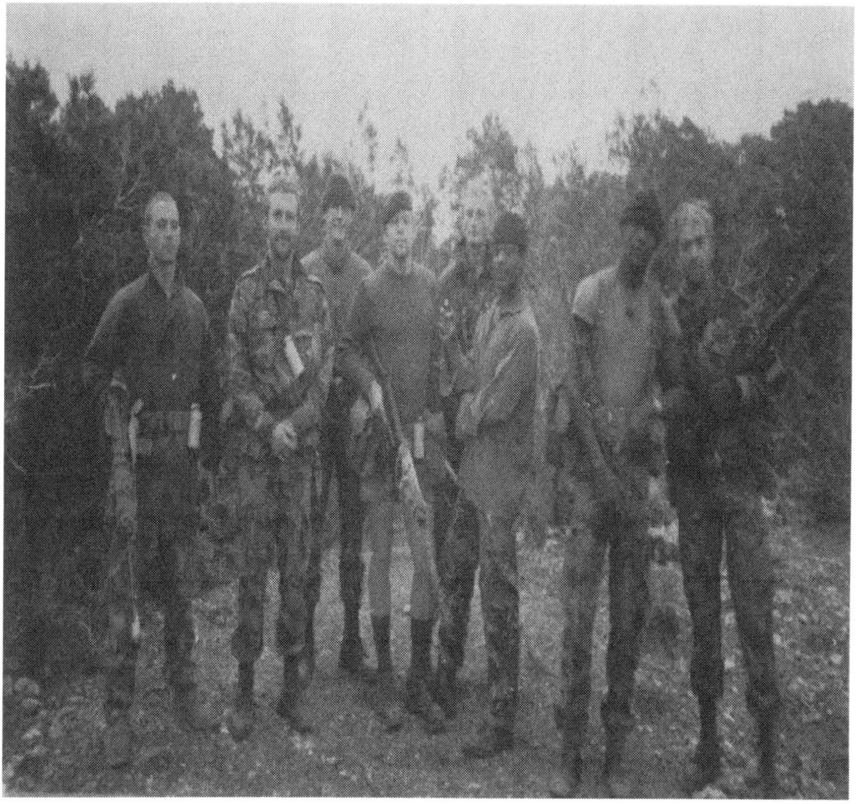

Back To The UK.

On our return to Norton Manor Camp the galley had taken on a new look. There were tablecloths, music and even a lounge area. This was the brainchild of Colour Sergeant Wickman, the head chef. Had he stolen these ideas from RAF camps in Cyprus? The similarity was uncanny. He held a Christmas competition where the most festive looking grot on camp would win a Christmas cake and guess what? We won! However if he had known what we had been up to we would have never received the cake. Little did Sgt Wickman know while still drunk after runs ashore we had been raiding his stores. Several times we broke into the galley, turned on the ovens and cooked ourselves some egg banjo's or ate any food that was left out, leaving a total mess behind.

In 1985 I unexpectedly met Sharon in Taunton for the second time in my life and at least there was some communication between us unlike previously in Plymouth. She had decided to visit her brother (remember he was also a Marine) and go out for a drink with him. It was an early Saturday afternoon and they found me sitting alone on a wall with a can of beer as my only company looking across the river Tone in the Goodland Gardens in the centre of Taunton. I had been drinking at lunch time in the Light Bob and was just hanging around waiting for the pubs to open at 17.00. Micky, my future brother-in-law, Sharon and myself went to the nearest pub, the Turks Head and had a few drinks. At the end of the night, all three of us found ourselves in Kingston's night club. Before we departed to go home, Sharon and I agreed to meet each other the next day. And guess what? Neither of us turned up! Later in the following week I managed to get her telephone number from her brother and contacted her to meet up in the future.

Rod and Burger decided to join Recce Troop and others I had known for some time were being drafted from 40 Commando to other units or sent on courses. For those of us still in the unit it was a case of doing similar exercises and returning to familiar places such as Sennybridge, Dartmoor and Salisbury Plain. It felt like time to move on from Charlie Company, so I put myself down to do a Drivers 3 (D3) MT course in Poole. On the D3 course I met up with several Marines that I had previously served or been in training with. We had most nights off and went on several runs ashore in Poole's town centre. There was one lad who on every run ashore, would trap a gronk and leave us without getting one single round in. We threatened him that if he did this one more time, we would throw all of his kit out of his grot window which was located on the first floor. He did, so we did. Yet again I found myself in trouble. The next morning the camp Adjutant saw clothing, bedding and shoes strewn across the grass outside our accommodation block and went ballistic. I ended up with restricted duties and very nearly got taken off the D3 course and RTUd.

9. BELIZE.

On completion of passing my D3's in 1985, I was drafted back to 40 Commando R.M'.s MT department only to find out that the Unit was about to go on a six-month tour to Belize, in Central America.

Because there was a shortage of men on the ground I was taken out of MT and put in a troop that had just been formed, from Marines straight out of training, again just like rear party! I couldn't believe it, I was fuming. I had lost all hope and decided enough was enough and handed my notice in to leave the Royal Marines in eighteen months' time. Also, Sharon and myself had decided to get married and I thought it was unfair for Sharon to live in Ipswich on her own.

During the tour in Belize, I was nearly killed when a Land Rover I was in, rolled. I was returning back to Airport Camp from being out on patrol, sitting in the front passenger's seat, while three other lads were in the back. The driver decided not to slow down at a T junction and tried to turn the ninety degrees in one go and at great speed, rolled the vehicle. I ended up upside down, with the front part of the vehicle slowly collapsing onto my head, petrol spilling on to me out of the fuel tank under my seat and the battery was hanging down near my face with the ignition light still on. The windscreen was splintering glass as it slowly submitted to the weight of the engine. I shouted to the stunned driver 'Get the fuck out of here!' Somehow I managed to crawl out of a tiny gap in the side window. The three lads in the back had been thrown out of the Land Rover. Unluckily for one Marine, Ivan, he ended up with a nasty break in his arm. We were miles from anywhere, but luckily another land rover was passing and took us back to camp. Poor Ivan must have suffered without having any pain killers. Driving on rough tracks at first, it took nearly two hours to get back. He had an open fracture, and I could see his ulna and radius protruding from his skin at the wrist. When we eventually got back to camp, we heard a helicopter lift off; apparently it was being sent to pick us up!

I was told later by the RMP's that the only thing that saved me from being crushed to death was my Armalite. The rifle, stored on a rack behind and in the middle of the driver and front passenger had wedged itself in, taking most of the weight of the front part of the vehicle. To be able to dislodge the Armalite by hand was impossible, so the RMP's had to tie one end of a rope to the middle of the weapon and the other end to the tow bar of a different Land Rover and drive.

Today the emotional tremors still reverberate through me every time I get into the front passenger's seat of someone else's car and they go to turn a corner.

The only things I brought back from Belize were some tools I had 'borrowed' from a drug dealers van, (but wisely not the drugs), mosquito and, their cousins in arms, sand fly, bites and a case of ring worm that blighted my skin for a long time. Unlike some other Marines I hadn't succumb to the local brothel, 'Raul's Rose Garden', who awkwardly returned home with an embarrassing STD! My lasting memory of Belize is a vision of hundreds of mosquito's dancing around a bare light bulb as I checked in my baggage for the flight back to the UK.

However all had not been bad in Belize. I was lucky enough to meet and befriend some fantastic lads, who had been thrown together and turned a bad situation to good. One Marine, Fabien Sommerville-Cotton or 'stitch' was one such character. As his double barrelled name suggests he was brought up well. Apparently, he was taken out of boarding school for poaching salmon from a nearby river and then trying to sell it. His father, who was a high ranking officer in the army, sent him off to join the Royal Marines. Whether this was to teach him a lesson or stop him from getting a criminal record I do not know; possibly a mix of the two. Stich was a step ahead of everyone else, potentially a great leader. He should have joined as an officer and I am sure if he had he would have achieved a very fruitful career in the Royal Marines.

Within a couple of weeks after my return from Central America, Sharon and I were married. Sharon and my best man, Robert had done a fantastic job of getting things ready and I did feel a little guilty. On the day, I remember walking into the church and the Marines, dressed in their 'Blues' sitting at the back, let out a barrage of friendly banter. The priest, not impressed, asked them to quieten down. What also made the day special was that my lifelong school friend, Michael Nellie, was the head chef for the sit-down reception meal. The day went well until the wedding cake collapsed. It had been made by a friend and transported down from Manchester to Ipswich with my in laws. Just after the first photographs were taken of the cutting of the cake, the cake decided enough was enough and crumpled from the top tier downwards, taking two other levels with it, leaving only the base standing in its original place. As cool as a cucumber, Michael walked out from the kitchen to see the destruction and salvaged what he could to be shared out amongst the guests.

For a prank the Marines at our wedding reception venue, decided to sabotage the bed legs, springs and almost demolish the rest of the interior fixtures and fittings of a room on the ground floor, because they thought it was the bridal suite where we would be sleeping. Unknown to the Marines, Sharon and I had been given for the night, by the hotel management, an executive room on the top floor. I have no idea what happened to the unfortunate people staying in that room on the ground floor that night, suffice to say I hope they received a full refund!

Sharon and I had just bought a house in Ipswich about half a mile from my parents. Before we went off to Paris on our honeymoon, we needed some belongings to be moved from my parents' house to ours. My parents were worried about moving some large items. Rod Roden, to the astonishment of my family, lifted our washing machine up on his back and marched off down the road, just like he had done in 1982 during the Falklands War while on 45 Commando's epic yomp.

After my wedding I was just biding my time in the Marines, waiting for the day of my release. The eighteen months since I put my chit in to leave seemed to drag on and what made it more uncomfortable was that I had to be away from Sharon on several occasions on exercises to places such as Norway and Denmark. Eventually, the day came for my release and I happily handed back my kit. As I went to return my mattress, the grumpy old civilian in the stores only comment was' It's not all a bed of roses out there you know'. For my final interview, I had to march into 40 Commando's CO's office and salute. The only thing going through my mind was that I just couldn't wait to get out. The last thing the CO said to me was a question 'Is there anything I can do to make you stay?' For a second the thought of me taking up this offer and re-joining 9 Troop crossed my mind, but no, deep down I knew it would never be the same. As I drove out of Norton Manor Camp for the last time I thought, I'd be back in a year. I never was.

Belize 1986. People asked me why I didn't come home with a suntan. The simple answer is because most of the time we were under the canopy of the jungle.

What was left of the Land Rover. Ivan Baker standing next to the collapsed vehicle.

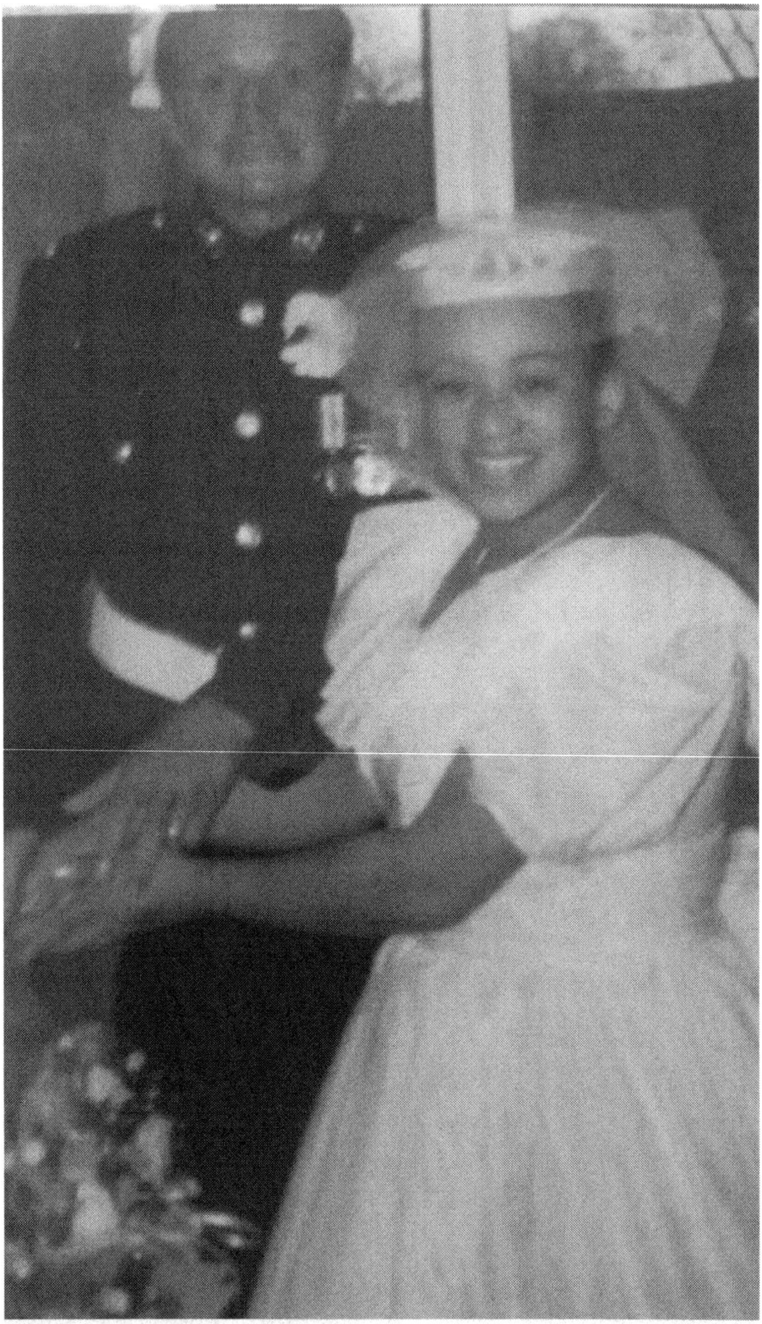

The collapsible wedding cake, tumbles off to the left!

10. BACK TO THE FALKLANDS.

For the 25th anniversary of the Falklands War I did several things to commemorate it. During the Parade at Horse Guards on June 17th, 2007, I met several old friends from 9 Troop, including Ged Herd. After the march from Horse Guards up to Buckingham Palace, all the veterans from the Royal Marines, with families and friends, went on for drinks at a reception in Lancaster House.

At another event, with my family, we were invited to St James' Palace for afternoon tea with Prince Charles and Camilla, where I also had the chance to speak to retired Major General Sir Jeremy Moore, Royal Marines.

I was privileged to be chosen to go, on the 25th Anniversary of Operation Corporate for a pilgrimage to the Falkland's. The trip was organised and sponsored by the South Atlantic

Medal Association (SAMA) and Combat Stress. On 4th November 2007 I travelled, unaccompanied by train from Ipswich to the Union Jack Club, (UJC), near Waterloo Station, London. My room on the seventeenth floor was a single for one night. I had a great view of St Pauls Cathedral and on across the City. I sat in my room feeling some excitement because of the possibility of meeting old friends and seeing the locations on the Falklands Island where I had personally been during the war in 1982. In my room I got dressed into smart trousers, polished shoes, Shirt, Corps tie, Blazer with medals and went down to the ground floor to find the bar. It was easy to locate because of the loud noise emanating from there. I had previously been sent a list of the people going but hadn't checked it through thoroughly. When entering the bar, I bumped into one veteran from 9 Troop, Ian Johnson and two others from C Charlie Company, Wayne McGregor and Max Burgess. There were a few other Royal Marines I recognised from either different Companies in 40 or 42, and 45 Commando.

Margaret Thatcher came to see us that night in the UJC bar. Even if you didn't agree with all of her political choices, it was just good to see her in the flesh, this historic figure, the 'Iron Lady' and after all, she had sent me to war. I spoke to her and asked if she wouldn't mind being in a photograph with me, she was very accommodating saying 'of course'. Thatcher was given a rapturous arrival and departure from the UJC. After the Iron Lady left, I decided to have an early night.

On the 5th November, two hundred and fifty three veterans of the Falklands War, including myself, from all of the services, boarded five coaches and headed for the airport. At Gatwick we boarded a specially commissioned A330 Airbus ready for the longest flight, so far, in my life. It was planned to take eighteen-hours, with a stop off in Rio de Janerio, just to stretch our legs. In 1982 the journey had taken over four weeks on the Canberra, stopping off at Sierra Leone and the Ascension Islands.

We couldn't leave the Airport in Rio and it was night time when our plane landed, so I didn't see a thing. It was such a shame as I would have loved to have gone to, and had a swim, at the famous Copacabana beach. On the plane, I was initially sat next to a Scots Guard. He constantly snored and apart from being deafening, it was also annoying for everyone nearby. When he was awake, he informed me that he had severe psychological problems and his carer was sitting next to him. I thought great, thanks for telling me at forty thousand feet with no escape; I immediately moved seat!

Day One.

After we landed at RAF Mount Pleasant Airport, in the Falklands and stepping off the plane in day light, I experienced the four seasons in a space of an hour; clear blue sky, misty cloud, rain and then squalls of snow flurries. The temperature was 5 °C as we landed but dropped even more after a while even though it was getting towards the summer in the southern hemisphere. The one thing that really took me back to 1982 and was currently slapping me in the face, was the constant wind. It rarely eased off in 1982 and unsurprisingly it was still the same. I had completely forgotten how out in the field, sometimes it was challenging to just do the basics of living in these conditions. Trying to put up tents was difficult. However, lighting Hexi blocks out in the open was impossible. It was so frustrating sometimes that I gave up and ate cold rations straight from the tins. In 1982, having hot food and a wet, was a great comfort psychologically. If this luxury was taken away it could quite easily affect your morale. I often had to either crawl behind a rock or make a circle of stones to try and cut the wind out. Regrettably, these places were often on uneven ground and sometimes I would knock the mess tin over, spilling the scran or wet and extinguishing the fire at the same time.

The coach driver on our journey from RAF Mount Pleasant Airport to Port Stanley, was Patrick Watts. Patrick was working at the Radio Station in Port Stanley at the time of the Falklands invasion by the Argentines and was forced, at gun point by an Argentinian soldier, to make broadcasts to the Islanders. He gave us a guided tour as we travelled along the road eastwards. As we approached the base of Mount Harriet, Patrick pointed to the right hand side of the road, on the downslope of the mountain and said 'This is where some lads were stuck in a mine field for up to seven hours'. To the astonishment of the contingent from Charlie Company, some Welsh Guards said 'Yes, we were there'. Sitting behind me, Wayne McGregor, Max Burgess, Ian (Jono) Johnson and myself shouted we were there too, leading the column, Royal Marines! Also, we made it known that one of our party had stepped on a mine and lost his foot on that dreadful night. Patrick asked, 'What unit were you from 42 or 45 Commando?' We replied no, 40! He looked surprised. The untrue story that all of 40 Commando had been left back at San Carlos in 1982 had not, and still has not been correctly reported in the history books.

On arrival at Port Stanley, I was met by Colleen Alazia, a Falklander who kindly put myself and another veteran up in her bungalow during our stay.

I found the Islanders to be very friendly at our first gathering in the evening, at the Falkland Islands Defence Force (FIDF) Hall in Port Stanley. I listened to a special message from HRH Prince of Wales that was read out.. Afterwards we had drink and food generously provided by the Falklanders. The next day during a reception at Government House, I met the then Governor, Alan Huckle, and his wife Helen. Also, attending the reception was Gary Clement, representing The Royal Marines Association (RMA). Gary was a resident in the Falklands, had served in the Royal Marines and spent a lot of time and effort organising our visit.

One person that I spoke to and to my surprise I hadn't noticed before now, even on the long flight down, was Chris Stubbing's. Chris had been in Charlie Company the same time as me. As a Colour Sergeant in 40 Commando RM's Assault Engineers he was responsible for the locating and making safe of the Argentinian mines. A job that required not only intelligence but a great deal of mental strength and yes, I'm going to use the word 'bravery'.

Feeling tired from the flight, I left the reception early on my own. As I exited, I felt the cold air hit me but for a change there was no wind, it was uniquely still. I started to walk back to my accommodation. I stopped, looked up at the clear night sky and because of the little light pollution, all of the southern hemisphere constellations were visible. I took this amazing vista in and stood there in awe, just as I had done during the landings at San Carlos back in 1982. After a few minutes I started to get cold and thought I had better head back to Colleen's bungalow. In the dark and after having had a few beers I lost my bearings. I couldn't find the bungalow as all of the buildings looked the same! I eventually stumbled through the front door about half an hour later, leaving in my wake several upset islanders I had woken up as I climbed over garden fences and set their dogs off into a barking frenzy.

Day Two.

On the morning of 7/11/07 I woke up, had breakfast left the bungalow, and then tried to orientate myself, by having a walk around Port Stanley. But first, to be sure I wasn't dreaming and definitely was in the southern hemisphere, I filled a sink and watched which way the water went down the plug hole; good it was going anticlockwise!

In 1982 Charlie Company were stopped from advancing into the Capital and spent the night of the Argentine surrender on top of Sappers Hill, the last high ground before Port

Stanley. So, strolling around Port Stanley was a new experience for me. All of the buildings, shops, post office, road signs and more importantly, the people, were a true reflection of the UK. Port Stanley and its surrounding topography could have been scooped up, taken, then dropped and fitted comfortably into the hamlets and villages of the Western Isles of Scotland.

Later on in the day I the accompanied my fellow Charlie Company veterans, Max and Wayne, in a 4x4 vehicle that was gratefully loaned by a Falklander to use as they wished for two days. We travelled through the interior of the East Island as we headed for San Carlos Settlement, the 45 miles took 2.5 hours. At San Carlos Blue Beach War Cemetery there was an act of remembrance. It was a moving event not only to see the graves, but also the names and the Corps badge on head stones of fellow Royal Marines and other service men. I wore my Green Beret and with another Royal Marine Veteran, laid wreaths of poppies at the war memorial and saluted . After the service I went for a walk to find the individual monument, located close by on a hill, for Marine Stephen Mc Andrews of 40 Commando RM.

We continued on and drove in a convoy, to the Argentine Cemetery at Fish Creek, east of the Darwin Settlement, where 236 remains are buried. Although it was an isolated location, with no buildings, it appeared stark in contrast to the brown colours of the local foliage and soil. The Cemetery was very well maintained, with an almost manicured appearance and rows of white crosses with grey granite chippings at their base and a central cenotaph. I immediately set off on my own to try and find the headstones of those that had died at Sappers Hill, but to my dismay I could not find them. I felt quite sombre as I read the inscription on some of the crosses, 'Soldado Argentino Solo Conocido Por Dios' (Argentine Soldier Known Only By God). I thought that perhaps the remains of those that died at Sappers Hill were possibly not identified and lay in one of these unmarked graves.

I spoke to some other veterans and they suggested looking for the names on the wall which formed a boarder around the top end of the Cemetery. On the walls were glass plaques with inscriptions of over 600 Argentine service men that had died in 1982. I did manage to find one of the names of the Argentine soldiers killed at Sappers Hill, but not the other two, due to the lack of time.

On the way back to Port Stanley, Max, Wayne, and I stopped off at Fitzroy where the only thing I could vaguely remember was the bridge that had been there back in 1982.

Day Three.

On the 8/11/07, Wayne, Max and myself in the same loaned Land Rover, drove from Port Stanley towards our final objective Ajax Bay, passing by San Carlos, then stopping at Wreck Point. We arrived at Wreck Point Farm and spoke to the farmer and his wife who informed us it was too difficult to get a vehicle down to Ajax Bay. So, we left the Land Rover and walked the short distance.

When we reached the Bay, we headed straight for the old refrigeration building that was still standing strong, where in 1982, the field hospital called 'The Red and Green Life Machine' was located. After reading the metal plaque on an outside wall of the building, dedicated to The Commando Logistic Regiment Royal Marines, I stepped through the main doors and had a look around the inside. It was now a cold, damp, empty and black void. A place that I had seen previously back in 1982 and to be honest I really didn't want to be in there again. It brought back memories of carrying the injured in off helicopters and seeing bodies lying on gurneys, as operations were being carried out by medical staff.

Also, I remembered the night 9 Troop slept in an outbuilding right next to a UXB, the thought made my insides twist. As I walked out of the building and made my way to the water's edge of Ajax Bay, another thing made me want not to be here. It was my first sighting of Gentoo Penguins and my god, did they stink! The smell was overpowering and as we approached them, they took on an aggressive posture. My perceptions of them being friendly, fluffy, cuddly creatures as portrayed in the animated film Penguins of Madagascar, soon evaporated. In 1982 the only ones I had seen from a distance were those on a rocky outlet near Port Stanley, as we departed from the Falklands heading home on the Canberra. At least back then they were too far away for me to smell them!

We left the buildings and made our way up on to the ridge that looks down onto Ajax Bay. Max and Wayne found their old positions, where they had dug in on the approach to the ridge line. Because I had only spent a couple of nights in this location, my memory failed me. I had some difficulty finding where I had stayed as I could only remember it being lower down the slope than Max and Wayne's' site. Disappointingly I never found it.

While walking around this area we found old empty ration tins, bivvy pegs and trenches half filled in with soil and water, just as they had been left all those years ago. As all three of us stood on the top of the ridge line above Ajax Bay and gazed down into San Carlos Waters, there was absolutely no sound, not even from the wind. The silence was almost deafening as my ear drums throbbed and my brain tried to comprehend what was happening. It was a very perplexing phenomenon to encounter. This was in stark contrast to 1982 when the noise was constant from the offloading of stores from ships to land by landing craft, helicopters buzzing around ferrying stores and personnel, both British and Argentine fighter jets, their engines screaming as they flew passed with an array of missiles and small arms fire chasing after the latter.

We got back to the Wreck Point Farmstead and were invited in to share tea and cakes with the farmer and his wife. I told them that I had really wanted to walk to the end of Wreck Point and find 33 C's old sangar but again, a lack of time let me down. Whilst I was speaking to the farmer, he assured me that the Sangar was still there (as was later proved by zooming in on Google Maps) but it was a good twelve miles away from the farm and unapproachable by vehicle. The only way was by foot or horse, as he had done several times to check the area and his livestock. I was saddened by this news and disappointed that I may never again have the opportunity to get to our Sangar.

We signed their visitors' book, said our thanks and goodbyes to the farmer and his wife and then headed straight back for Port Stanley. I got Max and Wayne to drop me off on the road, at the base of Sappers Hill just outside the capital. I spent approximately an hour on the hill trying to find the exact location of where I had taken cover in the firefight in 1982 but couldn't. I strolled around the old Argentinian positions and found a variety of old clothing, but strangely, within myself, I found no feelings or emotions. I felt nothing, only numbness, even at the positions where the Argentine soldiers had looked down on us and opened fire from and possibly died.

As dusk started to arrive, I got back onto the road and started to walk back into Stanley. Several people kindly stopped and asked if I needed a lift, but I declined. I wanted to walk on my own and try to reflect on why I didn't feel anything. I had no answer. It was a place I had never stopped thinking about in the past 25 years, but now, I felt zilch. Perhaps it was because I had nobody with me from 9 Troop that had been there in 1982 to share the experience. Was it a reflection of the reaction I had had at the time of shooting at the enemy and just a memory of the physical mechanics, with no emotions, a blackness, nothing? It took me several days to acknowledge that I was actually in the place where, as a nineteen-year-old, I had been so scared and frightened. And now, I had to confess to myself, that yes, the sights I saw and had been involved in were real. I was back here reflecting on the truth, no deflecting or hiding from the thoughts, no denial of, 'It wasn't me, it was somebody else' or seeing it as if I was watching the memories through a camera, portrayed as a film. It had been real, and I had to try to admit to what I saw and did and stop hiding from it.

For years after the war people have repeatedly asked me questions like 'what was it like down in the Falklands?' and 'How many did you kill?' I rarely answered and I used to shrug it off with a quick witty comment of anything I could think of at the time, but deep down I was angry. Angry because people didn't understand what it was like to be scared, to be in life threating situations, at such a young age, with very little experience of life.

Day Four.

On the Friday (9/11/07) again, I went with Max and Wayne in the Land Rover, this time to climb up to the top of Mount Harriet from the base. On the way up we met Jono. As we walked, we followed the exact route that some of 42 Commando RM had taken on the night of 11/12th June 1982. There were large craters, increasing in their number as we progressed up the mountain side. This was a legacy from the devastating effect of the Naval gun fire put down on the Argentine positions which I had witnessed. From a distance, we could see a large white cross placed to mark the summit. Eventually on top, and feeling out of breath, I found still lying around, spent rounds, Argentinian clothing, and shoes. Some of the shoes were plimsolls. This just proved to me how inadequately prepared the enemy soldiers must have been for the climatic conditions. I had suffered terribly as the result of poor footwear; these deprived sods were wearing plimsolls.

At the summit of Mount Harriet, the sky had cleared, there was not a cloud in sight and although cold, I could feel the sun starting to burn my face, due to the strong UV light at this latitude. We had a fantastic view, east towards Two Sisters and west, to the Falklands Sound. Jono had previously met and been given a detailed map by a Royal Engineer who had been responsible for clearing the mines on the path Charlie Company had taken in 1982, to and from Mount Harriet. This map showed the route north of a lake, which we should have taken and the actual way we went. We spent some time orientating the map and by sight, trying to pick out the route we took. I felt sorry for Wayne as he looked on, because it was twenty-five years since the explosion when he had lost his foot in a minefield below from where we now stood. All he said was in typical Bootneck fashion 'To think that bits of my foot could still be out there, I wonder where and what state it's in?'

Below the white cross at the summit, there was a brass plaque dedicated to the two Royal Marines killed, Cpl Jeremy Smith and Cpl Laurence Watts. At the base of the cross was a plastic container and inside was cleaning material used for visitors to buff up the brass. I took it out and gave the plaque a good clean. Also, there was a memorial visitors' book in a sealed waterproof bag, I took it out and wrote a few words of condolences directed to Cpl Watts' family. As I have already mentioned, Laurence Watts had taken me through training and had an influence on me as a recruit. I spent a couple of minutes remembering the last time I had seen him on the Canberra and also the advice he had given me as a seventeen-year-old nod. While we were stood on the Mount, looking west, a Hercules flew past about half a mile away at the same altitude as we were. A coincidence or a fitting tribute to those two Royal Marines who had died taking Mount Harriet, I hope the latter.

Before our drive back to Port Stanley I showed Max and Wayne the photographs I had taken during and directly after the firefight at Sappers Hill in 1982. As we approached Sappers Hill, sitting in the front passenger's seat, Wayne's keen eye managed to match up the old photograph I had shown him, with the current topography. How the hell he did this I do not know. We slowed down, pulled off the road, and stopped. All three of us got out of the Land Rover and walked up an incline to the Argentine positions. Again, just like on Mount Harriet, I found an extraordinary amount of clothing and equipment that had been abandoned by the enemy as they fled in 1982. I got into one of their trenches and looked down onto the track where I had taken cover and could not believe how lucky we had been. If 9 Troop had been in these defensive positions, we would have wiped out any infantry offensive, especially if we had been alerted by the sight of three huge enemy helicopters flying towards our trenches and having the audacity to land right in front of us! I recalled that during the firefight I could hear an Argentine 0.5 gun firing at us from our 11.00 o'clock as we lay at the base of the hill. I found the place where this gun had been positioned and it made me cringe thinking that if it had been placed a few metres to their left, they would have had a clear sight and therefore an easy target, us! We had been so fortunate that more of 9 Troop had not been shot or possibly killed. A single 0.5 round could rip a human body in two.

I had a macabre feeling that I wanted to find the exact spot where at least one of the Argentine Marines had been shot and killed. To see where he stood in the flesh and try to get an insight to his thoughts, what he had, perhaps for the last time, seen and experienced. It was possible for me to do this physically by standing as close as I could to what I thought was his final, fatal, position and see what he had possibly witnessed before he died. To attempt to get into his psychological state was a challenge. I tried, and retrospectively still do, but failed. I could only envision the sensations I had gone through: fear, panic, excitement, dread, relief, revenge and anger. Did this Argentine soldier encounter and wrestle with these same emotions? It seemed inconceivable that he hadn't, but at what intensity, the same as I had experienced? As I walked slowly back downhill towards the road and Land Rover, I concluded that ultimately it was probably only him and God that would ever know.

For my future perusal I took several photographs before I left Sappers Hill, thinking this was possibly my only ever, and/or last, visit back to the Falklands. I even managed to photograph a vivid picture that I had had in my mind since 1982. The scene was etched into my memory, remembering that I had wanted to go there for a swim after the fighting had stopped. The picture I wanted was a view looking downwards from Sappers Hill in a south easterly direction, across the flat moorland, to the shoreline and the waves crashing in and then eventually back out to sea.

On our return to Port Stanley at lunch time I managed to sneak into the FIDF galley for some scran with an old friend, Tim Jerman, who I had served with in Charlie Company and was staying on their camp for our pilgrimage. He had been on a ship's detachment in 1982.

In the afternoon, with Tim, I went to visit the War Museum in Port Stanley. As I was looking at some of the displays of the kit and weapons, I was especially drawn to one showing British ration packs. I laughed out loud as I thought to myself, was it that long ago to warrant being in a museum? 1982 seemed like only yesterday to me. Deep down I was pleased that this museum was built and hopefully, will be standing here for a very long time after me. With any luck it will at least serve to inform and remind the younger generation of the sacrifices made in 1982. I just wished there was something as comprehensive as this exhibition back in the UK.

Day Five.

Saturday the 10/11/07 I did a quick visit with Jono to Mount Pleasant Airfield to see the site where a Gazelle helicopter from the Army Air Corps 656 Squadron had been shot down, by one of our Sea Dart missiles in a blue-on-blue accident, killing all four on board. I believe it took fifteen years for the truth to be told. Traveling back to Port Stanley we stopped off at Sappers Hill so I could pick up some memento stones to take back to the UK with me and place them in my rockery.

With Jono and Dave Jones, we drove some of the way up the Two Sisters Mountain. The track just ran out and the going would have been too difficult for the vehicle to make it to the peak so we parked up and walked the rest of the way. In 1982 during this night assault on Two Sisters by 45 Commando RM, in which Dave had taken part, seven Royal Marines Commandos and a Sapper from 59 Independent Commando Squadron, Royal Engineers were, killed.

The Two Sisters Mountain consists of the east and west twin peaks. Dave showed us the path where in 1982 he had advanced, heading for the top of one peak, along an inclined slope of wet moorland bog and the occasional granite boulders. As the men from 45 Commando advanced up the slope, they came under heavy fire from Argentine soldiers in positions above. I stayed at the eastern peak and Dave went off on his own for a stroll along the ridge to the western. On Dave's return I could see it had been an emotional experience for him. Together with Jono we had a chat, and he went into some detail about what had experienced.

Because Dave had heard from us about our exploits and seen my photographs of Sappers Hill, I think he felt uninhibited, free to express his feelings to us and I was pleased to listen to him. I remember him saying that if he heard anyone saying that 40 Commando did nothing 'Down South' he would put them right, which pleased me.

That Saturday afternoon was a special occasion, the remembrance main parade and march passed in Port Stanley. I think nearly all of the capital, if not the whole Falklands Islands population turned out to watch the ceremony at the Liberation Memorial. For the event, all veterans turned out immaculately, wearing blazers, shirts, ties, polished shoes and medals. Typically of the unpredictability of the weather in the South Atlantic as soon as the parade halted at the memorial the heaven's opened and it poured down with rain. The only blessing was having my beret on which gave me some protection from the rain and a little warmth to my head. As I felt the rain soak through the shoulders of my blazer, shirt and eventually on to my skin, I said to the guy standing next to me, in pure Victor Meldrew style 'I don't believe it!'

Near the end of the religious service a Tornado flew overhead, at what seemed to be a very low height and scared the hell out of me, reminding me of my similar experience with a Harrier near Mount Harriet in 1982. I'm glad that no one saw me flinch because their perception of me being a hardened ex Royal Marine would have evaporated.

As we marched back along Ross Road towards the East Jetty, we stopped at Victory Green, for a dedication read by a vicar, and the giving of two new benches bought by us, the members of the 25th Pilgrimage. To be honest I was happy when we had started to march again from the Liberation Memorial as it warmed me up. I was even more excited when we were ordered to fall out and there was free tea, coffee and biscuits waiting for us in a nearby hall.

Day Six.

At 09.00 on the 11/11/07 there was a Service of Remembrance in Christchurch Cathedral, Port Stanley. Apart from Veterans and Falklanders it was also attended by the Under Secretary for Defence and the Veterans Minister. I arrived about twenty minutes before the service began, thinking I had plenty of time to find a seat. However, I poked my head through the main doors to find it was already packed full of people. So, I back tracked and walked to a side entrance and found a room attached to the Cathedral, where the service was being streamed live on a screen.

A middle aged, Falklander woman approached me, saw that I had my medals on and was a veteran. She grabbed me by the hand and led me directly back into the Cathedral. Once inside the woman took a look around and saw a couple of American tourists that had been visiting for the day on a cruise ship, sitting on pews right at the front, near the altar. She approached them with me being dragged along like a shy, embarrassed kid by his parents, with the rest of the congregation watching. 'Can you please move, this seating is for veterans only' she bellowed at the unsuspecting Americans. I ended up with one of the best seats in town!

That night after a meal, kindly prepared by my host, Colleen, we went out for a drink, first to the infamous Globe and then on to the Victory. You could mistakenly have been in a pub in any town or village in the UK. The only difference was the overwhelming amount of military plaques on the walls and the smoke from cigarettes. In the Falklands, public smoking was still permitted in bars in 2007.

My penultimate day was spent taking 'Buster,' Colleens dog, for a walk with another ex-Marine, to a cove (at the time the only, non-mined beach), near the old airport just outside Port Stanley. As I stood on the beach, I felt that there was a freshness, in both the air and from the clear, cold sea water, that I had not come across before. Large waves, directly from the Antarctic came crashing into the white sand and rocks giving the place an illusion of being on a tropical paradise, apart from the temperature of course!. However, this freshness evaporated after I chased after Buster, who was running off in the distance to find the burrows used for nesting by Magellanic Penguins. As I approached where the dog was digging and sniffing, the pungent aroma of penguins' droppings and decaying fish knocked me back. How the hell Buster didn't pass out after sticking his nose down these burrows, god only knows (or nose, please excuse the pun!)

As we headed back to Port Stanley, along the Airport Road, we stopped to take a look at the old airfield that was put to great use by the Argentine Air Force in 1982 for resupply of food, kit and personnel. When I was up in the observation tower, signing the visitors' book, a woman stopped me and asked if I was an I.T.F.C. supporter. I said with some hesitation, 'Yes I am'. She told me her whole family had heard about me and were supporters too. Apparently, she had been looking for me since I had arrived six days ago.

There was one last place I wanted to visit during my stay on the Falklands and that was the Memorial Woods in Port Stanley. In the woods individual trees had been planted to commemorate every British serviceman that had died in 1982. It was only a short walk from where I was staying so I went on my own. I found it moving that the citizens of the Islands had not only put a memorial in stone in the middle of Port Stanley but also a green one. I thought this was a way of saying look, yes, these service men did die, but they are still living in your and our memories and in the symbolic form of a tree. They must not and should not be forgotten because of the ultimate sacrifice they gave.

During the early evening of the 11/11/07 I walked from Colleens home to the FIDF Hall for a Veteran's leaving party organised by the people of the Falkland Islands. As I entered and looked straight down the hall, I saw something I automatically recognised, which gave me a feeling of joy and put a smile across my face too. Four individuals stood together, two children and their parents, the mother I recognised from my visit to the old airport earlier on in the day. Three of them were wearing Ipswich Town football club shirts. I wanted to go up to them and give them an enormous hug. I moved towards the family, through the crowd. They must have seen me laughing as I approached because they smiled back. Migs, Aniya, Reuben and Dan Cofre introduced themselves and I spent some time with them chatting about I.T.F.C.. They had, in fact, been to Portman Road as special guests the last time they had visited England. I made a mental note to send them some gifts from the I.T.F.C. shop when I got home. The Cofre family had made me feel so welcome and their kind act travelled with me back to the UK as a highlight in my memory.

During the leaving party I also had a chat with Malcom Hunt, 40 Commando RM Commanding Officer in 1982. I had met him before at reunions at Norton Manor Camp and always found him entertaining. He was trying to get myself and more ex Royal Marines involved in SAMA because he feared it was being overrun by Pongos!

On a wall display in the FIDF Hall, primary school aged children that lived on the Falklands had made a collage of hand drawn pictures with some very heart touching, personal comments. I spent some time reading these messages and felt very happy, almost intoxicated, because they had gone to so much effort and really did appreciate what we had done in 1982.

Day Seven.

On my final morning in the Falkland Islands, as I was leaving Colleens home, she gave me a commemorative coin. A very thoughtful and appreciated gift. It was 06.30 and to say it was to be the start of a hellish journey back would be an understatement. The first drama was when the Plane was delayed leaving RAF Mount Pleasant. In Rio we had to wait an additional four hours for the Boeing 767 plane to arrive that was taking us on to the UK. At Gatwick I caught the express train to Victoria and then travelled by underground, where there were delays due to 'security reasons'. Eventually I reached Liverpool Street Station thinking it couldn't get worse; could it? I then boarded the train to Ipswich and found out via an announcement onboard that there was a replacement bus service for half the journey thus increasing arrival time by one hour. The gods where certainly having a laugh at my expense! All in all, from leaving Colleens bungalow in Port Stanley to stepping through my front door in Ipswich at 15.56, it had taken over thirty hours. I was shattered but pleased to get home.

Although the UK is only three hours ahead, my circadian rhythm was out of sync. It took me several days to recover from this ordeal, and very quickly I developed a heavy cold. I am sure this was caused by germs that had been spread again and again by the aircrafts recycled air conditioning system as we flew back to the UK. However, there was one part of the journey that I shall never forget. As the plane was rolling down the runway gathering speed for take-off from Mount Pleasant Airport, on our port side there was a RAF Guard of Honour saluting us. Forward of them a Sea King was hovering, and it tipped its nose as we passed. The icing on the cake was just after take-off. Two Tornadoes appeared off each of our plane's wings and escorted us, for some distance before peeling off at great knots of speed. I was so happy when several months later SAMA sent in the post to my home address a DVD of our pilgrimage, capturing this momentous send off and some of the other main events during my visit.

Was I pleased that I went on the Pilgrimage? Yes, I was. I was privileged to be able to go on the 25th reunion and thankful for the considerable amount of effort by individuals and organisations to make it happen. The one thing I missed was the companionship of those I had served with. In an ideal world, I would have been accompanied by all my fellow Royal Marines from 9 Troop, especially 33.C section. These were the people that I shared both happy and horrendous experiences with. I would particularly like to go to three places with my section: Sappers Hill, the Mine field near Mount Harriet (hopefully cleared by now) and Wreck point to see the infamous 'Sangar'. The first two locations were where frightening, life changing events occurred. The final was where we spent some time as a section, left on our own from the rest of the Troop and we bonded. Chris Pretty recently went on Google Earth, located Wreck Point and told me to take a look. I did the same and found that the 'Sangar' was clear to see, still standing after all these years, as has my friendship with the lads from 9 Troop Charlie, Company.

In 1982 it had taken over six weeks on the Canberra to reach the Falkland Islands, stopping of at Sierra Leone and the Ascension Islands. It would have been nice to sail down again and appreciate the distance with a few, if not all, from 9 Troop.

Back to San Carlos, 2007 Pilgrimage. Below left, L-R Jono Johnson, Wayne McGregor and me.

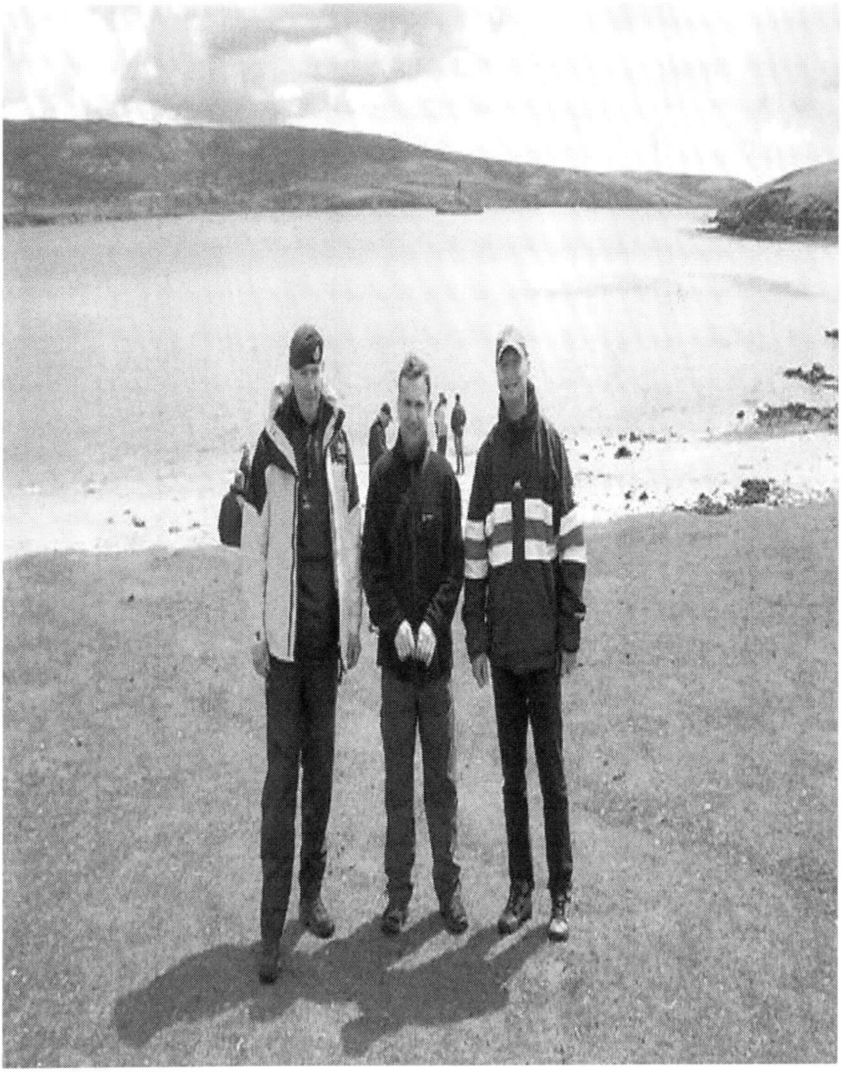

Part of the still uncleared minefield at the base of Mount Harriet where Charlie Company spent a horrendous night back in 1982.

Sappers Hill 2007. Argentine equipment from 1982 can still be found lying out in the elements. This picture displaying a pair of discarded Argentine plimsolls.

11. PADDY ASHDOWN (LORD ASHDOWN) GCMG, CH, KBE, PC (RIP).

People sometimes ask me if I ever served with Paddy Ashdown. My reply is quite swift, 'No, he was way before my time', although I did have an encounter with him! Paddy Ashdown was doing a tour of the UK in 2010 to promote his new book 'A fortunate life', an autobiography. He was going to do a talk in the Ipswich Council Chambers, so I thought I would go along and have a listen to what he had to say. I obviously knew about his time serving in the Royal Marines Commandos and his specialisation in the SBS as an officer.

I was a bit apprehensive going along because I thought much of his dialogue might be about his political career as leader of the Liberal Democrats. The talk began at 18.30 on

30th June 2010. It was a rare, pleasant, summers evening so I thought I would arrive early to take in the atmosphere. As I got to the town hall, I saw Paddy walking up the steps to the front door, accompanied by his 'minders'. I caught his eye by shouting 'Hello Royal'. He stopped and I approached him and introduced myself. We had a long chat about the Corps. I looked at my watch and realised that it was 18.25 and said to him, 'Haven't you got to start your talk at 18.30?' He looked down at his watch too and then at the door entrance and replied, 'Oh yes, of course', as if he had forgotten. As he was just about to leave I said, 'And there's one more thing.' He looked back at me with a puzzled expression, 'Your flies are undone'. He burst out laughing and said, 'Thanks Royal'. I went into the large Victorian chamber of the town hall, where Paddy was giving his talk and sat down on one of the fifty or so chairs laid out in rows of approximately ten. Two minutes later Paddy walked out onto the stage with a pint of beer in one hand and moved a stool to the centre with the other. He took a seat, a sip of his beer, looked up, saw me in the audience and gave me a thumbs up.

From the start I found his life story intriguing. I hadn't known that like my father, he had been born in India and that he had been to Ipswich several times before. Once to do a reconnaissance on the Ipswich docks for an exercise with the SBS.

To be honest after his discourse on his visits to Bosnia and

Herzegovina I started to lose interest because it edged towards his time as a politician. However, Paddy did come out with some very funny stories. He recalled while working for the government, when he had been sent on an interpreter's course in Chinese. He said that he had difficulty with the Chinese language because in some cases it was the tone of speech that made a difference to the meaning of a word. Paddy had once tried to engage in conversation with a Chinese lady sitting next to him on a plane. He thought that he had asked her if she had ever flown before. Paddy had got the pitch wrong and instead he had enquired if she had ever sat on a flying penis!

Paddy Ashdown was doing a book signing session after his lecture. I went and bought the book (he didn't give me a discount!) but he signed it 'To Terry, once a bootie, always a bootie'! Paddy Ashdown, a gentleman through and through and of course, OARMAARM.

12. A LITTLE PIECE ON TEACHING.

I knew it was time for me to leave teaching when I found the new wave of 'educators' was not of my liking or thinking. One particular individual aged in his mid to late twenties was the epitome of this. His hair was tied in a ponytail, and his body covered in tattoos. This appearance I had no issue with. What did annoy me was the fact that he had no sports related degree and frequently thought he knew everything on the subject. He was from somewhere in the southern part of the African Continent. He brought with him an attitude of arrogance, sometimes associated with the dreadful times of apartheid. The world according to him was 'me,me,me (or I,I,I) and he thought himself to be god's gift to teaching, no doubt inherited in his genes from his parents' who were (oh dear lord!), also alleged educators. In any meetings, he was the type of person that would continue the discussion way past the prescribed end time, simply because he would put his point forward and his point was the right point, and nobody else's was. If you disagreed, he would act like a spoilt child by not talking to you and ignore you totally at other meetings and passing's in the corridor. It was getting to be too much for me. He behaved worse than a disruptive student – what an arse!

To make it worse our new, middle management was just as bad and ignorant. Most, with very little experience, and at least twenty years younger than me, took control. Their only aim was to save money. I will not go 'all political' but education and teaching were last on their agenda. 'On the cheap' was their mantra and any method of cutting the financial cost was celebrated. The management did very little teaching, and most, none at all. They were just administrators, and this annoyed me the most. The management had a hidden agenda, their career progress, pay and pension. Well, there's my moan finished, at least for now; sorry reader!

I did have the opportunity to meet some fantastic students who I can only hope I guided in the right direction. Many, after all these years, keep in contact with me, in fact some have gone on to join the Royal Marines.

One benefit I had while I was teaching was that I organised several five day 'Look at Life' courses at CTCRM for twelve of our students. I took a teaching colleague with me for company, but if the truth was to be told, it was because of health and safety requirements. We drove down with our baggage, in a very cramped minibus. If the students dared to misbehave on the trip down to Devon I used an old trick I had learnt many years ago from a seasoned teacher. By putting the heating on full blast they would slowly but surely fall asleep!

Walking around the camp at CTCRM as a civilian and after so many years was novel. Even though I was accompanied by other staff and students, inside I felt lonely. It was a bit like returning to your primary school, knowing the fabric of the buildings but not recognising anyone there. All your friends and teachers had gone; you were history.

The idea of the visit was to give an insight to the students of what the Royal Marines did and for them to sample some of the fitness and academic levels required to enter. One of the entry tests for recruits which was attempted by our students was carried out in the swimming pool at CTCRM. It was a case of simply jumping off a 3-metre-high diving board and swimming 50 metres. The students were lined up at the swimming pool edge and one at a time carried out the test, got out of the pool and immediately got changed. This procedure was done so that no one felt intimidated by the others watching. Most of the group went through with no problems, a few of the anxious ones tried to hide at the back of the queue, but credit to them that they eventually did it. However, one lad got to the top of the steps of the diving board and refused to go any further. The Royal Marine PTI tried in vain to help the student build up the courage to jump, initially by verbal persuasion. When this method of motivation was exhausted, as was the patience of the PTI and to be frank, my colleagues' and mine, the student was given an ultimatum by the Royal Marine. 'Either you jump or I'll come up there and push you off'. The young lad thought it was just an idle threat, unfortunately it was not to be. The Royal Marine climbed up the steps, casually walked up to the student, grabbed him by the arms and threw him off the diving board into the water below. Deep in my heart and from my experience as a Nod, I knew the PTI wasn't bluffing. My teaching colleague, who had no experience of the military, especially the Royal Marines, stood there, gob smacked and said, 'For god sake I hope nobody filmed that because if OFSTED got hold of it our days of teaching would be numbered!'

My time as an undergraduate and living in Canterbury, teaching in the heart of Suffolk and early retirement, intermixed with my travels abroad and in the UK, I shall leave for another book. I hope you have enjoyed reading my stories as much as I have in writing them.

I must conclude by mentioning a tale about parenthood. Before the birth of my beautiful daughter, Sarah, I asked for some tips/guidance from people I knew that had children of their own. Once I was shopping in the centre of Ipswich and bumped into an ex-marine who was then a serving police officer. Seeking some serious advice, I posed the question to him on bringing up a child. He chuckled and replied, 'It's like a sixteen year old who wants to join the Royal Marines asking you what's it like in training as a nod; an eternal bloody nightmare'! He walked off, now in fits of laughter and shaking his head in disbelief, as if I had asked him for a loan! I stood there for a while bewildered and naïve just as I had as a sixteen year old waiting for the train to take me to CTCRM for the first time.

My little Angel Sarah at the age of three.

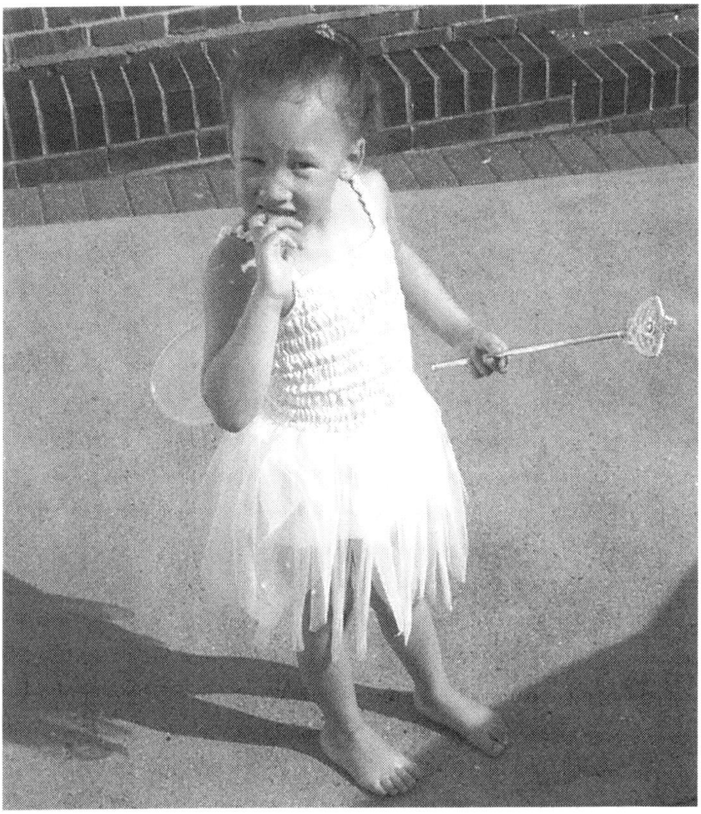

How can I not include a picture of my other daughter, Duchess (AKA The Fox).

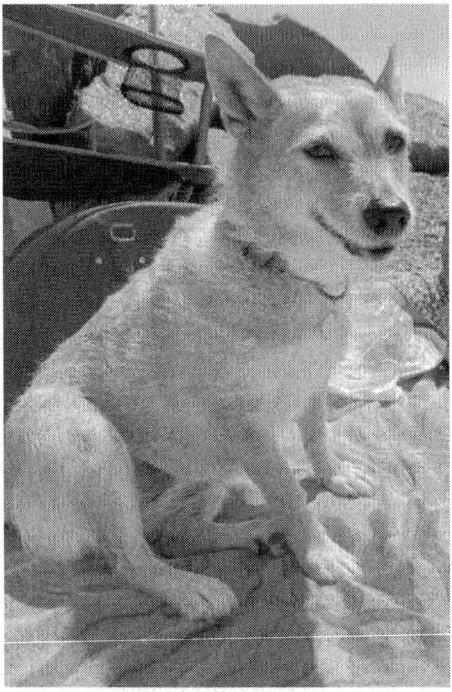

Finally, I would like to wish you well and leave you with the phrase the Irish comedian Dave Alan would conclude with on all of his TV shows, **'May your god go with you'**.

BIBLIOGRAPHY.

Delves Cedric (2018), **Across the Angry Sea: The SAS in The Falklands War**. Hurst & Company, 2018. London.

Hastings and Jenkins (1983) The **Battle For The Falklands.** Michael Joseph Ltd. London.

Van Der Biji. N (2007) **Victory in The Falklands** Pen and Sword Books, UK.

https://www.britannica.com/ (2020), britannica.com/place/Falkland-Islands.

GLOSSARY OF TERMS.

A Glossary of Royal Marines terms used in this book (There are many more). Please note that the term 'Hoofing' (Fantastic, brilliant) was not used when I was in the Corps, it was Wazza!

Arc of fire – Sighting of weapons.

Beasting – A form of physical exercise to discipline a Marine for bad behaviour.

Biff – Useless.

Bimble – To walk casually or wonder slowly with no purpose.

Bivvy – Temporary shelter normally made out of a poncho.

Blues – Ceremonial blue No.1 uniform, worn with either beret and gold cap badge or Peaked Cap. Occasionally with a Pith Helmet and a long coat for ceremonies.

Bootneck – A Royal Marines Commando. From the Nelsonian era when the Marine guard on ships wore a leather sleeve around their necks to prevent garrotting.

Brick – Four-man team.

C.O. – Commanding Officer

Chit – Service request.

Company Lines – The location for the Company headquarters, stores and for parade.

Chopper – Helicopter.

CSM – Company Sergeant Major.

CTCRM– Commando Training Centre Royal Marines.

Dhobi – To wash or to do your laundry.

Dhobi-dust – Washing powder.

DPM – Disruptive Pattern Material.

Dig-out (blind) – To make an all-out effort.

Drip – Moan.

Duchy's – Late night food hut.

Essence – Good Looking Person.

Fell in – To take your place in line.

FIDF – Falklands Island Defence Force.

Flap – Or Flapping, to worry or panic.

FN FAL – 7.62mm rifle, can be used in semi or fully automatic mode, made under licence in Argentina.

Forty– 40 Commando Royal Marines.

GPMG – General Purpose Machine Gun.

Galley – Kitchen and mess hall.

Gash – Rubbish.

Globe & Buster – The Globe & Laurel. The official Royal Marines bimonthly publication.

Goffers – Soft drinks.

Goffer Wallah – The operator of a small shop or stand.

Gopping – Nasty, horrible, unenjoyable.

Going outside – Leaving the Corps.

Gongs – Medals.

Gopping – Dirty.

Gronk – An ugly woman.

Gronk board – A display of photographs of gronks'.

Grot – Bedroom/accommodation on camp.

Honking – Dirty.

LMA – Leading medical assistant (Royal Navy).

LMG – Light Machine gun.

LAW 66 – Light Anti-Tank Weapon.

ML– Royal Marines Mountain Leader Cadre, who are specialists in long range reconnaissance, arctic Warfare and mountain climbing.

NAAFI – Navy, Army and Air Force Institute.

N.C.O – Non-commissioned officer.

Nod – The nickname given to recruits and Jnr Mne's.

Nutty – Sweets.

'O' Group – Meeting/ briefing.

OARMAARM – Once A Royal Marine, Always A Royal Marine.

Oppo – Friend.

Pinged – To be chosen for a course or job without your consent.

Pit – Bed.

Plums rating – One who is continually unsuccessful with women.

Poncho - Waterproof coat used to make a Bivvy.

Pongo – Anybody in the Army. Wherever the Army goes, 'pongos'. A dig at their standards.

Proffed – Finding things that won't be missed, through dubious means.

Pussers – MOD issued kit and clothing. Sticking to orders or how things are done to perfection; by the book.

RTUd – Returned to unit.

Racing snake – Fast runner.

Rigid raider – A small high powered attack boat made of fibre-glass.

Run ashore – Short leave or a night out on the town.

RM – Royal Marine(s).

Royal – a Royal Marine or Royal Marine Veteran.

Sad-on – To be unhappy.

SB – Special Boat Squadron.

Scran – Food.

Sit Rep – Situation Report.

SLR – The L1A1 Self Loading Rifle firing 7.62 rounds.

Sprog – Young Royal Marine or child.

Stand Easy – Official break.

Sunshine Commando – Slang for 40 Commando Royal Marines.

Swamp – Soaking wet or to urinate.

Threaders – Angry, fed up.

Thunder Flash – A pyrotechnic used to simulate battlefield artillery landing.

Trap/ Trapped – To chat up a woman ashore, or to be ensnared by one.

V.C.P. – Vehicle check point.

Wings – To become parachute trained.

Wet – A hot drink.

Woolly Pully – Issued heavy weight jumper.

WREN – A woman in the RN service.

Yomp/yomping – A forced march or load carry.

Zap/zapped – To shoot or be shot at or have been shot.

Zeds – To sleep.

2i/c - Second in command.

APPENDICES.

The Commando tests are done one day after the other. The only rest day is between the Endurance and Tarzan Assault courses. These final Commando tests are not exclusive. Constant assessments both academic, administrative and physical are carried out throughout recruit training. If recruits do not reach the standards required at any stage of the 32-week training schedule they may be put into Hunter Troop for rehabilitation or given extra military training to help them pass.

The Nine Mile Speed March, is done carrying full fighting order, and must be completed in 90 minutes.

The Endurance Course is six-mile in total that starts with a two-mile run across Woodbury Common over obstacles that include tunnels, concrete pipes, wading pools, and an underwater culvert. The test ends with a four-mile run back to CTCRM. The course has to be completed in 73 minutes (71 minutes for Royal Marine officers). The Endurance Course finishes with a shooting test, the recruit must hit 6 out of 10 shots at a 25m target simulating a 200m shoot. If he fails the shooting, the whole Endurance test is failed.

The Tarzan Assault Course. This is an assault and Tarzan course combined into one and completed at CTCRM. It starts with a death slide and ends with a rope climb up a thirty-foot near-vertical wall. It must be completed with full fighting order and rifle in 13 minutes, (12 minutes for officers).

The 30 Miler. This is a 30-mile Yomp across Dartmoor, wearing full fighting order. It must be completed in eight hours for recruits and seven hours for Royal Marine officers.

After the 30-mile march, any recruit who has failed any of the tests may attempt to retake them within a seven day window.